LIVING IN THE SHADE OF ISLAM

HOW TO LIVE AS A MUSLIM SERIES

LIVING IN THE SHADE OF ISLAM

Ali Ünal

NEW JERSEY • LONDON • FRANKFURT • CAIRO

New Jersey

18 17 16 15   4 5 6 7

Published by Tughra Books
335 Clifton Avenue, Clifton
New Jersey 07011, USA

www.tughrabooks.com

Library of Congress Cataloging-in-Publication Data Available

Unal, Ali.
Living in the shade of Islam / Ali Unal.
p. cm. -- (How to live as a Muslim series ; 2)
Includes bibliographical references and index.
ISBN 978-1-59784-211-2 (pbk.)
1. Islam--Doctrines. 2. Islam--Customs and practices. I. Title.
BP165.5.U53 2009
297.2--dc22

2009016362

ISBN 978-1-59784-211-2

Printed by
Imak Ofset, Istanbul - Turkey

Contents

INTRODUCTION

Islam, which literally means peace, submission, and obedience, is the religion of the whole universe. The universe is orderly, a cosmos whose parts are linked together and work together for the same purpose and goal.

Islam and the Universe

Everything is assigned a place in the grand scheme of the universe, which works in a magnificent way. The sun, moon, stars, and all heavenly bodies are knit together in a splendid system, follow unalterable laws, and never deviate from their ordained course.

The universe, although seemingly monotonous and blindly obeying a set of laws, is neither a factory, as eighteenth-century theists thought, nor a chaos, as conceived by Existentialist philosophers. Rather, it is like a lively and dynamic organism, each part of which works according to the position it occupies and fulfills its role in the system of mutual relationships. In addition, God is not a passive power that set up the universe to work automatically, but an "ever-active" Power Who unceasingly reflects His Names in the mirror of the universe. Each such reflection renews the universe, meaning that a new one is manifested each moment. But this renewal depends upon certain immutable principles that allow us to regulate our lives and, therefore, make human life possible. These principles, which we deduce by observing "natural" events and call "natural" laws, have only nominal existence. The universe's Creator and Ruler established them; creation obeys them.

This is why Islam is the universe's religion, for Islam is nothing other than obedience and submission to God, the Lord of the universe. The sun, the moon, the earth, and all heavenly bodies are *muslim*, as are air, water, heat, stones, trees, and animals, for everything in existence obeys God by submitting to His laws. Even unbelievers and atheists are *muslim* as far as their bodily existence is concerned, for each part of their bodies follows the course God established for it, from birth until death and dissolution.

Islam teaches that God, nature, and humanity are not remote from, alien to, or opposed to each other. God makes Himself known to humanity through nature and humanity itself, and nature and humanity are two books (of creation) that make God known. Islam is the name of the code according to which nature functions in perfect obedience and by which humanity is required, but not forced, to live by using its free will.

Islam Defined with Respect to the Universe

Islam, derived from *silm* (submission, salvation, and peace), is the expression of God's Grace flowing in the universe's arteries. Being the Divine system to which all creation, except humanity, has submitted willingly, the universe contains no disorder. Islam is the firm, unbreakable rope stretched from Heaven to which all creatures hold fast and by which humanity will ascend to Paradise, our original home. Islam connects all creatures in a single unity, and thus is the religion of universal brotherhood and solidarity.

Tawhid (monotheism), which is the bedrock of Islam, implies the necessity of humanity's harmony with nature. The universe, which has submitted to God, displays a coherence and harmony of which our world is also a part. Although our world is subject to the general laws of "nature" as well as its own unique set of laws, it is in harmony with other laws governing those phenomena beyond it. Humanity, which alone does not tread the path of "nature," has free will and the gift of freedom, as well as the obligation to harmonize its life with the rest of nature. This harmony, moreover, is also the path of human exaltation and progress, the path upon which God originated human nature:

> So set your whole being upon the Religion (of Islam) as one of pure faith (free from unbelief, polytheism, and hypocrisy). This is the original pattern belonging to God on which He has originated humankind. No change can there be in God's creation. This is the upright, ever-true Religion, but most of the people do not know. (30:30)

Islam seeks to unite us with the vast domain of being, and strives to create an absolute unity between us and the universe. We are the most essential partner in the realm of existence, and each Muslim is the co-religionist of all creatures:

> Do they now seek a religion other than God's, when to Him submits whoever is in the heavens and on the earth, willingly or unwillingly, and to Him they are being returned? (3:83)

> Do you ever consider that all who are in the heavens and all who are on the earth prostrate themselves to God, and so do the sun, the moon, the stars, the mountains, the trees, and the beasts, and so do many among human beings? (22:18)

Islam Does not Accept Contradictions

Tawhid implies the equality and unity of all people in their relation with God, and thus indicates homogeneity, equality, and the unity of human origin. Humanness is the one element ingrained in the nature of all individuals. People of different social strata were not created by separate deities with varying levels of power, for this would violate *tawhid* by allowing possible disparity in their essential nature and erecting insuperable barriers between them. The same God created everyone, and so all people have the same fundamental essence: *O humankind! In due reverence for your Lord, keep from disobedience to Him Who created you from a single human self* (4:1).

Given this, Islam rejects legal, physical, class, social, political, racial, national, territorial, genetic, or even economic factors in measuring people's worth. *Tawhid* means considering humanity as a unity and working to eliminate all efforts at division based upon such factors as color, social status, occupation, education, geography, and ideology. All such divisions are reconcilable only by replacing *shirk* (dualism, trinitarianism, or polytheism, secular humanism and/or existentialism) with *tawhid*.

The Qur'an declares:

> O humankind! Surely We have created you from a single (pair of) male and female, and made you into tribes and families so that you may know one another (and so build mutuality and co-operative relationships, not so that you may take pride in your differences of race or social rank, or breed enmities). Surely the noblest, most honorable of you in God's sight is the one best in piety, righteousness, and reverence for God. Surely God is All-Knowing, All-Aware. (49:13)

In fact, the noblest person in God's sight is the one who is the most pious, righteous, and God-revering. The Prophet is reported to have said, "Your Lord is One. You are from Adam and Adam is from dust. An Arab is not superior to a non-Arab, nor a white person to a black person, except for his or her piety, righteousness, and reverence for God."[1] This is what the Qur'an calls *taqwa* and a Muslim's daily life centers around it. Bediüzzaman Said Nursi defines *taqwa* as follows:

> The human conscious nature, which we call conscience, and which distinguishes between what is good and evil, feeling pleasure and exhilaration in what is good, and suffering from and grieved at what is evil, has four basic elements, namely the spiritual intellect, willpower, the mind, and the power of perceptiveness. These four elements are also regarded as the senses of the spirit. In addition to their different duties and functions, each of these senses has an ultimate purpose for its existence. The ultimate purpose for willpower is worshipping God; for the mind, it is having knowledge of God; for the power of perceptiveness, love of God; and for the spiritual intellect, "vision" of God. What we call taqwa (piety and righteousness), which is the perfect form or degree of worship, is the result of the functions of all of these four senses. The Divine Law, included in the Divine Religion, feeds them to develop, equips them with the necessary material, and directs them to the ultimate purposes for the existence of each.[2]

Chapter 1

Cardinal Articles of Islamic Faith and Virtues of Belief

CARDINAL ARTICLES OF ISLAMIC FAITH AND VIRTUES OF BELIEF

In the first volume of the "How to live as a Muslim" series, we tried to give a general outline of Islamic faith, thought, and worldview. In this second volume, we will try to present the daily life of a Muslim. Here, we deem it useful to summarizc a Muslim's faith and thought in a list of articles of faith.

> The Archangel Gabricl came to God's Messenger, upon him be peace and blessings, in the form of a man dressed in white to teach the Companions about Islam. He sat beside the Messenger and said, "Muhammad, inform me about Islam?" The Messenger replied, "Islam means that you testify that there is no deity but God and that Muhammad is God's Messenger, and that you establish the Prayer, pay the Zakah, observe the fast of Ramadan, and perform pilgrimage to the (House—the Ka'ba) if you are capable enough to do so (in respect of wealth and security of travel)." He (Gabriel) said, "You have told the truth." ....Then, he said, "Inform me about iman (faith). He (the Messenger) replied, "That you affirm your belief in God, in His angels, in His Books, in His Messengers, in Judgment Day, and you affirm your belief in the Divine Decree about good and evil."[1]

Cardinal Articles of Faith

1. God is One, without any partners. The name "Allah," His special Name, cannot be used for anybody or anything else.
2. He eternally exists without coming into existence. He is the Eternal without a beginning and endures without end.
3. There is nothing like Him. He is the Creator, neither created nor a part of His creation. He neither begets nor is begotten.

4. He cannot be conceived of in any human terms and qualities, and does not become incarnate. He is different from any created being. He knows, but not as we know; He has power, but not as we have power; He sees, but not as we see; He hears, but not as we hear; and He speaks, but not as we speak. We speak via speech organs and sounds, whereas God the All-High and Transcending speaks without organs or sounds. He has neither body nor substance, neither accidental property nor limit, neither opposite, nor like, nor similitude.
5. There is no god other than Him. He is One, not in a numerical sense, but in the sense that He is unique and has no partner nor like. He is the Eternal Refuge. He has absolute control over everything, and nothing has any control over Him. Nothing can be independent of Him, even for the blink of an eye.
6. Nothing can overwhelm Him. No limits or restrictions can be placed upon Him. He has no parts or limbs, and cannot be contained by the six directions, as all created things are.
7. He is the All-Worshipped One, having the exclusive right to be worshipped. No entity in the universe is worthy of worship besides Him.
8. Nothing happens except that He wills it to happen.
9. He is the All-Living and never dies, is eternally active and never sleeps nor slumbers. He is never wearied and never feels the need to rest.
10. He creates without being in need to do so, and provides for His creation without any effort.
11. He causes death without fear, restores to life without difficulty.
12. He has the power to do everything. Everything is dependent upon Him, and yet He needs nothing. There is nothing like Him.
13. He ordered His creatures to obey Him and forbade them to disobey Him.

14. He is the All-Exalted beyond having opposites or equals.
15. No one can ward off His decree, delay His command, or overpower His affairs.
16. He is the All-Merciful, the All-Compassionate, and the All-Loving. After His proper Name, "Allah," He introduces Himself as the All-Merciful (*ar-Rahman*), meaning that He has mercy for the whole creation and provides for it, and as the All-Compassionate (*ar-Rahim*), meaning that He has particular compassion for each creature, and will include the believers into Paradise in the Hereafter out of His particular compassion for them.
17. He is the All-Forgiving, and we pray to Him exclusively. He answers all prayers according to His Wisdom. He either gives what is requested, or what is better, or does not give it at all because what is requested is not in the best interest of the one who prays. He sometimes accepts prayers by rewarding in the Hereafter the one who prays.
18. Muhammad, upon him be peace and blessings, is His chosen Servant, elect Prophet, His Messenger with whom He is well pleased, and the Seal of the Prophets.
19. Every claim to Prophethood after Prophet Muhammad is falsehood and deceit.
20. Prophet Muhammad has been sent to the jinn and humanity with truth, guidance, light, and illumination.
21. We believe in all the Prophets without making any discrimination between them in respect of believing in them. The Prophets, peace and blessings be upon them, are free of all major and minor sins, unbelief, and everything that is repugnant. Any insignificant lapses and errors that they might commit cause them to be corrected immediately by God.
22. God took Prophet Abraham as an intimate friend, and spoke to Moses in a special way, and created Prophet Jesus without a father. Jesus' mother, the Virgin Mary, was ab-

solutely chaste, and gave birth to Jesus without the hand of any man having touched her.

23. The Qur'an is God's word, which He revealed to His Messenger Muhammad, upon him be peace and blessings. All Muslims accept it as absolute truth.
24. We believe in all the other Divine Books in their original, revealed forms to the Messengers, and we bear witness that they were all following the manifest Truth.
25. Belief consists of belief in God, His angels, His Books, His Messengers, the Last Day (along with the Resurrection and the Day of Judgment), and belief in Divine Destiny and Decree (including human free will). So, we believe in the bodily resurrection and the Hereafter, and also in the Final Judgment, the Balance, the Records of Deeds, the Bridge, and in Paradise and Hell.
26. God, the Guardian of those who recognize and believe in Him, will not treat them in the Hereafter in the same way as He treats those who deny Him, who are bereft of His guidance, and who have failed to obtain His protection. O God, You are the Protector of Islam and its people. Make us firm in Islam until the day we meet You.
27. God loves all the believers, and the noblest of them in His sight are those who are the most righteous and the most obedient to Him, and who follow Islam most closely.
28. People's actions are created (given external existence in the material world) by God, but earned (done) by people themselves.
29. We believe in the Unseen, and in the existence of the incorporeal entities and beings such as the Divine Supreme Seat, the Divine Supreme Throne, and the angels, the jinn, and Satan.
30. We call the people of our *qibla* Muslims and believers as long as they acknowledge what Prophet Muhammad brought and accept as true everything that he said and told us about.

We do not consider any of them unbelievers because of any religiously wrong or forbidden action they have done, as long as they do not consider that action religiously lawful.

31. A person enters unbelief only by disavowing what led him or her to belief.
32. Whatever the Prophet, upon him be peace, said about the Shari'a (Islamic belief, thought, and way of of life) and the explanation (of the Qur'an and of Islam) is true.
33. We follow the *Sunna* of the Prophet and the Muslim community, and avoid deviation, difference, and divisions.
34. We do not accept as true anything said by soothsayers and fortune-tellers, nor do we accept the claims of those who affirm anything that goes against the Book, the *Sunna*, and the consensus of the Muslim Community.
35. We agree that holding together is the true and right path, and that separation is deviation and torment.[2]

The Importance and Virtues of Belief

Bediüzzaman Said Nursi explains in his *Words* five out of the thousands of virtues of belief in the following four points:[3]

First point. Through the light of belief, we reach the highest degree of perfection and become worthy of Paradise. The darkness of unbelief reduces us to the lowest level so that we deserve Hell. Belief connects us to our Majestic Maker, and our value derives from using our belief to demonstrate the Divine art and manifest the Divine Names. Unbelief breaks this relation, thereby veiling the Divine art and reducing our value to that of a mere physical entity with almost no value (a physical entity is perishable and is no more than a transient animal). We will explain this through a parable.

The value of the iron (or any other material) from which a work of art is made differs from the value of the art expressed in it. The art's worth is usually far more than its material. An antique may fetch as much as a million dollars, while its material is not even worth a few cents. If taken to the antiques market, it may be sold for its true value because of its art and the brilliant artist's name. If taken to a blacksmith, it would be sold only for the value of its iron.

Similarly, each person is a unique, priceless work of God Almighty's Art. We are His Power's most delicate and graceful miracles, beings created to manifest all His Names and inscriptions in the form of a miniature specimen of the universe. If we are illuminated with belief, these meaningful inscriptions become visible. Believers manifest these inscriptions through their connection with their Maker, for the Divine art contained in each person is revealed through such affirmations as, "I am the work of the Majestic Maker, the creature and object of His Mercy and Munificence." As a result, and because we gain value in proportion to how well we reflect this art, we move from insignificance (in material terms) to beings ranked above all creatures. We communicate with God through worship and prayer, are His guests on the earth, and are qualified for Paradise.

But if unbelief is ingrained in us, all of the Divine Names' manifestations are veiled by darkness and thus unexpressed. If the artist is unknown or denied, how can the aspects expressing the worth of his art be identified? Thus, most meaningful instances of that sublime art and those elevated inscriptions are concealed. In material terms, unbelievers attribute such art and inscriptions to trivial causes, nature and chance, thereby reducing them to plain glass instead of sparkling diamonds. Unbelievers render themselves and other humans no more significant than any other material entity, self-condemned to a transient and suffocating life, and no better than a most impotent, needy, and afflicted animal that eventually will become dust. Unbelief thus spoils our nature by changing our diamond into coal.

Second point. Just as belief illuminates human beings and reveals all the messages inscribed in their being by the Eternally-Besought-of-All, it also illuminates the universe and removes darkness from the past and future. We will explain this truth through what I experienced regarding the meaning of: *God is the Guardian of those who believe, bringing them out from all kinds of darkness into the light, and keeping them firm therein* (2:257).

I saw myself standing on an awe-inspiring bridge set over a deep valley between two mountains. The world was completely dark. Looking to my right, I imagined I saw a huge tomb. Looking to my left, I felt as if I were seeing violent storms and calamities being prepared amid tremendous waves of darkness. Looking down, I imagined I was seeing a very deep precipice.

In that darkness, my torch's dim light revealed a dreadful scene. All along the bridge's length were such horrible dragons, lions, and monsters that I wished I had no torch. Whichever way I directed it, I got the same fright. "This torch brings me only trouble," I exclaimed, throwing it away and breaking it. Suddenly, darkness was replaced by light, as if I had switched on a huge light by breaking my torch. I saw everything in its true nature.

I discovered that the bridge was a highway on a smooth plain. The huge tomb was a green, beautiful garden in which assemblies of worship, prayer, glorification, and discourse were being led by illustrious persons. The turbulent, stormy, frightening precipices now appeared as a banqueting hall, a shaded promenade, a very beautiful resting place behind lovely mountains. The horrible monsters and dragons were, in fact, camels, sheep, and goats. "Praise and thanks be to God for the light of belief," I said, and then awoke reciting, *God is the Guardian of those who believe, bringing them out from all kinds of darkness into the light, and keeping them firm therein*.

The two mountains are this life's beginning and end, and the life between death and the Resurrection. The bridge is the lifespan, between the two phases of the past (on the right) and the future (on the left). The torch is our conceited ego that, relying on its own achievements, ignores Divine Revelation. The monsters were the world's events and creatures of all kinds.

Those who have fallen into the darkness of misguidance and heedlessness because of their confidence in their egos resemble me in the former state—in the dim light of a torch. With their inadequate and misguided knowledge, they see the past as a huge tomb in the darkness of extinction and the future as a stormy scene of terror controlled by coincidence or chance. The torch shows them events and creatures as horrible dragons, lions, and monsters. In reality, these are subjugated to the All-Wise and All-Merciful, fulfill specific functions, and serve good purposes in submission to His Decree. However, they see such things as harmful monsters. These are the people referred to in "*And those who disbelieve, their guardians are the "taghut" (false deities and powers of evil): bringing them out from the light into all kinds of darkness*" (2:257).

If, however, people are favored with Divine guidance so that belief enters their hearts and their Pharaoh-like egos are broken, thereby enabling them to listen to the Book of God, they will resemble me in my later state. Suddenly the universe will fill with Divine Light, demonstrating the meaning of "*God is the Light of the heavens and the earth*" (24:35).

Through the eye of their hearts, such people see that the past is not a huge tomb; rather, each past century is the realm of authority of a Prophet or a beloved friend of God, where the purified souls, having completed the duties of their lives (worship) with "God is the Greatest," flew to higher abodes on the side of the future. Looking to their left and through the light of belief, they discern, behind the mountain-like revolutions of the intermediate world and the next life, a feasting place set up by the All-Compassionate One at palaces of bliss in gardens of Paradise. They understand that what seems to be storms, earthquakes, epidemics, and similar events serves a specific function, just as the spring rain and winds which, despite their apparent violence, serve many agreeable purposes. They even see death as the beginning of eternal life, and the grave as the gateway to eternal happiness.

Third point. Belief is both light and power. Those who attain true belief can challenge the universe and, in proportion to their belief's strength, be relieved of the pressure of events. Relying upon God, they travel safely through the huge waves of events in the ship of life. They voyage through the world comfortably until their last day, since they have entrusted their burdens to the Absolutely Powerful One's Power. The grave will be a resting place, after which they will fly to Paradise to attain eternal bliss. If they do not rely upon God, their worldly life will force them down to the lowest depths.

Belief, therefore, consists of affirming Divine Unity, which requires submitting to God, which requires relying upon God, which yields happiness in both worlds. Such reliance upon God should not be misunderstood as ignoring cause and effect. Rather, it means that one should think of causes as a veil covering Power's hand. One observes them by seeking to comply with the Divine Will, which is a sort of worship in action. However, such desire and seeking is not enough to secure a particular effect. We must understand that, in accordance with right belief, the result is to be expected only from God, the All-Mighty. As He is the sole producer of effects, we always should be grateful to Him.

To understand the truth and meaning of trust in God, consider this parable: Once two people boarded a ship with heavy burdens. One put his burden on the deck immediately after boarding and sat on it to keep it safe. The other one, even after being told to lay his burden down, refused to do so and said, "I won't put it down, for it might get lost. Besides, I'm strong enough to carry it." He was told:

> This reliable royal ship is stronger and can hold it better. You will most probably get tired, feel dizzy, and fall into the sea with your burden. Your strength will fail, and then how will you bear this burden that gets heavier every moment? If the captain sees you in this state, he might say you are insane and expel you from the ship. Or maybe he will think you do not trust our ship and make fun of us, for which he will imprison you. Also, you will be marked out and become the butt of jokes. Your vanity reveals your weakness, your arrogance reveals your impotence, and your pretension betrays your humiliation. And so you have become a laughing-stock—look how everybody is laughing at you.

These words convinced him to follow his companion's example. He told him, "May God be pleased with you. I have obtained relief and am no longer subject to imprisonment or becoming a laughing-stock." So, trust in God and come to your senses, as the man in the parable did. Put your trust in God so that you may be delivered from begging from creation and trembling in fear at each happening. Doing so will deliver you from self-conceit, being ridiculous, the pressures of this life, and the torments of the Hereafter.

Fourth point. Belief enables us to attain true humanity, to acquire a position above all other creatures. Thus, belief and worship are our most fundamental and important duties. Unbelief, by contrast, reduces us to the state of a brutal but very impotent beast.

A decisive proof for this truth is the difference between how human beings and animals come into existence. Almost from the very moment of birth, an animal seems to have been trained and to have perfected its faculties elsewhere. Within a few hours or days or months, it can lead its life according to its particular rules and conditions. A sparrow or a bee is inspired with the skill and ability to integrate into its environment within a matter of twenty days, while it would take a person twenty years to do so. This means that an animal's basic obligation and essential role does not include seeking perfection through learning, progress through scientific knowledge, or praying and petitioning for help by displaying its impotence. Rather, its sole purpose is to act within the bounds of its innate faculties, which is the mode of worship specified for animals.

People are born knowing nothing of life and their environment and so must learn everything. As we cannot do this even within twenty years, we must continue to learn until we die. We appear to have been sent here with so much weakness and inability that we might need two years to learn how to walk steadily. Only after fifteen years can we distinguish good and evil to a certain extent. Only by living in society can we become smart enough to choose between what is good and what is bad.

Thus the essential and intrinsic duty of our existence is to seek perfection through learning and to proclaim our worship of and servanthood to God through prayer and supplication. We should look for answers to such questions as, "Through whose compassion is my life so wisely administered? Through whose generosity am I being so affectionately trained? Through whose favors and benevolence am I being so solicitously nourished?" Then we should pray and petition the Provider of Needs in humble awareness of our needs, none of which we can satisfy on our own. This understanding and confession of our impotence and poverty will become two wings on which to fly to the highest rank: being a beloved servant of God.

And so our purpose here is to seek perfection through knowledge and prayer. Everything is, by its nature, essentially dependent on knowledge. The basis, source, light, and spirit of all true knowledge is knowledge of God, of which belief is the very foundation. After belief, prayer is our essential duty and the basis of worship, for despite our infinite impotence, we are exposed to endless misfortune and innumerable enemies. And despite our infinite poverty, we suffer limitless need and demands.

Children express their need for something they cannot reach with words or tears. Both are a sort of plea or prayer, in word or deed, in the tongue of weakness. Eventually, they get what they want. Similarly, we are quite like a beloved child, for at the Most Compassionate and Merciful Being's Court we either will weep (due to our weakness and impotence) or pray (due to our poverty and need) so that our need may be satisfied. In return, we should perform our duty of gratitude and thanksgiving for this provision. Otherwise, the ingratitude of those who claim to have so much intelligence and power over everything that they can meet their own needs finally will come to the point where they resemble mischievous children moaning about irritating flies despite their claim of absolute power. Such ingratitude is against our essential nature and makes us worthy of severe punishment.

Chapter 2

at-Tahara
(Cleanliness or Purification)

AT-TAHARA
(CLEANLINESS OR PURIFICATION)

Islam is based on five pillars: Bearing witness to God's Existence and Oneness and the Messengership of Muhammad, upon him be peace and blessings, praying five times a day, fasting during the month of Ramadan, paying the *Zakah* (the prescribed purifying alms), and performing the *Hajj* or pilgrimage. The first pillar includes all the essentials of belief which are discussed in the first book of this series.

The Importance of Cleanliness

Islam requires physical and spiritual cleanliness. On the physical side, Islam requires Muslims to clean their bodies, clothes, houses, and community, and they are rewarded by God for doing so. While people generally consider cleanliness desirable, Islam insists upon it and makes it indispensable to religious life.

Prophet Muhammad, upon him be peace and blessings, advised Muslims to appear neat and tidy in private and in public. Once when returning home from battle, he advised his army, "Soon you will meet your brothers, so tidy your saddles and clothes."[1] On another occasion he said, "If I had not been afraid of overburdening my community, I would have ordered them to use a *miswaq* (to brush and clean their teeth) for every prayer."[2] He also declared:

> Cleanliness is half of belief. Praising God (saying "All praise and gratitude are for God") fills the Balance. Glorifying and praising God (saying "All-Glorified is God, and all praise and gratitude are for God") fills what is between the heaven and earth. Prayer is a light, and charity is proof (of one's belief), and patience is

> brightness, and the Qur'an is evidence in favor of or against you. All people go out early in the morning and sell themselves, thereby either setting their selves free (to save them from Hellfire) or destroying them.[3]

Imam Ghazzali mentions four kinds of cleanliness:

> Physical cleanliness (of the body, clothes, and residence);
>
> Cleanliness of the bodily organs (from the sins committed by them);
>
> The cleanliness of the heart (from unbelief, association of partners with God, hypocrisy, and all evil moral qualities);
>
> The cleanliness of the innermost dimension of one's existence from attachment to anything other than God).[4]

Moral hygiene also was emphasized, for the Prophet, upon him be peace and blessings, encouraged Muslims to make a special prayer upon seeing themselves in the mirror, "God, You have endowed me with a good form; likewise bless me with an immaculate character."[5] He advised modest clothing for men as well as for women on the grounds that it helps one maintain purity of thought.

Being charitable is a way of purifying one's wealth. A Muslim who does not give charity (*sadaqa*) and pay the required annual *Zakah* (the prescribed alms), contaminates his or her wealth by hoarding that which rightfully belongs to others: *Of their wealth take alms so that you may purify them* (9:103).

All the laws and injunctions given by God and His Prophet, upon him be peace and blessings, are pure. Any law established by Divine guidance is just and pure.

The Purity of Water

Pure water is used essentially in matters of purification or *wudu'* (minor ablution) and *ghusl* (major ablution). Hence the necessity to investigate water's purity. Water has four essential attributes: smell, color, taste, and fluidity. Any water is judged according to these attributes.[6] As a result, water is classified into two categories: *mutlaq* and *muqayyad* water.

Mutlaq water is "natural" water, such as that which comes from rain water, snow, hail, sea water, and water from the Zamzam well.

It is subdivided as follows:

- Water that is both pure and purifying (e.g., rain water, snow, hail, sea water, water from the clean reservoirs and water from the Zamzam well).
- Used water: Water that drips from a person after he or she has washed any part of his or her body or performed the minor or major ablution, and therefore is considered used. It is considered pure, but cannot be used for another minor or major ablution, for God's Messenger forbade the spouses to wash with the water either used to be cleaned of canonical impurity.[7] Abu Hurayra also reported the Messenger to have said, "None of you must wash in standing water when he is in a state of canonical impurity."[8] Scholars inferred from these and similar *hadith*s that the water which has been used for minor or major ablution is no longer purifying afterwards.
- Leftover water: This is the *mutlaq* or natural water which remains in a pot after some has been drunk. It has some types:
    - Water that is both pure and purifying. This is the water from which a human being who has a clean mouth because he or she has not vomited or taken something impure such as alcohol, or from which a horse or an animal whose flesh is religiously edible has drunk.
    - Water which is both pure and purifying but whose usage is disliked (*makruh*) (e.g., water left in a container after a cat, birds of prey, or other "allowed" animals such as hens that eat filth, and donkeys, and mules have drunk from it). God's Messenger, upon him be peace and blessings, declared that cats are not impure,[9] and his wife 'A'isha, Mother of Believers, reports that the Messenger took ablution with the water from which a cat had drunk.[10]

- Water remaining in a pot after some of it has been drunk by a pig or a dog or wild animals such as lions and tigers is impure and must be avoided.[11]
- Water mixed with impure elements. A small amount of water whose taste, color, or smell has been altered by an impure substance cannot be used for purification. However, if the water is flowing water, or as much as about $0.7m^3$, or is still considered water, meaning that if the impure substance has not altered its taste, color, or smell, it can be used for purification. God's Messenger declared that any running water which carries away impurity,[12] or any water of at least two *qullas* (approximately $0.7m^3$) will not become impure.[13]

Muqayyad water includes naturally *muqayyad* water, such as fruit juices, and water that has been mixed with various substances (e.g., soap, saffron, flowers) or any objects that the Shari'a considers pure. Such water is considered pure until, due to being mixed with other substances, one can no longer call it water. In this case, the water is still considered pure, but it cannot be used for purification (minor and major ablution). If the water is mixed with any impure substance which changes its nature, then it is no longer pure and purifying. Abu Hurayra reports from God's Messenger that he forbade urinating into standing water (which is less than about $0.7m^3$), as it would no longer be purifying.[14]

Types of Impurities

Najasa refers to impure substances that Muslims must avoid and wash off after coming into contact with them. God says, *Keep your clothing clean!* (74:4) and, *God loves those who turn to Him in sincere repentance, and He loves those who cleanse themselves* (2:222).

- Animals that died naturally (e.g., not killed in the Islamic manner) are impure (5:3), as is anything cut off a live animal. God's Messenger declared that anything cut off a live animal is impure and cannot be eaten.[15] However, dead sea animals and those that have no flowing blood (e.g., bees and ants) are not impure.[16] The bones, horns, claws, fur, feathers, and skin of dead animals, except for pigs, are pure.[17] When asked about the forbidden foods, Ibn 'Abbas recited verse 5:3, and according to the report of Ibn Mundhir and Ibn Abi Hatem, added, "What is forbidden is the meat (of a dead animal). As for its skin, skin used for waterskins, teeth, bones, fur and wool, they are permissible."

- Any blood that flows from a person's or an animal's body (e.g., blood from a killed animal or menstrual blood) is impure (5:3; 6:145). However, blood that remains in the veins is permissible. Also, any blood that remains in edible meat, livers, hearts, and spleens is not impure, provided that the animal was sacrificed in the Islamic way.[18]
- A person's vomit, urine, excrement, *wadi* (a thick white secretion discharged after urination), *mazi* (a white sticky fluid that flows from the sexual organs when thinking about sexual intercourse, foreplay, and so on), prostatic fluid, and sperm is impure. However, according to some, based on a *hadith* reported by 'A'isha, Mother of Believers, sperm is not impure but should be washed off if it is still wet, and scratched off if it is dry.[19] Any part of human flesh is impure.
- The urine, saliva, and blood of all animals whose meat is prohibited, and the excrement of all animals except birds whose meat is allowable, are impure.
- The excrement of poultry (i.e., geese, hens, ducks) is impure. They are creatures that eat the waste of other living beings. Ibn 'Abbas reports that even God's Messenger forbade eating their meat.[20] However, if they are kept away from filth and other animals for three days and are given clean food to eat, their meat becomes permissible to eat.
- Pork and alcohol are impure.
- Dogs are considered impure. Any container that a dog has licked must be completely washed and sterilized. God's Messenger ordered it to be washed three times with the first or last

washing being with soil.[21] If a dog licks a pot that has dry food in it, what it touched and what surrounds it must be thrown away. The remainder may be kept, as it is still pure. A dog's hair is considered pure.

- The impurities mentioned are considered "gross impurity" (*najasat al-ghaliza*). Any amount of them contaminates whatever it touches. However, if it is on a person's body or clothes when he or she is praying, or on the ground or mat where he or she is praying, its amount is taken into consideration. Any solid filth weighing about four grams, and any liquid more than the amount that spreads over a person's palm, invalidates the prayer.
- The urine of horses and domestic or wild animals whose meat one is allowed to eat is "weak impurity" (*najasat al-khafifa*). When more than one fourth of a limb or one fourth of one's clothes are smeared with it, the prayer is invalidated.

Ways of Purification

Purifying the body and clothes. If these are contaminated, they must be washed with water until no impurity remains. Water is the basic element of purification. The Qur'an states, *He sent down water upon you from the sky, that thereby He might cleanse you (of all actual or ritual impurities, by enabling you to do the minor and major ablution)* (8:11). This is especially so if the impurity is visible, such as blood. If some stains remain after washing, such as those that would be extremely difficult to remove, they can be overlooked. If the impurity is not visible, such as urine, wash it away (three times) and then wring the clothing. If it cannot be wrung, then wait until the water is completely removed. Al-Bukhari ("Hayd," 9) and Muslim ("Tahara," 110) relates from Asma bint Abu Bakr that a woman came to the Prophet, upon whom be peace and blessings, and said, "Our clothes are contaminated with menstrual blood. What should we do about this?" He said, "Scrape it, rub it with water, pour water over it and then pray in it."

Purifying the ground. Purify the ground by pouring water over it. If the impurity is solid, the ground will become pure only by the removal or decay of the impurity. God's Messenger ordered keeping yards clean.[22] When a man from the desert urinated in the mosque, the Companions said, "Stop, stop!" However, the Messenger, upon him be peace and blessings, warned them, saying, "Do not interrupt him; leave him alone." They left him alone, and when he finished urinating, the Messenger told him, "These mosques are not places meant for urine and filth, but are only for the remembrance of God, prayer, and the recitation of the Qur'an." Then he told the Companions to pour a bucket of water to clean away the urine.[23] According to some narrations, he also ordered them to remove the contaminated part of the soil and pour water upon the place.[24]

Purification with soil. Soil is one of the elements of purification. Abu Hurayra reports God's Messenger to have said, "When one of you steps on some filth, soil will clean it."[25]

Purifying contaminated butter and similar substances. God's Messenger, upon him be peace and blessings, was asked regarding ghee (cooking butter) into which a mouse had fallen. He said, "Take out the mouse and throw away the ghee around it and use the rest."[26] If a dead animal has fallen into solid matter but has not swollen or disintegrated, whatever the corpse touches and what is around it must be thrown away, provided that one can make sure that it did not touch the rest of the matter. If it fell into a liquid substance, the majority say that the entire liquid becomes impure.[27]

Purifying a dead animal's skin. Tanning purifies a dead animal's skin and fur except those of pigs. The Prophet said, "If the animal's skin is tanned, it is purified."[28]

Purifying mirrors and similar objects. Mirrors, knives, swords, nails, bones, glass, painted pots, and other smooth surfaces that have no pores are purified by removing the impurity.

Chemical change purifies. For example, when alcohol changes into vinegar, it becomes pure.[29]

Useful Points

- If an unknown liquid falls on a person, there is no need to ask about it or to wash one's clothes.
- If a person finds something moist on his or her body or clothes at night and does not know what it is, he or she does not need to smell it in order to identify it.
- Clothes that have street mud on them do not have to be washed.
- If a person finishes praying and sees some previously unseen impurity on his or her clothes or body, or was aware of but forgot about it, his or her prayer does not have to be repeated.
- If a person cannot determine what part of his or her clothes contains the impurity, the whole garment should be washed, for "if an obligation can be fulfilled only by performing another related act, that act also becomes obligatory."
- If a person mixes pure clothes with impure clothes (and cannot tell them apart), he or she should investigate the matter and can pray once in one of the clothes.
- It is not proper to carry something that has God's Name upon it while going to the bathroom, unless he or she is afraid of losing it or having it stolen.
- One should not talk in the bathroom, respond to a greeting, or repeat what the *muadhdhin* is saying. One may speak if there is some necessity. In the event of sneezing, one should praise God silently by moving one's lips.[30]
- One should neither face nor turn one's back to the *qibla* while answering a call of nature, especially if in an open area.[31]
- When urinating, one should seek a soft and low piece of ground to protect against any impurity. One should also seek a place away from people. The Prophet said, "When one of you urinates, he should choose the proper place to do so."[32]
- One should avoid shaded places and places where people walk and gather. One should not answer a call of nature in bathing places or in still or running water either.[33] At-Tabarani reports

in his *al-Mu'jam al-Kabir* that God's Messenger strictly forbade troubling people.

- One should avoid urinating while standing, though some allow it in case of the inability to avoid doing so.[34]
- One must avoid any urine spattering one's clothes, clean oneself with water and dry oneself after relieving oneself, and remove any impurities from one's clothes and body.[35] This is called *istinja'* (seeking complete deliverance from dirt and trouble).
- One should not clean oneself with the right hand.[36]
- One should enter the bathroom with the left foot, saying, "I seek refuge in God from noxious male and female beings (devils)," and exit with one's right foot, saying, "O God, I seek your forgiveness."[37]
- One should remove any bad smell from one's hands after cleaning oneself.[38]
- After a man has relieved himself, he should wait until the urine stops completely and make sure that none of it has fallen onto his clothes. This is called *istibra* (seeking full purification). Ibn 'Abbas related that the Messenger of God, upon him be peace and blessings, passed by two graves and said, "They are being punished, but not for a great matter (on their part). One of them did not clean himself from urine, and the other used to spread slander."[39] To erase all doubt, a person should sprinkle his or her private parts and underwear with water.[40]

Acts That Correspond to Human Nature

God has chosen certain acts for all of His Prophets and their followers to perform. These acts, known as *sunan al-fitra* (acts required by human nature) and mentioned in some Prophetic Traditions,[41] are as follows:

Circumcision.[42] This prevents dirt from getting on one's penis and also makes it easy to keep clean. The Shafi'i scholars maintain that it should be done on the seventh day after birth, although it is permissible to do it later.

Shaving pubic hair and pulling out underarm hair. Doing so is *sunna*. However, it is enough to trim or pull it out.

Clipping fingernails, trimming and shaving the moustache, and keeping the beard tidy. A moustache should not be so long that food particles, drink, and dirt accumulate in it. If one grows a beard, it should not be untidy.

Honoring and combing one's hair. Abu Hurayra reported that the Prophet, upon whom be peace and blessings, said, "Whoever has hair should honor it."[43] Cutting one's hair off is permissible, and so is letting it grow if one honors it, that is, one combs it or keeps it tidy.

Leaving gray hairs in place. This applies to both men and women. 'Amr ibn Shu'ayb related, on the authority of his father from his grandfather, that the Prophet said, "Do not pluck the gray hairs, as they are a Muslim's light. A Muslim never grows gray in Islam except that God writes for him, due to that, a good deed, raises him a degree, and erases for him, due to that, one of his sins."[44]

Using a tooth-stick or toothbrush. God's Messenger, upon him be peace and blessings, said, "Were it not that I might overburden the believers, I would have ordered them to brush their teeth with *siwaq* for every Prayer."[45] This shows the importance of keeping the teeth clean.

Dyeing one's gray hair. According to the accepted opinion, dyeing one's gray hair with henna or yellow dye, and so on is permissible, provided that the dyes are religiously allowable.[46]

Using musk and other kinds of perfume. Using musk and other perfumes that are free of alcohol and similar forbidden things is highly advisable,[47] for they are pleasing to the soul and beautify the atmosphere. Women are not supposed to wear perfume outside the home or to the mosque.

Menstruation and Post-Childbirth Bleeding

Menses is a natural type of blood that flows at regular intervals from a woman's uterus after puberty. God has laid down certain rules in connection with this, as a concession to the woman, in consideration of her condition.

The menstrual flow usually lasts three to ten days and nights, varying from woman to woman. Most women have a regular number of days for their monthly menstrual period. The number of days may fluctuate and the period might come a little early or a little late. So when a woman sees her menstrual blood, she should consider that it is her menstrual period. When it stops, and after she has taken *ghusl*, she should consider herself clean. If more blood appears after her menstrual period has ended, but does not have the same color as menstrual blood, it should not be considered as menses. It is called *istihadha* (non-menstrual vaginal bleeding).

Post-childbirth bleeding is the blood that comes during and after childbirth. It may begin to come two or three days before delivery and be accompanied by labor pains. There is no minimum limit as to how long a woman will bleed, but generally the upper limit falls within forty days.

A woman is prohibited from performing certain acts during her menstrual period and post-childbirth bleeding. They are as follows:

- She cannot pray (*Salah*) after she begins to bleed.[48] She does not have to make up any prayers she missed when she was bleeding.
- She cannot observe any obligatory (Ramadan) or supererogatory fasts. She must make up the obligatory fasting days after regaining her ritual cleanliness. If bleeding begins during a supererogatory fasting day upon which she had intended to fast, she must stop fasting and make it up later. 'A'isha, Mother of Believers, explains, "We passed through this (period of menstruation during the Messenger's time), and we were ordered to make up the fasts, but were not ordered to make up the Prayers."[49]
- She can do all pilgrimage rites except circumambulating the Ka'ba (*tawaf*). 'A'isha, Mother of Believers, says, "I was menstruating when I reached Makka. So, I neither performed *tawaf* of the Ka'ba nor the *tawaf* between Safa and Marwa. Then I in-

formed God's Messenger about it. He replied, 'Perform all the ceremonies of *Hajj* like the other pilgrims, but do not perform *tawaf* of the Ka'ba till you get clean (from your menses).'"[50] Ibn 'Abbas reports, "God's Messenger decreed that a menstruating woman and the one who delivered a child should bathe, put on *ihram* and perform all the rites of *Hajj* except circumambulation of the House (Ka'ba)."[51]

- She should avoid mosques or places of worship, and cannot touch the Qur'an. She cannot recite it from memory, but can recite the verses of prayer and supplication with the intention of praying. (She cannot perform *Salah* but can supplicate and recite the prayers mentioned in the Qur'an with the intention of saying prayers or making supplications.) The Qur'an declares, *None except the purified ones can touch it* (56:79). God's Messenger declared that a woman in menses or post-childbirth bleeding could not recite the Qur'an.[52] Women stayed away from the places of Prayer while in these conditions.[53]
- A man cannot have sexual intercourse with his wife while she is having her menstrual period or having post-childbirth bleeding, for she is not allowed to make herself available to him. The Qur'an declares, *They also ask you about (the injunctions concerning) menstruation. Say: "It is a state of hurt (and ritual impurity), so keep away from them during their menstruation and do not approach them until they are cleansed. When they are cleansed, then (you can) go to them inasmuch as God has commanded you (according to the urge He has placed in your nature, and within the terms He has enjoined upon you). Surely God loves those who turn to Him in sincere repentance (of past sins and errors), and He loves those who cleanse themselves* (2:222). However, a man can kiss, hug, or touch his wife anywhere except the pubic region.[54] It is better and highly advisable to avoid the area between the navel and the knees.[55]

When a menstruating woman stops bleeding, she must perform a complete *ghusl* (major ablution).[56] After this, she must resume praying and fasting, can enter the mosque, make *tawaf*, recite the Qur'an, and engage in allowable sexual intercourse. She must make up the fasting days that she missed during Ramadan, but not the Prayers. The same rules apply to women in post-childbirth bleeding.

Istihadha (Non-Menstrual Vaginal Bleeding)

In some women, bleeding never stops; in others, it continues for longer than normal. This blood is called *istihadha*. Likewise, any blood coming before puberty and after menopause is also considered *istihadha*.

A woman with this condition should calculate when her period would normally end, and then stop praying during the days of her calculated period and follow all of the other menstruation-related rules. For the rest of the days, her bleeding should be treated as *istihadha*. If she does not have a regular period or does not remember when it used to occur, but can distinguish between the two kinds of blood based on color, thickness, and smell (i.e., menstrual blood is dark, thick, and has a strong odor, while *istihadha* is bright red, thin, and less disagreeable in smell), she must act accordingly. If she does not have a regular period and cannot distinguish between the two types of blood, she must consider the blood coming for three to ten days every month as menses and calculate it from the time she first noticed her vaginal bleeding.

There is no difference between a woman beset by *istihadha* and one who has a complete cessation of menstrual flow, except as follows:

- If the first woman wants to perform *wudu'* (ritual ablution), she should wash the blood from her vaginal area and then apply a menstrual pad or wrap the area with a clean rag on top of a wad of cotton to catch the blood. Any blood coming out after that is of no account.[57]
- She must perform *wudu'* for every obligatory prayer.[58]

Ghusl (Major Ablution)

Ghusl means major canonical ablution or a complete washing of the body. It is obligatory after sexual intercourse (Qur'an, 5:6), even if only the head of the penis disappears into the vagina,[59] after any discharge of semen,[60] and after the completion of menses and post-childbirth bleeding. The Qur'an declares, *And if you are in the state of major ritual impurity (requiring total ablution), purify yourselves completely (by taking a bath)* (5:6), and, *When they (menstruating women) are cleansed, then (you can) go to them inasmuch as God has commanded you ....* (2:222). Umm Sulaym came to God's Messenger and said, "Surely God is not ashamed of (telling you) the truth. Is it necessary for a woman to take a bath after she has a wet dream?" The Prophet replied, "Yes, if she notices a discharge." Umm Salama, Mother of Believers, covered her face and asked, "O Messenger of God! Does a woman get a discharge?" He replied, "Yes, may you achieve goodness, and that is why the son resembles his mother."[61] If one has a wet dream but does not find any traces of ejaculation, there is no need for *ghusl*.[62] If ejaculation occurs owing to such other causes as lifting a heavy thing or cold, without any stimulation, *ghusl* is not needed then either.

Taking *ghusl* every Friday before the congregational Prayer is highly advisable, for the Prophet always did so.[63] Before beginning *ghusl*, one should make the intention to perform it to be purified of canonical impurity and, if one will pray after performing it, also to perform the Prayer. It is also a *sunna* act to take *ghusl* before putting on the *Hajj* attire and beginning to stay (*waqfa*) in 'Arafat until sunset on the ninth of *Dhulhijja* during the *Hajj*.

Things Forbidden to a Ritually Impure Person

People who are in this state cannot perform Prayer,[64] fast,[65] do *tawaf*,[66] enter a place of worship unless necessary,[67] or recite the Qur'an or touch it or any of its verses except with a clean cloth or something similar.[68]

What Makes One's Ghusl Valid?

- Rinsing the mouth thoroughly so that it is cleaned properly.
- Rinsing the nose right up to the nasal bone.
- Washing all bodily parts thoroughly, including the hair.

The order, "purify yourselves completely" in the verse, *And if you are in the state of major ritual impurity (requiring total ablution), purify yourselves completely (by taking a bath)* (5:6), and the Prophetic Traditions, "Pour water over yourselves",[69] and "Rinsing the mouth and nose is obligatory for a ritually impure person,"[70] led the Hanafi scholars particularly to regard rinsing the mouth and nose as among the obligatory acts of *ghusl*.

The best way to perform *ghusl* is as follows:

- Having the intention (*niyyah*) to cleanse the body from (ritual) impurity while washing oneself.
- Washing the hands up to the wrists three times.
- Washing the private parts thoroughly.
- Removing all filth from all bodily parts.
- Performing ablution. Rinsing the mouth and nose particularly three times.
- Washing all bodily parts three times, including the hair thoroughly. No part, even the size of a pinpoint, is allowed to remain dry. Rubbing and pressing the body is not obligatory. However, women are not obliged to unbraide their hair; provided the hair is washed .[71]

Tayammum (Ablution with Clean Soil)

When a person is too sick to use water or the water is too cold to use or there is no water around when it is time to pray, he or she can perform *tayammum* in place of *wudu'* and *ghusl*. The Qur'an declares:

> And if you are in the state of major ritual impurity (requiring total ablution), purify yourselves (by taking a bath). But if you are ill, or on a journey, or if any of you has just satisfied a want

> of nature, or if you have had contact with women, and can find no water, then betake yourselves to pure earth, passing with it lightly over your face and your hands (and forearms up to and including the elbows). God does not will to impose any hardship upon you, but wills to purify you (of any kind of material and spiritual filth), and to complete His favor upon you, so that you may give thanks (from the heart, and in speech and action by fulfilling His commandments). (5:6)

The requirements are as follows:

- Intending to perform *tayammum* to remove any impurity.
- Striking the pure soil lightly with the palms of both hands and passing the palms over the face one time.
- Striking the pure soil again with one's palms and rubbing the right and left arms alternately from the fingertips to the elbows.[72]

Tayammum is nullified as soon as the cause for performing it is removed (i.e., the sick person recovers or pure water is found). If a person performs *tayammum* and then prays, he or she does not have to repeat the Prayer if the conditions for it are removed before the time for that particular prayer ends. Abu Sa'id reports that two people went on a journey. When the time of a Prayer came, they could not find any water and did *tayammum*. However, later they found water before the time of the Prayer ended. One of them did not repeat the Prayer, while the other did. When they were back home, they told God's Messenger about what they had done. The Messenger told the one who had not repeated the Prayer, "You acted according to the *Sunna*," and the other, "There are double rewards for you."[73]

Wudu' (Ablution)

Wudu' is a very virtuous act of worship. Nu'aym Al-Mujmir relates:

> Once I went behind the Mosque, along with Abu Hurayra. He performed ablution and said, "I heard the Prophet say, 'On the

> Day of Resurrection, my followers will be called those with shining faces and radiant hands and feet from the trace of ablution. Whoever can increase the area of his radiance should do so (i.e. by performing ablution regularly)."[74]

Abu Hurayra reports:

> God's Messenger, upon him be peace and blessings, said, "Shall I suggest to you that by which God obliterates the sins and elevates the ranks (of a person)." They (the hearers) said, "Yes, O Messenger of God." He said, "Performing the ablution thoroughly despite odds, taking more steps towards the mosque, and waiting for the next Prayer after observing a Prayer, and that is mindfulness (like the mindfulness of a warrior on guard in God's cause); that is mindfulness."[75]

Wudu' involves, in its obligatory acts, washing with water at least once the usually exposed bodily parts, namely, the face, hands and arms up to (and including) the elbows, and feet, and wiping one quarter of the head.[76] It is obligatory before any obligatory or supererogatory Prayer, circumambulating the Ka'ba, and touching the Qur'an with bare hands.

Wudu' is performed in the following manner:

- Ensure that the water to be used is pure, and use it economically.
- Intend to perform *wudu'* to offer Prayer, if you plan to pray after taking it.
- Recite, "*Bismillahir-Rahmanir-Rahim*" (i.e., in the Name of God, the All-Merciful, the All-Compassionate).
- Wash the hands up to the wrists three times, and do not miss the parts between the fingers.
- Clean your mouth with a brush or a finger, and gargle with water three times.
- Rinse the nostrils with water three times.
- Wash the face from the forehead to the chin and from ear to ear three times.

- Wash the right arm followed by the left up to the elbows three times.
- Wipe at least a quarter of the head with wet hands, pass the wet tips of the little fingers inside and the wet tips of the thumbs outside the ears, and pass the palms over the nape and sides of the neck.
- Finally, wash the feet up to (and including) the ankles, the right foot first and then the left, taking care to wash in between the toes, each three times.[77]

The following acts nullify *wudu'*:

- Whatever comes out from the two private parts (front and back): waste matter, urine, wind, *wadi* (a thick white secretion discharged after urination), *mazi* (a white, sticky fluid that flows from the sexual organs when thinking about sexual intercourse or foreplay, and so on), and prostatic fluid.[78] Semen, menstrual blood, and post-childbirth blood require *ghusl*.
- Emission of blood, pus, or yellow matter from a wound, boil, pimple, or something similar to such an extent that it flows beyond the wound's mouth.[79]
- Vomiting a mouthful of matter.[80]
- Physical contact for pleasure between men and women without any obstacle (e.g., clothes). Simple contact or kissing does not invalidate *wudu'* according to the Hanafis.[81] If the head of a man's penis disappears into a woman's vagina, *ghusl* is required for both man and woman.
- Loss of consciousness through sleep, drowsiness, and so on.[82]
- Temporary insanity, fainting, hysteria, or intoxication.[83]
- Audible laughter during the Prayer. God's Messenger, upon him be peace and blessings, said, "One among you who laughs loudly during their Prayer should repeat both their ablution and Prayer."[84]

Wiping Over Clean, Indoor Boots (Khuffayn)

While performing ***wudu'***, one can wipe over (the top of) clean, indoor boots once with wet hands instead of washing the feet. Several companions of God's Messenger, upon him be peace and blessings, such as 'Ali ibn Abi Talib, Mughira ibn Shu'ba, and Safwan ibn 'Assal reported that the Messenger wore indoor boots and wiped over them with wet hands during ablution.[85]

- The boots should be waterproof and cover the whole foot up to (and including) the ankles. They must have no holes wider than three fingers in width. It does not matter if their mouths are so wide that the feet can be seen when looking down at them.
- They must fit, and be strong, and tough enough so that they should allow no water into them, and the feet do not come out of them, and they should not fall apart when walked in for three miles.
- They cannot be made out of wood, glass, or metal.
- One must put on the boots after washing one's feet while performing ablution. One can wear them for a whole day if one is resident. If traveling, one can wear them for three consecutive days.[86]

CHAPTER 3

as-Salah (The Prayer)

AS-SALAH (THE PRAYER)

The Prayer is the most important type of worship, for it displays a person's sincerity and loyalty to God. God ordered it to all the communities of humankind through the Prophets (Qur'an, 2:83; 10:87; 11:87; 14:37, 40; 20:14; 21:72–73; 31:17).

The Qur'an orders and encourages the Prayer in many of its verses, such as 2:238; 4:103; 7:205; 22:78, and 98:5. For example, it says:

> Establish the Prayer (O Messenger) at the beginning and the end of the day, and in the watches of the night near to the day. Surely good deeds wipe out evil deeds. This is advice, and a reminder for the mindful who reflect. (11:114)

It also declares:

> Recite and convey to them what is revealed to you of the Book, and establish the Prayer in conformity with its conditions. Surely, the Prayer restrains from all that is indecent and shameful, and all that is evil. Surely God's remembrance is the greatest (of all types of worship, and not restricted to the Prayer). God knows all that you do. (29:45)

God's Messenger says that the Prayer is the pillar or main support of religious life.[1] Abu Hurayra narrates:

> I heard God's Messenger saying, "If there was a river at the door of anyone of you and he took a bath in it five times a day, would you notice any dirt on him?" They said, "Not a trace of dirt would be left." The Prophet added, "That is the example of the five Prayers with which God blots out sins."[2]

God's Messenger also says, "God, the Almighty, has made five Prayers obligatory. If anyone performs ablution for them well, offers them at their (right) time, and observes perfectly their bowing and submissiveness in them, it is the guarantee of God that He will pardon him; if anyone does not do so, there is no guarantee for him on the part of God; He may pardon him if He wills, and punish him if He wills."[3]

Abu Hurayra reports from the Messenger, "The first thing for which the people will be called to account out of their actions on the Day of Judgment is the Prayer. Our Lord, the Almighty, will say to the angels—though He knows better, 'Look into the Prayer of My servant and see whether he (or she) has offered it perfectly or imperfectly.' If it is perfect, that will be recorded perfect. If it is defective, He will say, 'See if there are some optional (supererogatory) Prayers offered by My servant.' If there are optional Prayers to his (or her) credit, He will say: 'Compensate the obligatory Prayer by the optional Prayer for My servant.' Then all the actions will be considered similarly."[4]

The Prayer's Meaning and Importance

"The prescribed Prayers (*Salah*) are Islam's pillars. To fully understand their importance, and with what little expense they are gained, and how foolish and at what great loss is the person who neglects them, consider this parable: A ruler gives each of his two servants twenty-four gold coins and sends them to settle on one of his beautiful farms that is two months' journey away. He tells them, 'Use this money to buy your ticket, your supplies, and what you will need after you arrive. After traveling for a day, you will reach a transit station. You can proceed from there either by car or by train or by ship or by plane. You can choose one according to your capital.'

"The servants leave. One spends only a little money before reaching the station. He uses his money so wisely that his master increases it a thousandfold. The other servant gambles away twenty-three of the twenty-four coins before reaching the station. The first servant advises the second one, "Use this coin to buy your ticket, or else you'll have to walk and suffer hunger. Our master is generous. Maybe he'll forgive you. Maybe you can take a plane, so we can reach the farm in a day. If not, you'll have to go on foot and endure two months of hunger and loneliness while crossing the desert." If he ignores his friend's advice, and instead of buying a ticket, which is like the key to a treasury, spends his remaining one coin on passing pleasures, anyone can understand how foolish and senseless he is.

"Now, those of you who do not pray, as well as you, my soul that is not inclined toward the Prayer. The ruler is our Lord, our Creator. One servant represents religious people who pray with fervor; the other represents people who do not like to pray. The twenty-four coins are the twenty-four hours of a day. The farm is Paradise, the transit station is the grave, and the journey is human life from birth to the grave, and therefrom to eternal life. People cover the part of the journey from the grave at different times according to their deeds and reverence for and obedience to God. Some of the truly devout pass, in a day, one thousand years like lightning, while others pass, like imagination, fifty thousand years. The Qur'an alludes to this truth in 22:47 and 70:4.

"The ticket is the prescribed Prayers. What a great loss one suffers who spends twenty-three hours a day on this brief, worldly life and does not reserve the remaining hour for the prescribed Prayers, and to what extent he or she wrongs himself or herself; how unreasonably he or she behaves. Would not anyone who considers himself or herself to be sensible understand how contrary to reason and wisdom and how far from good sense it will be, if, considering it reasonable, one uses half of one's money for a lottery being played by a thousand people and in which the possibility of winning is 1:1,000, but he does not spend one twenty-fourth part of it on an eternal, inexhaustible treasure where the possibility of winning has been confirmed to be ninety-nine out of a hundred?

"Prayer comforts the soul, the heart, and the mind, and is not burdensome or trying for the body. Furthermore, if we pray regularly, correct, sincere intention transforms our daily deeds and conduct into worship. Thus, our short lifetime is spent for the sake of eternal life in the other world, and our transient life gains a kind of permanence."[5]

The prescribed Prayer is the pillar of the religious life and the best of good deeds. One who does not perform it cannot construct the building of the Religion on the foundation of faith. Any foundation on which a building was not built is liable to removal. The Messenger, upon him be peace and blessings, taught that it is like a river running by one's house. One who bathes in it five times a day is cleaned of all dirt (which may have smeared him or her during the periods between them). He also taught that the prescribed Prayers can serve as an atonement for the minor sins committed between them.[6]

The Qur'an declares that the prescribed Prayer prevents one from committing indecencies and other kinds of evil deeds (29:45). Also, it serves as repentance and asking God for forgiveness. Similarly, any good deed done just after an evil one may cause it to be forgiven. So it is highly advisable that one should do good immediately after doing an evil deed. Like the prescribed Prayer, this manner of action may also restrain one from doing further evil.

The Prayer seems to be a strenuous demand, but in reality gives indescribable peace and comfort. Those who pray recite *ashhadu an la ilaha illa'llah* (I bear witness that there is no deity but God). Only God Almighty can give harm and benefit. He is the All-Wise, Who does nothing useless; the All-Compassionate, Whose mercy and bounty are abundant and encompass the whole creation. Having faith, believers see in every event a door to the wealth of God's Mercy, and knock on it via supplication. Realizing that their Lord and Sustainer controls everything, they take refuge in Him. Putting their trust in and fully submitting to God, they resist evil. Their faith gives them complete confidence.

As with every good action, courage arises from faith in and loyal devotion to God. As with every bad action, cowardice arises from misguidance. If the earth were to explode, those servants of God with truly illuminated hearts would not be frightened—they might even consider it a marvel of the Eternally-Besought's Power. Yet, a rationalist but nonbelieving philosopher might tremble at the sight of a comet, lest it should strike the earth.

Our ability to meet our endless demands is negligible. We are threatened with afflictions that our own strength cannot withstand. Our strength is limited to what we can reach, yet our wishes and demands, suffering and sorrow, are as wide as our imagination.

Anyone not wholly blind to the truth understands that our best option is to submit to God, to worship, believe, and have confidence in Him. A safe road is preferable to a dangerous one, even one with a very low probability of safe passage. The way of belief leads one safely to endless bliss with near certainty; the way of unbelief and transgression, meanwhile, is not profitable and has a near certainty of endless loss. Even its travelers agree on this truth, as do countless experts and people of insight and observation.

In conclusion, just like the other world's bliss, happiness in this world depends upon submitting to God and being His devoted servant. So always praise Him, saying, "Praise be to God for obedience and success on His way," and thank Him that we are His believing and worshipping servants.

Kinds of Prayer

There are several kinds of Prayer, as follows:

- *Obligatory* (*fard*). The five daily prescribed Prayers and the *Jumu'a* (Friday congregational) Prayer. The latter is not obligatory for women, but they can pray it if they wish. The funeral Prayer is obligatory, but not upon every individual. If some people in the community perform it, others do not have to.
- *Necessary* (*wajib*). The *'Iyd* (religious festive days) Prayers and the *witr* Prayer (performed after the late evening or night Prayer at any time until dawn).

- *Sunna* (those performed or advised by the Prophet). Those performed before or after the daily prescribed Prayers, *tahajjud* (performed after the late evening Prayer and before the *witr* Prayer), *tarawih* (performed after the late evening Prayer during Ramadan), *khusuf* and *kusuf* (performed during solar and lunar eclipses), and the Prayer for rain (*salatu'l-istisqa'*).
- *Supererogatory* or *optional*. *Salat al-ishraq* (performed some three quarters of an hour after sunrise), *salat ad-duha* (forenoon or broad daylight Prayer, performed until some three quarters of an hour before the noon Prayer), and *salat al-awwabin* (performed between the evening and late evening Prayers). There are some other supererogatory prayers, such as *salat at-tawba* (performed before asking God to forgive us), *salat al-istikhara* (performed to ask God to make something good for us), *salat at-tasbih* (the Prayer of glorifying God), the Prayer performed when leaving on a journey, and the Prayer performed when returning from a journey.

Who must pray?

The Prayer is obligatory upon every sane Muslim who has reached the age of puberty. Only women having their menstrual period or post-childbirth bleeding do not perform it. Prepubescent children do not have to pray, but God's Messenger, upon him be peace and blessings, advises us to tell them to pray when they reach the age of seven in order to prepare their hearts for it.[7]

The Times of the Five Daily Prescribed Prayers

Every sane, adult Muslim must perform the five daily prescribed Prayers each within its own time. The Qur'an mentions these times. For example:

> Establish the Prayer at the beginning and the end of the day, and in the watches of the night near to the day. Surely good

> deeds wipe out evil deeds. This is advice, and a reminder for the mindful who reflect. (11:114)
>
> Establish the Prayer in conformity with its conditions, from the declining of the sun to the darkness of the night, and (be ever observant of) the recitation of the Qur'an at dawn (the dawn Prayer). Surely the recitation of the Qur'an at dawn is witnessed (by the angels and the whole creation awakening to a new day). (17:78)
>
> Therefore, be patient with whatever they say, and glorify your Lord with praise before sunrise and before sunset, and glorify Him during some hours of the night—as well as glorifying (Him) at the ends of the day—so that you may obtain God's good pleasure and be contented (with what God has decreed for you). (20:130)
>
> So glorify God when you enter the evening and when you enter the morning—and (proclaim that) all praise and gratitude in the heavens and on the earth are for Him—and in the afternoon, and when you enter the noon time. (30:17–18)

These verses circumscribe the five prescribed Prayers. The Prayers to be established at the sides of the day, at its beginning and end from the declining of the sun to the darkness of night, are the noon and afternoon Prayers. The original word for "watches of night near to the day" is *zulaf*, which is plural. In Arabic, plural includes at least three things, so it can be concluded that it refers to the three Prayers to be established during the night (i.e., the evening, late evening, and dawn [early morning] Prayers). These five Prayers were prescribed for Muslims during the Messenger's Ascension in the eleventh year of his Messengership.[8]

Verse 17:78 also alludes to the daily five prescribed Prayers and each one's time. *Declining of the sun* means the sun's passing its zenith, and therefore refers to the noon Prayer. After the noon Prayer comes the afternoon Prayer. Immediately after sunset and after night has fallen, the evening and late evening Prayers are performed, respectively. The verse specifically mentions the dawn Prayer because of its importance, and draws attention to reciting the Qur'an during it, for the Messenger, under Divine Revelation, used to lengthen his recitation during that Prayer.

Concerning the times of the daily five Prayers, God's Messenger explained:

> (The Archangel) Gabriel (upon him be peace) led me in prayer at the House (i.e., the Ka'ba). He prayed the noon Prayer with me when the sun passed its zenith to the extent of the thong of a sandal; he prayed the afternoon Prayer with me when the shadow of everything was as long as itself; he prayed the evening Prayer with me when one who is fasting breaks the fast; he prayed the night Prayer with me when the twilight ended; and he prayed the dawn Prayer with me when food and drink become forbidden to one who is keeping the fast.
>
> On the following day he prayed the noon Prayer with me when the shadow of everything was as long as itself; he prayed the afternoon Prayer with me when the shadow of everything was twice as long as itself; he prayed the evening Prayer at the time when one who is fasting breaks the fast; he prayed the night Prayer with me when about a third of the night passed; and he prayed the dawn Prayer with me when there was a fair amount of light.[9]

According to another report from God's Messenger, upon him be peace and blessings, the Messenger performed the evening Prayer when the twilight had almost ended.[10] According to these and similar other *hadiths*, as well as the practice of the Prophet and his Companions, the time of each Prayer is as follows:

- The *fajr* (dawn or early morning) Prayer is performed from the break of dawn until sunrise.
- The *zuhr* (noon) Prayer is performed when the sun passes its zenith until a person's shadow is the same length as his or her height.
- The *'asr* (afternoon) Prayer is performed when a person's shadow is the same length as his or her height and continues until the yellowing of the sun.
- The *maghrib* (evening) Prayer is performed as long as twilight lasts following the sunset. However, when the *hadith* quoted

above, in which Gabriel led the Prayers, is considered, it is greatly preferred to perform the evening Prayer as early as possible when the sun has just set.

- The *'isha'* (night) Prayer begins when twilight completely ends and darkness has utterly fallen, and continues until a short while before the break of dawn, based on the *hadith* related by Muslim that "There is no negligence in sleeping, but the negligence lies in not performing a Prayer until the time of the next Prayer has come."[11] This *hadith* shows that the time of every Prayer continues until the beginning of the time for the next one, except for the dawn or early morning Prayer, as all scholars agree that its time lasts only until sunrise.
- The *Jumu'a* Prayer is performed during the time of the noon Prayer on Friday. The time of the *'Iyd* (religious festive days) Prayers is some three quarters of an hour after sunrise on *'Iyd* days. Their time continues until the sun reaches its zenith.

The Times When Prayers Cannot Be Performed

- During sunrise and sunset.
- From sunrise until the sun has completely risen to the length of a spear above the horizon (approximately three quarters of an hour after sunrise).
- When the sun is at its zenith until it moves slightly to the west.
- After the time for the afternoon Prayer till the sun sets.[12]

However, if one has not been able to perform the afternoon Prayer during its time, one can perform it until the sun begins to disappear in the west.

Praying in the Polar or Similar Regions

God's Messenger, upon him be peace and blessings, said, "The Dajjal will stay in the world for forty days. But his first day will be like one year, his second day one month, his third day one week, the rest of his days will be like your days." The Companions asked, "O

God's Messenger, would one day's Prayer suffice for the Prayers of one day equal to one year?" The Messenger answered, "No, but you must make an estimate of time (and then observe the Prayer)." Based on this *hadith*, the scholars concluded that those living in the polar or similar regions where days and nights are much longer than normal days and nights in most of the world or the time of a Prayer does not occur, should make an estimate of time considering the times of the Prayers in other regions where every day is twenty-four hours, and perform the Prayers.[13]

Combining the Two Prayers

Every Prayer is and must be performed during its own time. However, it is unanimously agreed by the scholars that during the pilgrimage, God's Messenger, upon him be peace and blessings, performed the noon and afternoon Prayers together in 'Arafat during the time of the noon Prayer, and the evening and night Prayers together in al-Muzdalifa during the time of the night Prayer.[14] *Iqama* (i.e., the call which announces that the obligatory Prayer is about to begin) is made before each Prayer.

Based on certain *hadiths*,[15] there are some scholars who are of the opinion that when in a hurry during a journey or due to some pressing need, it is permissible to combine the noon and afternoon Prayers, and the evening and night Prayers during the time of either. However, 'Abdullah ibn Mas'ud says that he did not see God's Messenger perform a Prayer save during its own time except that during the *Hajj*, he combined the noon and afternoon Prayers in 'Arafat, and the evening and night Prayers in al-Muzdalifa.[16] Therefore, the Hanafi scholars say that the Messenger did not combine any of these two Prayers, but while in a hurry during journeying or due to some pressing need, he postponed the noon and evening Prayers until the final end of the time of each, and performed the afternoon and night Prayers just at the beginning of the time of each. They are insistent that except in 'Arafat and al-Muzdalifa during the *Hajj*, any two Prayers cannot be combined.

The Meaning of Different Prayer Times[17]

Each Prayer time is the opening of a significant turning point, a mirror to the Divine acts of disposal as well as the universal Divine bounties therein. We are told to pray at those specific times to give more adoration and glory to the All-Powerful One of Majesty, and to give more thanks for the bounties accumulated between any two periods. To comprehend this subtle and profound meaning a little better, consider these five points:

First point. Each Prayer stands for praising, glorifying, and feeling grateful to God. We glorify Him by saying *subhana'llah* (All-Glorified is God) by word and action in awareness of His Majesty or Glory. We exalt and magnify Him by saying *Allahu akbar* (God is the All-Great) through word and action in awareness of His Perfection. We offer thanks to Him by saying *al-hamdu li'llah* (All praise and gratitude are for God) with our heart, tongue, and body, in awareness of His Grace. From this, we conclude that the heart of Prayer consists of glorification, exaltation, praise, and thanksgiving. Thus, these three phrases are present in all words and actions of those who pray. Further, following each Prayer, they are repeated thirty-three times each to confirm and complete the Prayer's objectives. The meaning of the Prayer is pronounced consecutively with these concise utterances.

Second point. We are God's servants. Aware of our defects, weakness, and poverty in the Divine presence, we prostrate in love and awe before His Lordship's perfection, His Divine Might on which every creature relies, and His Divine Compassion. Just as His Lordship's sovereignty demands devotion and obedience, His Holiness requires us to see our defects and seek His pardon, to proclaim that He has no defect, that the false judgments of the ignorant are meaningless, and that He is beyond all the failings of His creatures.

His Might's Perfection requires that, realizing our weakness and the helplessness of all creatures, we proclaim, "God is the All-Great" in admiration and amazement before the majesty of the Eternally Besought One's works. Bowing humbly, we are to seek refuge in Him and place our trust in Him. His Compassion's boundless treasury demands that we declare our need and that of all creatures by praying and asking for His help, and that we proclaim His blessings through praise and gratitude by uttering *al-hamdu li'llah*. In short, the Prayer's words and actions comprise all these meanings, and so were ordered and arranged by God.

Third point. Each person is a miniature of the universe. In the same way, the Qur'an's first *sura* (chapter), *Surat al-Fatiha*, is an illumined miniature of the whole Book, and the Prayer is a bright index involving all ways of worship, a sacred map hinting at the diverse kinds of worship practiced by all living entities.

Fourth point. The consecutive divisions of day and night, as well as the years and phases of our life, function like a huge clock's wheels and levers. For example:

The time for *fajr* (before sunrise) may be likened to spring's birth, the moment when sperm takes refuge in the protective womb, or to the first of the six consecutive "days" during which the earth and the heavens were created. It recalls how God disposes His Power and acts in such times and events. The time for *zuhr* (just past midday) may be likened to the completion of adolescence, the middle of summer, or the period of humanity's creation in the world's lifetime. It also points to God's compassionate manifestations and abundant blessings in those events and times.

The time for *'asr* (afternoon) resembles autumn, old age, and the time of the Last Prophet (the Age of Happiness). It calls to mind the Divine acts and the All-Compassionate's favors in them. The time for *maghrib* (sunset or evening) reminds us of many creatures' decline at the end of autumn and also of our own death. It thus forewarns us of the world's destruction at the Resurrection's beginning, teaches us how to understand the manifestation of God's Majesty, and wakes us from a deep sleep of neglect.

The time for *'isha'* (nightfall or late evening) calls to mind the world of darkness, veiling all daytime objects with its black shroud, and winter covering the dead earth's surface with its white shroud. It brings to mind the remaining works of the dead being forgotten, and points to this testing arena's inevitable, complete decline. Thus, *'isha'* proclaims the awesome acts of the Overpowering One of Majesty. Night reminds us of winter, the grave, the Intermediate World, and how much our spirit needs the All-Merciful One's Mercy. The late-night *tahajjud* Prayer reminds and warns us of how necessary this Prayer's light will be in the grave's darkness. By recalling the True Bestower's infinite bounties granted during these extraordinary events, it proclaims how worthy He is of praise and thanks.

The next morning points to the morning following the Resurrection. Just as morning follows night and spring comes after winter, so the morning of the Resurrection or "spring" follows the intermediate life of the grave.

We understand that each appointed Prayer time is the beginning of a vital turning point and a reminder of greater revolutions or turning points in the universe's life. Through the awesome daily disposals of the Eternally Besought One's Power, the Prayer times remind us of the Divine Power's miracles and the Divine Mercy's gifts regardless of time and place. So the prescribed Prayers, which are an innate duty, the basis of worship, and an unquestionable obligation, are most appropriate and fitted for these times.

Fifth point. We are created weak, yet everything involves, affects, and saddens us. We have no power, yet are afflicted by calamities and enemies. We are extremely poor, yet have many needs. We are indolent and incapable, yet the burden of life is very heavy. Being human, we are connected with the rest of the world, yet what we love and are familiar with disappears, and the resulting grief causes us pain. Our mentality and senses inspire us toward glorious objectives and eternal gains, but we are unable, impatient, powerless, and have only a short lifetime.

Given all of this, several things become quite clear:

The *fajr* Prayer is essential, for we must present a petition before the day's activities begin. Through prayer and supplication, we must beseech the Court of an All-Powerful One of Majesty, an All-Compassionate One of Grace, for success and help. Such support is necessary to bear and endure the troubles and burdens waiting for us.

The *zuhr* Prayer is essential, for this is when the day starts to move forward to complete its course. People take a break from their activities. The spirit needs a pause from the heedlessness and insensibility caused by hard work, and Divine bounties are fully manifest. Praying at this time is good, necessary, agreeable, and proper. This Prayer gives relief from the pressures of daily life and heedlessness. We stand humbly in the presence of the Real Bestower of blessings, express gratitude, and pray for His help. We bow to demonstrate our helplessness before His Glory and Might, and prostrate to proclaim our wonder, love, and humility before His everlasting Perfection and matchless Grace.

The *'asr* Prayer resembles and recalls the sad season of autumn, the mournful state of old age, and the distressing period at the end of time. The day's tasks are brought toward completion, and the Divine bounties received that day (e.g., health, safety, and good service in the cause of God) have accumulated to form a great total. It is also the time when the sun fades away, proving that everything is impermanent. We, who long for eternity, are created for it and show reverence for favors received, are also saddened by separations. So we stand up, perform *wudu'* (ablution), and pray.

Thus, praying *'asr* is an exalted duty, an appropriate service, a reasonable way of paying a debt of gratitude, and an agreeable pleasure. We acquire peace of mind and find true consolation and ease of spirit by supplicating at the Eternal Court of the Everlasting, the Eternally Self-Subsistent One, and by seeking refuge in His infinite Mercy, offering thanks and praise for His countless bounties, bowing humbly before His Lordship's might and glory, and prostrating humbly before His Eternal Divinity.

Evening reminds us of winter's beginning, the sad farewells of summer and autumn creatures, and our sorrowful separation from loved ones through death. The sun's lamp is extinguished, and the earth's inhabitants will migrate to the other world following this one's destruction. It is also a severe warning for those who adore transient, ephemeral beloveds, each of whom will die.

By its nature, the human spirit longs for Eternal Beauty. During this Prayer, it turns toward the Eternal Being, Who creates and shapes everything, Who commands huge heavenly bodies. At this time, the human spirit refuses to rely on anything finite and cries *Allahu akbar* (God is the All-Great). Then, in His presence, we say *alhamdu li'llah* (All praise and gratitude are for God) to praise Him in the awareness of His faultless Perfection, matchless Beauty and Grace, and infinite Mercy.

Afterwards, by declaring, *You alone do we worship, and from You alone do We seek help* (1:5), we offer our worship of, and seek help from, His unassisted Lordship, unpartnered Divinity, and unshared Sovereignty. Bowing before His infinite Greatness, limitless Power, and perfect Honor and Glory, we demonstrate, with the rest of creation, our weakness and helplessness, humility and poverty by saying, "All-Glorified is my Lord, the Mighty." Prostrating in awareness of the undying Beauty and Grace of His Essence, His unchanging sacred Attributes, and His constant everlasting Perfection, we proclaim, through detachment from all that is not Him, our love and servanthood in wonder and self-abasement. Finding an All-Beautiful Permanent, an All-Compassionate Eternal One to Whom we say, "All-Glorified is my Lord, the All-Exalted," we declare our Most Exalted Lord free of any decline or fault.

After that, we sit reverently and willingly offer all creatures' praises and glorifications to the Eternal, All-Powerful, and All-Majestic One. We also ask God to bestow peace and blessings on His holy Messenger in order to renew our allegiance to him, proclaim our obedience to His commands, and renew and strengthen our belief. By observing the universe's wise order, we testify to the Creator's Oneness and the Messengership of Muhammad, upon him be peace and blessings, herald of the sovereignty of God's Lordship, proclaimer of what pleases Him, and interpreter of the Book of the Universe's signs or verses.

Given this, how can we be truly human if we do not realize what the evening Prayer represents: an agreeable duty, a valuable and pleasurable service, a fine and beautiful act of worship, a serious matter, a significant conversation with the Creator, and a source of permanent happiness in this transient guest-house?

The time of *'isha'* (nightfall), when night covers the earth, reminds us of the mighty disposals of God's Lordship as the Changer of night and day. It calls to our mind the Divine activities of the All-Wise One of Perfection as the Subduer of the sun and the moon, observed in His turning the white page of day into the black page of night, and in His changing summer's beautifully colored script into winter's frigid white page. It recalls His acts as the Creator of life and death in sending the dead entity's remaining works to another world. It reminds us of God's majestic control and graceful manifestations as the Creator of the heavens and earth, and that this narrow, mortal, and lowly world will be destroyed. The same is true for the unfolding of the broad, eternal, and majestic world of the Hereafter. It also warns that only the One Who so easily turns day into night, winter into summer, and this world into the other world can be the universe's Owner and True Master. Only He is worthy to be worshipped and truly loved.

At nightfall our spirits, which are helpless and weak, poor and needy, tossed to and fro by circumstances and whirling onward into the dark veils of the future, perform the *'isha'* Prayer. We say, like Abraham, *I do not love those that set* (6:76). We seek refuge at the Court of the All-Living, the Ever-Worshipped, the Eternal Beloved One. From our transient life in this dark, fleeting world and dark future, we beseech the Enduring, Everlasting One. For a moment of unending conversation, a few seconds of immortal life, we seek the All-Merciful and Compassionate's favors. We ask for the light of His guidance that will illuminate our world and our future, and bind up the pain from the decline of all creatures and friends.

We forget the world, which has left us for the night, and pour out our heart's grief at the Court of Mercy. Before death-like sleep comes, after which anything can happen, we perform our "last" duty of worship. To close our day's activities on a favorable note, we pray and enter the Eternal Beloved and Worshipped One's presence, rather than the mortal ones we loved all day; the All-Powerful and Generous One's presence, rather than the impotent creatures from which we begged all day; and the All-Compassionate Protector's presence in the hope of being saved from the evil of the harmful creatures before which we trembled all day.

We start the prayer with *Surat al-Fatiha*, which extols the Lord of the worlds, Perfect and Self-Sufficient, Compassionate and All-Generous. We move on to *You alone do We worship* (1:5). That is, despite our insignificance and being alone, our connection with the Owner of the Day of Judgment, the Eternal Sovereign, causes us to be treated like an indulged guest and important officer. Through *You alone do we worship and from You alone do we seek help* (1:5), we offer Him the worship of all creatures and seek His assistance for them. Saying *Guide us to the Straight Path* (1:6), we ask to be guided to eternal happiness and the radiant way.

Saying, "God is the All-Great," we bow down and contemplate the Grandeur of the Majestic One, Who orders hidden suns and waking stars, that are like individual soldiers subject to His command just like the plants and animals that have now gone to sleep, and are His lamps and servants in this world.

We think of the universal prostration of all creatures. That is, like the creatures that have gone to sleep at night, when all creation living in a certain age or period is discharged from the duty of worship by the command of *"Be!" and it is* like a well-ordered army of obedient soldiers, and is sent to the World of the Unseen, it prostrates on the rug of death or decline in perfect orderliness saying, "God is the All-Great." They are resurrected in the spring by a rousing, life-giving trumpet-blast from the command of *"Be!" and it is*, and rise up to serve their Lord. Like this, insignificant humanity makes the same declaration in the presence of the All-Merciful One of Perfection, the All-Compassionate One of Grace, in wonder-struck love, eternity-tinged humility, and dignified self-effacement. We then prostrate and achieve a sort of Ascension by performing the night Prayer. So you understand what an agreeable, beautiful, lovely, elevated, precious, pleasant, reasonable, and proper duty and act of worship performing the night Prayer is; how serious a truth it is!

Thus, each prescribed Prayer time points to a mighty revolution, is a sign indicating the Lord's tremendous activity, and a token of the universal Divine bounties. And so, carrying out the duty of the prescribed Prayers at those times is pure wisdom.

Adhan (Call to the Prayer)

The *adhan* calls Muslims to the Prayer. Although it consists of few words, it covers the essentials of faith, expresses Islamic practices, is a form of worship, and one of Islam's collective symbols or marks. God's Messenger, upon him be peace and blessings, said, "If people knew what virtue there is in the *adhan* and the first row (of the Prayer), and that they could not get it save by drawing lots, they would draw lots. If they knew the reward for praying the noon Prayer early in its time, they would race to it. And if they knew the reward for the night and the early morning Prayers in congregation, they would come to them even if they had to crawl."[18]

The call to Prayer is made at the beginning of each prescribed Prayer's time, and should be made by the man who can perform it in the best way possible. Even if one is performing the Prayer alone, he is strongly advised to make it before beginning to pray. Abdurrahman al-Mazini reports from his father: "Abu Sa'id Al-Khudri told me, 'I see you like sheep and the wilderness. So whenever you are with your sheep or in the wilderness and you want to pronounce *adhan* for the Prayer, raise your voice in doing so, for whoever hears the *adhan*, whether a human being, a jinn or any other creature, will be a witness for you on Resurrection Day.' Abu Sa'id added, 'I heard this from God's Messenger.'"[19]

The words of *adhan* are as follows:

Allahu akbar (God is the All-Great): four times.

Ashhadu an la ilaha illa'llah (I bear witness that there is no deity but God): twice.

Ashhadu anna Muhammadan Rasululu'llah (I bear witness that Muhammad is God's Messenger): twice.

Hayya 'ala's-salah (Come to the Prayer): twice.

Hayya 'ala'l-falah (Come to salvation): twice.

Allahu akbar (God is the All-Great): twice.

La ilaha illa'llah (There is no deity but God): once.[20]

The *adhan* for the dawn (early morning) Prayer includes *as-salatu khayrun mina'n-nawm* (The Prayer is better than sleep [twice]) after *hayya 'ala'l-falah* (Come to salvation).[21]

It is a *sunna* act for those who hear the *adhan* to repeat each of its phrases after the one who calls to Prayer, except for the two *Hayya 'ala's-salah* and *Hayya 'ala'l-falah* phrases, after which they should say, "There is no might and strength save with God."[22] God's Messenger, upon him be peace and blessings, also encourages us strongly to make the following supplication after every call to the Prayer:

> O God! Bestow blessings on our master Muhammad, and on the Family of Muhammad![23] I am pleased with God as Lord and Muhammad as Prophet and Islam as religion.[24] O God, Lord of this perfect call and of the regular Prayer which is going to be established, give Muhammad the right of intercession and the highest virtue, and resurrect him to the best and highest position of praise, which You promised him.[25]

The Messenger promises that his intercession will be allowed on Resurrection Day for the one who says this prayer after every call to the Prayer.[26]

The Obligatory Acts before the Prayer

For the Prayer to be complete and acceptable to God, one must perform the following acts:

- Purify oneself from all major and minor impurity by performing *ghusl* (the major ablution) and *wudu'* (the minor ablution), respectively. One cannot perform any Prayer while in a state of canonical impurity requiring the major or minor ablution. The Qur'an orders:

> O you who believe! When you rise up for the Prayer, (if you have no ablution) wash your faces and your hands up to (and including) the elbows, and lightly rub your heads (with water), and (wash) your feet up to (and including) the ankles. And if you are in the state of major ritual impurity (requiring total ablution), purify yourselves (by taking a bath). But if you are ill, or on a journey, or if any of you has just satisfied a want of nature, or if you have had contact with women, and can find no water, then betake yourselves to pure earth, passing with it lightly over your face and your hands (and forearms up to and including the elbows). God does not will to impose any hardship upon you, but wills to purify you (of any kind of material and spiritual filth), and to complete His favor upon you, so that you may give thanks (from the heart, and in speech and action by fulfilling His commandments). (5:6)

If one has not broken *wudu'* between two Prayer times, it does not need to be renewed before the next Prayer. The Prophet strongly recommended that one should clean one's teeth with *miswak*, or at least something clean, while making *wudu'*.[27]

- Remove any impurity from one's clothes, body, and place of Prayer. The impurities that invalidate the Prayer were mentioned in the section on *tahara*. They are divided into two categories: gross impurity (*najasat al-ghaliza*) or weak impurity (*najasat al-khafifa*). Vomit, urine, excrement, *wadi* (a thick white secretion discharged after urination), *mazi* (a white sticky fluid that flows from the sexual organs when thinking about sexual intercourse or foreplay, and so on), and prostatic fluid, are included in gross impurity. Also included in this category are the urine, saliva, and blood of all animals whose meat is forbidden, the excrement of all animals (except birds) whose meat is allowable, the excrement of poultry (geese, hens, and ducks), any part of pigs, and alcohol. Any such solid filth that weighs about four grams, and any such liquid more than the amount that spreads over one's palm, invalidates the Prayer.

The urine of horses and domestic or wild animals whose meat is allowed is weak impurity. If such impurity covers more than one fourth of a limb or smears more than one fourth of one's clothes, the Prayer is invalidated.

- Covering the area of the body that cannot be shown in public. For the men, this is from the knee to the navel; for women, the whole body except the face, hands, and feet. Some scholars maintain that women should cover the top of their feet also.

  God's Messenger declared, "God does not accept the Prayer of an adult woman unless she is wearing a headcovering."[28] He considered the thighs as included in the part of the body which men should cover.[29] He even told 'Ali, his son-in-law and the fourth Caliph, to cover his knees and not to look at the knees of anybody.[30]
- Facing the *qibla* (the direction of the Sacred Mosque in Makka) during the Prayer. This is ordered by the Qur'an (2:144, 150). If one does not know its location, one must search for it. If one prays in another direction after searching, the Prayer is valid. If the chest is turned from the *qibla* during the Prayer, the Prayer is invalid. If the head is turned even for a moment, the person must immediately turn it back toward the *qibla*.
- Performing the Prayer in its time.
- Make the intention to perform a specific Prayer. 'Umar ibn al-Khattab, the second Caliph, reports that God's Messenger said, "Actions are judged according to intentions. One is rewarded for whatever one intends to do. Whoever emigrates for God

and His Messenger has emigrated for God and His Messenger; whoever emigrates to acquire something worldly or to marry has emigrated for what is intended."[31] Thus the intention is the aim and purpose of something. It is a condition of the heart and does not have to be spoken out loud.

The Obligatory Acts during the Prayer

- Say the opening *takbir* and begin the Prayer. When God's Messenger stood for the Prayer, he would stand straight, raise his hands as high as his ears, and, with his palms facing the *qibla*, say, "*Allahu akbar*." He said, "The key to the Prayer is purification; its beginning is *takbir* and its end is *taslim* (greeting)."[32]
- Stand while reciting *Surat al-Fatiha* (the Opening Chapter of the Qur'an) and a selection of verses. One must stand during the obligatory Prayers, if at all possible. But if this is not possible, the Prayer can be performed while sitting or, if even that is not possible, while lying on one's right side. For men, the feet should be kept about a span or a little more apart while standing in the Prayer. Women stand with their feet closer together. The voluntary (supererogatory) Prayers can be offered while sitting, although standing will bring a greater reward.[33]
- Recite *Surat al-Fatiha* and another portion from the Qur'an. This is obligatory in the first two *rak'a*s (cycles) of the obligatory Prayers and in every *rak'a* of necessary (*wajib*), recommended (*sunna*), and supererogatory (*nafila*) Prayers. God Almighty orders recitation of the Qur'an during the Prayer (73:20), and there are many *hadith*s concerning the necessity of reciting *Surat al-Fatiha* and an additional portion from the Qur'an after it.[34] In the last cycle (i.e., the third *rak'a* of the evening Prayer and the last two *rak'a*s of the obligatory noon, afternoon, and late evening Prayers), reciting *al-Fatiha* is preferable, but one can glorify (*Subhana'llah*), praise (*al-hamdu li'llah*), exalt (*Allahu akbar*) God, and declare His Unity (*La ilaha illa'llah*). The portion to be recited after *Surat al-Fatiha* should be at least as

long as the shortest *sura* (*Surat al-Kawthar*). Those who pray following an imam do not recite either *Surat al-Fatiha* or an additional portion from the Qur'an.[35] The recitation of the imam is sufficient for the congregation also, whether he is reciting loudly or not. God Almighty orders us to keep silent while the Qur'an is recited (7:204).

No translation of the Qur'an can be recited during the Prayer, for the Qur'an is composed of both its meaning and wording and is from God with both its meaning and wording. Everyone can memorize *Surat al-Fatiha* and another verse as long as *Surat al-Kawthar* or that *sura* itself within ten or so minutes.

- Bow down and remain in that position (*ruku'*) for some time (long enough to say *Subhana'llah* three times). The Qur'an orders *ruku'* (22:77) and we learn from it that the Prayer of the previous peoples of the Book also contained *ruku'* and *sujud* (prostration) (3:43). The position of *ruku'* consists of bending down and grasping the knees with the palms, and leaving the fingers partly spread apart. This position is maintained until one attains "calmness." The back must be kept straight while bowing. This is how God's Messenger both did and described *ruku'*.[36]
- Prostrate (*sujud*). God's Messenger explains, "Prostrate until you are calm in your prostration, then rise (and sit) until you are calm in your sitting, and then prostrate until you are calm in your prostration."[37] The first prostration, sitting afterwards, the second prostration, and calmness during all of these acts are obligatory in every *rak'a* of every type of Prayer offered.

  It is related from God's Messenger, concerning the parts of the body that must touch the ground during prostration, that he said, "I have been ordered to prostrate on seven bodily parts: the forehead (and he also pointed to his nose), the hands, the knees and the toes."[38]
- The final sitting. In the Prayer's last *rak'a*, one must sit long enough to recite the *tashahhud* before ending the Prayer by giving greetings by turning one's head to the right and then to

the left and saying: *As-salamu 'alaykum wa rahmatu'llah* (Upon you be peace and God's mercy). During this sitting, one recites *at-tashahhud* or *at-tahiyyat*. Reciting words of *salat wa salam* (God's peace and blessings) on Muhammad and his Family is also necessary.[39]

Necessary Things to Complete the Prayer

- The Prayer is the most valuable and important of the acts of worship. In praising the believers certain to prosper and be saved, God Almighty mentions first that they are in their Prayer humble and fully submissive, being overwhelmed by the awe and majesty of God (23:2). In this same passage, He once more stresses that they are ever mindful guardians of their Prayers, including all the rites of which they are constituted (23:9). So, to complete the Prayer, one must pray in utmost humility and overwhelmed by God's majesty. One must recite correctly, understandably, and distinctly; carry out all of the obligatory acts correctly and in the proper order; attain calmness; straighten the body while standing, bowing down, and prostrating; bow, prostrate, and stand after bowing and before prostrating and sit between prostrations as long as it takes to say *Subhana'llah* at least. God's Messenger, upon him be peace and blessings, strictly forbade turning one's head to the right or left or upwards, taking sideways glances or looking upwards, being busy with anything which is not a part or an act of the Prayer, cracking one's knuckles, and so on.[40]
- Unless there is an acceptable impediment, obligatory Prayers should be performed in congregation. God's Messenger, upon him be peace and blessings, said:

> The Prayer offered in congregation is twenty-five times superior (in reward) to the Prayer offered alone in one's house or in a working place or market because if one performs ablution and does it perfectly, and then proceeds to the mosque with the sole intention of praying, then for each

> step which a person takes towards the mosque, God upgrades them a degree in reward and forgives one sin till they enter the mosque. When they enter the mosque, they are considered in Prayer as long as they are waiting for the Prayer and the angels keep on asking for God's forgiveness for them and the angels keep on saying, "O God! Be Merciful to him [or her], O God! Forgive him [her], as long as he [she] keeps on sitting at his [her] praying place."[41]

- One who prays alone should recite *al-Fatiha* and a portion from the Qur'an inaudibly in both the prescribed or supererogatory Prayers performed during the day. One can recite loudly or inaudibly during the night Prayers. In congregation, the imam (the one leading the prayer) should recite audibly in all *rak'a*s of the morning, *Jumu'a*, *tarawih*, and *witr* Prayers, and the first two *rak'a*s of the evening and late evening Prayers. He should recite inaudibly in all *rak'a*s of the noon and afternoon Prayers, the last one *rak'a* of the evening Prayer, and the last two *rak'a*s of the late evening Prayer.
- Sitting between the second and third *rak'a*s of those Prayers having three or four *rak'a*s.
- Reciting *at-tashahhud* or *at-tahiyyat* when sitting in the second and fourth *rak'a*s, and in the third *rak'a*s of the evening and *witr* Prayers.[42]
- The acts of the Prayers should be done one after the other, without any break or delay.
- Ending the Prayer by giving greetings on both sides, saying *as-salamu 'alaykum wa-rahmatu'llah*.[43]
- If one recites during the Prayer any of the verses requiring prostration, one must do the prostration of recitation.

Sunna Acts

Each Prayer contains certain acts that are *sunna*, meaning that the Messenger, upon him be peace and blessings, performed them and advised Muslims to do likewise. They are extremely important for completing the Prayer and receiving a greater reward.

- *Adhan* and *iqama* are *sunna* for the five daily prescribed Prayers and *Jumu'a* congregational Prayer. Women are not required to say *iqama*.
- While beginning the Prayer and saying the opening *takbir*, men should raise their hands (according to the Hanafis) as high as the ears and the thumbs touch the earlobes. According to the reports from the Messenger by some Companions such as Anas ibn Malik, Bara' ibn 'Azib, and Wa'il ibn Hujr, God's Messenger, upon him be peace and blessings, used to raise his thumbs in the Prayer up to the lobes of his ears.[44] According to the Hanafi School, women raise their hands in front of the chest.
- According to the Hanafis, men should place their hands below the navel, (the Shafi'is say below the chest), and the right hand should grasp the wrist of the left arm.[45] Women place their hands on their chest, right hand over left.
- The Prayer should begin with a supplication used by the Prophet, upon whom be peace and blessings, to begin his Prayers. This is said after the opening *takbir* and before reciting *al-Fatiha*. The Hanafis prefer, *Subhanaka'llahumma wa bi-hamdik. Wa tabara-ka'smuk. Wa ta'ala jadduk. Wa la ilaha ghayruk.* (All-Glorious are You, O God, and to You is the praise. Blessed is Your Name and most high is Your honor. There is no deity other than You).[46] The Shafi'is prefer: *Inni wajjahtu wajhiya li'lladhi fatara's-samawati wa'l-ardi hanifan wa ma ana mina'l-mushrikin. Inna salati wa nusuki wa mahyaya wa mamati li'llahi Rabbi'l-alamin, la sharika lah; wa bi-dhalika umirtu; wa ana mina'l-muslimin* (I have turned my face [my whole being] with pure faith and submission to the One Who has originated the heavens and the earth each with particular features, and I am not one of those associating partners with God. My Prayer, and all my [other] acts and forms of devotion and worship, and my living and my dying are for God alone, the Lord of the worlds.

He has no partners; thus have I been commanded, and I am the first and foremost of the Muslims [who have submitted to Him exclusively]). Other supplications related from the Messenger also can be recited before *al-Fatiha*.

- Reciting silently, "I seek refuge in God from Satan, the accursed; in the Name of God, the All-Merciful, the All-Compassionate" in the first *rak'a*, and only "In the Name of God, the All-Merciful, the All-Compassionate" in the other *rak'a*s before *al-Fatiha* while standing.[47] The Qur'an orders, *When you recite the Qur'an, seek refuge in God from Satan, the accursed.* (16:98)
- Saying *Amin* after reciting *al-Fatiha*. God's Messenger, upon him be peace and blessings, strongly advised it.[48]
- Reciting fairly long passages from the Qur'an after *Surat al-Fatiha* in the morning (about one page or more in each *rak'a*, a longer section in the first one),[49] noon, and afternoon Prayers (about one page),[50] either somewhat long or shorter passages in the evening Prayers,[51] and somewhat short passages in the night Prayer.[52]
- Saying the *takbir* upon every bowing down, sitting down, moving to and rising from prostration, and standing up after sitting.[53] Upon rising from the bowing, all Muslims should say, *Sami'a'llahu li-man hamidah* (God hears the one who praises Him), and after it, *Rabbana wa-laka'l-hamd* (Our Lord, and to You is all praise).[54]
- Saying, *Subhana Rabiyya'l-'Azim* (All-Glorious is my Lord, the Mighty) three times while bowing, and, *Subhana Rabbiya'l-A'la* (All-Glorious is my Lord, the Most High) while prostrating.[55]
- Placing the hands on both knees with the fingers open and bending one's back straight while bowing; placing the knees on the ground before the hands while prostrating, and during prostration, placing the hands on the ground with the forearms away from the ground and away from one's body, with the toes facing the *qibla*, while prostrating. Sitting on one's left foot and propping up the right one.[56] According to the Hanafi

School, women perform the same movements keeping their feet closer together and their elbows closer to the body and to the ground.

- Calling God's blessings and peace upon our Prophet and his Family after *at-tahiyyat* in the final sitting.[57]
- Supplicating after the final *tashahhud* and before giving the final salutations (that end the Prayer). These may consist of any supplication mentioned in the Qur'an or reported from the Messenger.[58]
- Saying words of remembrance, asking forgiveness, and supplicating after the Prayer. The most famous and widespread one reported from the Messenger is: *Astaghfiru'llaha'l-'Azim* (I ask God, the Mighty, for forgiveness: three times), and *Allahumma anta's-Salamu wa minka's-salam. Tabarakta ya Dha'l-Jalali wa'l-Ikram* (O God, You are Peace, and from You is peace. You are the All-Blessed and One bestowing blessings, O One of Majesty and Munificence).[59] Reciting *Ayat al-Kursiyy* (the Verse of the Throne) (2:255) and saying words of glorification (*Subhana'llah*), praise (*al-hamdu li'llah*), and exaltation (*Allahu akbar*) each thirty-three (or thirty-four) times, at the end of the Prayer is highly advisable. In addition, reciting, "There is no deity but God, He is One, having no partners. For Him is sovereignty and for Him is all praise; and He is powerful over everything," ten times after the early morning and evening Prayers is also strongly encouraged.[60]

Disliked and Discouraged Things

God's Messenger, upon him be peace and blessings, and his Companions were extremely careful to perform the Prayer as perfectly as possible. They avoided any act, no matter how small, which would damage its perfect performance. When they saw anyone making a mistake in its performance, they would warn him or her. In the books of *Hadith*, there are many examples of this. The following are the disliked and discouraged things concerning the Prayer against which they warned:

- Beginning the Prayer while feeling the need to answer a call of nature.
- Omitting any *sunna* act.
- Thinking about worldly affairs while praying.
- Doing things that cannot be reconciled with being in God's presence (e.g., cracking one's knuckles, playing with any part of the body or clothes, smoothing the stones on the ground, putting the hands on the hips while bending down or standing up, yawning, blowing something, coughing, or cleaning the throat without a valid excuse).
- Leaning on a post, a wall, or something similar without a valid excuse.
- Praying while having something to eat or chew in the mouth, regardless of its size.
- Praying while angry or hungry, when food has been placed nearby, or wearing something that may distract one's attention.
- Praying in the path of people who are passing in front of one.[61]

Things That Invalidate the Prayer

- Omitting any of the Prayer's obligatory acts, whether doing so is intentional or out of ignorance or forgetfulness.
- Uttering a word, even if only two letters long, that is not included in the recitations of the Prayer.
- Weeping, sighing and complaining about worldly things, and making any noise (except clearing the throat, coughing, or yawning), and speaking, and laughing. Only weeping unintentionally out of fear or love of God and similar things does not invalidate the Prayer.
- Talking or answering any call or salutation.
- Reciting the Qur'an or supplications so incorrectly that what is said cannot be found in the Qur'an or among the reports from

the Messenger and transforms the meaning so that it violates Islamic truths and principles.

- Saying prayers that are not found in the Qur'an or reported from the Messenger, and concerning worldly things, such as, "O Lord, enable me to pay my debts," or "Lord, let me marry such-and-such a woman (or man)."
- Moving aside or changing places when asked or ordered to do so by one who is not praying.
- Doing something that makes someone else think that one is not praying.
- Doing something that invalidates ritual purity.
- Turning one's chest from the *qibla*.
- Eating or swallowing anything bigger than a chickpea grain that has remained between the teeth.[62]

How to Pray

The dawn (early morning [*fajr*]) Prayer)

Having done what is necessary to have the Prayer accepted, men recite the *iqama* even if praying alone. Women are not required to recite the *iqama*. The *iqama* is as follows:

Allahu akbar (God is the All-Great): four times.

Ashhadu an la ilaha illa'llah (I bear witness that there is no deity but God): twice.

Ashhadu anna Muhammadan Rasululu'llah (I bear witness that Muhammad is God's Messenger); twice.

Hayya 'ala's-salah (Come to the Prayer): twice.

Hayya 'ala'l-falah (Come to salvation): twice.

Qad qamatu's-salah (Now the Prayer is about to be performed): twice.

Allahu akbar (God is the All-Great): twice.

La ilaha illa'llah (I bear witness that there is no deity but God): once.

One should pause between each phrase of the *adhan*, but be quick when reciting the *iqama*.[63]

After the *iqama*, one intends to perform the dawn Prayer, and, while reciting the opening *takbir*, raises the hands with the palms facing the *qibla* to one's ears, with the thumbs touching the earlobes (or in front of the chest for women), and then puts them (according to the Hanafis) under the navel with the right hand grasping the left one at the wrist (or on the chest for women). Then, recite a supplication with which the Prophet, upon whom be peace, used to begin his Prayers. The Hanafis prefer, *Subhanaka'llahumma wa bi-hamdik. Wa tabara-ka'smuk. Wa ta'ala jadduk. Wa la ilaha ghayruk* (All-Glorious You are, O God, and to You is the praise. Blessed is Your Name and most high is Your honor. There is no deity other than You).

Then recite *Surat al-Fatiha*, say *Amin* at its end, and recite a portion from the Qur'an. Then bow down, saying, *Allahu akbar* and, attaining calmness with one's back straightened, say three times, *Subhana Rabiyya'l-'Azim* (All-Glorious is my Lord, the Mighty). Afterwards, rise up and say, *Sami'a'llahu li-man hamidah* (God hears him who praises Him), and then, *Rabbana wa-laka'l-hamd* (Our Lord, and to You is all praise). After a short pause, prostrate, saying, *Allahu akbar*, with one's palms, knees, toes, forehead, and nose touching the ground. While prostrating, recite three times, *Subhana Rabbiya'l-A'la* (All-Glorious is my Lord, the Most High). Then, sit up, saying, *Allahu akbar*, and, after a short pause while sitting, prostrate again and say, *Allahu akbar*. Recite the same things that were recited during the first prostration. This is the first *rak'a* in all Prayers except the *'Iyd* (religious festive day) Prayers and *salat at-tasbih* (the Prayer of glorification), which will be described below.

Rise from prostration saying, *Allahu akbar*, and then perform the second *rak'a* just as the first one was performed. After the second prostration, sit and recite *at-tashahhud* or *at-tahiyyat*, which is as follows: *At-tahiyyatu li'llahi wa's-salawatu wa't-tayyibatu as-salamu 'alayka ayyuha'n-nabiyyu wa-rahmatu'llahi wa-barakatuh. As-sal-*

amu 'alayna wa 'ala 'ibadi'llahi's-salihin. Ashhadu an la ilaha illa'llah wa ashhadu anna Muhammadan 'abduhu wa-rasuluh (All the worship [performed by all living creatures through their lives] is God's, and so is all the worship [particular to and performed by all the living beings with spirits] and the worship [performed by perfected members of humanity and the angels near-stationed to God]. Peace be upon you, O the [greatest] Prophet, and God's mercy and gifts. Peace be also upon us and God's righteous servants. I bear witness that there is no deity but God, and I bear witness that Muhammad is His servant and Messenger).[64]

Afterwards, one calls God's blessings and peace upon His Messenger together with his Family, saying, *Allahumma salli 'ala sayyidina Muhammadin wa 'ala Al-i Muhammad, kama sallayta 'ala Ibrahima wa 'ala Al-i Ibrahim. Innaka Hamidun Majid. Allahumma barik 'ala (sayyidina) Muhammadin wa 'ala Al-i Muhammad, kama barakta 'ala Ibrahima wa 'ala Al-i Ibrahim. Innaka Hamidun Majid* (O God, bestow Your blessings upon our master Muhammad and the Family of Muhammad, as You bestowed Your blessings upon Abraham and the Family of Abraham. Assuredly, You are All-Praiseworthy, All-Sublime. O God, send Your abundant gifts and favors upon our master Muhammad and the Family of Muhammad, as You sent them upon Abraham and the Family of Abraham. Assuredly, You are All-Praiseworthy, All-Sublime).[65]

Then, pray to God. Choose prayers from the Qur'an and the prayers of God's Messenger, upon him be peace and blessings. Then, give greetings, turning your head to your right and left, saying, *As-salamu 'alaykum wa rahmatu'llah* (Peace be upon you, and God's Mercy). While giving greetings to your right, direct them to those sitting at your right (if praying in congregation), and while giving greetings to your left, direct them to those sitting at your left (if praying in congregation).[66] According to scholars, the noble angels who record our deeds may also be intended additionally.

THE NOON, AFTERNOON, AND NIGHT (*ZUHR*, *'ASR*, AND *'ISHA'*) PRAYERS

Having done what is necessary to have the Prayer accepted, men recite *iqama* even if praying alone. Women are not required to recite *iqama*.

Then, perform the first two *rak'a*s just as in the dawn Prayer, except that after sitting in the second *rak'a* and reciting the *tashahhud*, one then stands up, saying, *Allahu akbar* (God is the All-Great). Perform another two *rak'a*s without reciting the opening *takbir*, and, while standing, recite only *al-Fatiha* preferably; although you can recite, instead of *al-Fatiha*, words of glorification (*Subhana'llah*), praise (*al-hamdu li'llah*), and exaltation (*Allahu akbar*) and declare God's Oneness (*La ilaha illa'llah*). 'Abdullah ibn Abi Qatada reports from his father Abu Qatada that God's Messenger recited only *Surat al-Fatiha* in the third and fourth *rak'a*s of the noon and afternoon Prayers.[67] While sitting in the last (fourth) *rak'a*, recite that which was recited in the dawn and all other Prayers. End the Prayer by giving salutations to the right and left.

THE EVENING (*MAGHRIB*) PRAYER

One begins the Prayer and prays the first two *rak'a*s as outlined above. After reciting the *tashahhud* while sitting in the second *rak'a*, perform the third *rak'a* in the same way as the third *rak'a* of the noon, afternoon, and late evening Prayers. However, after the second prostration, sit again, as in the second (or last sitting) of the other Prayers or in the second *rak'a* of the dawn Prayer. Do what is done in them.

Prostrations of Forgetfulness

If any of the obligatory acts of the Prayer are delayed or any of the necessary acts are omitted or delayed for some time due to forgetfulness (e.g., sitting between the second and third *rak'a*s of those

Prayers having three or four *rak'as;* stopping between the obligatory acts more than a few seconds; delaying standing up following the first sitting in the second *rak'a* after reciting *at-tahiyyat* by reciting as much as *Allahumma salli 'ala Muhammadin wa 'ala Al-i Muhammad* from the supplication of calling God's blessings on our Prophet and his Family; omitting the *qunut* in the *witr* Prayer; or an imam's reciting loudly in the Prayers in which he must recite silently or vice versa), after giving the salutations, make two prostrations just like the other prostrations and recite *at-tashahhud* (*at-tahiyyat*) and the supplications of calling God's peace and blessings on God's Messenger, upon him be peace and blessings. Then, give salutations and finish the Prayer. In the congregational Prayer, the imam recites only *at-tahiyyat* and the initial part of calling God's blessings and peace upon the Messenger and his Family (i.e., *Allahumma salli 'ala Muhammadin wa 'ala Al-i Muhammad*) before making the prostrations of forgetfulness, and does these prostrations after giving the salutation only to his right.

If one feels doubtful or forgets for the first time in one's life how many *rak'as* one has prayed, it is best to perform the Prayer anew. But if one falls into doubt from time to time, one thinks about how much one might have prayed and completes one's Prayer. On completing the Prayer, one makes the prostrations of forgetfulness before giving the salutations. God's Messenger decreed:

> When any one of you feels doubtful about his Prayer, he should aim at what is correct and complete his Prayer in that respect and then make two prostrations after giving the salutations.[68]

The Messenger also decreed:

> When any one of you feels doubtful about his Prayer and he does not know how many *rak'as* he has prayed, whether three or four (*rak'as*), he should cast aside his doubt and base his Prayer on what he is sure of, and then perform two prostrations before giving salutations. If he has prayed five *rak'as*, they will make his Prayer an even number for him, and if he has prayed exactly four, they will be humiliation for Satan.[69]

If one cannot arrive at a fairly certain decision about how much one has prayed, one should base one's Prayer on the lesser number of *rak'a*s, and then complete one's Prayer. Before giving salutations, one must perform the prostrations of forgetfulness.[70]

If one forgets to sit in the second *rak'a* of Prayers of three or four *rak'a*s, one completes the Prayer and does the prostrations of forgetfulness at the end. If one forgets to sit at the end of any Prayer of two or three or four *rak'a*s, and stands up for an extra third or fourth or fifth *rak'a*, and remembers not having sat before going to the prostrations, one immediately sits down, completes the Prayer and does the prostrations of forgetfulness. But if one remembers when or after one prostrates in the next, extra third or forth or fifth *rak'a*, one completes the Prayers of two or three *rak'a*s to four *rak'a*s, and the Prayers of four *rak'a*s to six. One does not have to do the prostrations of forgetfulness, but one must perform the Prayer anew if it is an obligatory Prayer. If one is praying a Sunna Prayer, he or she does the prostrations of forgetfulness at the end of the Prayer.

If one stands up forgetfully for a third *rak'a* in a Prayer of two *rak'a*s after the *tashahhud* before giving the salutations, or for a fourth in a Prayer of three *rak'a*s, or for a fifth in a Prayer of four *rak'a*s, and if one remembers before the prostrations in the next *rak'a*, one sits down, completes the Prayer and does the prostrations of forgetfulness. But if one remembers after the prostrations in the next *rak'a*, one completes the Prayers of two and three *rak'a*s to four, the Prayers of four *rak'a*s to six, and does the prostrations of forgetfulness in the end before giving the salutations, without having to perform the Prayer anew.

If one who is praying following an imam makes an error requiring the prostration of forgetfulness, he or she does not have to do it. If the imam errs, he does the prostration of forgetfulness together with the congregation. One who arrived late to follow the imam in the first *rak'a* does the prostration of forgetfulness together with the imam, but stands up to complete his or her Prayer while the imam is giving salutations without giving salutations himself or herself.

Prostrating While Reciting

Whoever recites a verse of prostration or hears it, whether during a prayer or outside it, should pronounce the *takbir*, prostrate, recite *Subhana Rabbiya'l-A'la* three times, and rise from the prostration. There are fifteen such verses in the Qur'an. If one of them is recited during a Prayer, prostrate without interrupting the Prayer and then continue it.[71]

The Prayer of the Sick (*Salatu'l-Marid*)

Whoever cannot stand due to illness or another valid reason can pray sitting. If this is not possible, one can pray while lying on one's right side by making gestures. In such a case, the gestures for *sajda* should be lower than those for *ruku'*. The Prophet, upon him be peace and blessings, described to 'Imran ibn Husayn how to pray while he was ill, saying, "Pray while standing and if you cannot, pray while sitting, and if you cannot do even that, then pray lying on your side."[72]

The Prayer in Times of Fear or Danger (*Salatu'l-Khawf*)

All scholars agree about the legality of such Prayers. The Qur'an decrees as follows:

> When you are among the believers (who are on an expedition and in fear that the unbelievers might harm them) and stand to lead the Prayer for them, let a party of them stand in Prayer with you and retain their arms with them (while the other party maintain their positions against the enemy). When the first party have done the prostrations (finished the *rak'a*), let them go to the rear of your company (and there, hold positions against the enemy), and let the other party who have not prayed

> come forward and pray with you, being fully prepared against danger and retaining their arms. Those who disbelieve wish that you should be heedless of your weapons and your equipment, so that they might swoop upon you in a single (surprise) attack. But there will be no blame on you if you lay aside your arms (during the Prayer), if you are troubled by rain (and the ground impedes your movement), or if you are ill; however, be fully prepared against danger. Surely God has prepared for the unbelievers a shameful, humiliating punishment. (4:102)

The Prayer of a Traveler (*Salatu'l-Musafir*)

God's Messenger, upon him be peace and blessings, decreed that the upper limit of wiping over indoor boots for residents is one day and one night, and for travelers is three days and three nights.[73] He also decreed that a woman should not go on a journey to last more than three days without being accompanied by her husband or by another man who is a relative whom she cannot legally marry.[74] The scholars deduce from these Prophetic decrees that the lowest limit of a journey requiring the shortening of a prescribed Prayer is three days. If one begins a journey of at least three days, one shortens the prescribed Prayers of four *rak'as* (the noon, afternoon, and night Prayers) and offers them as two *rak'as*, just like the dawn Prayer. Since at that time travel was generally on foot and a day's travel was counted as six hours, the distance of three days on foot was regarded as ninety kilometers (fifty-six miles). However, many contemporary scholars maintain that since many people now travel by bus or train, the above-mentioned prayers can be shortened only if the distance is around 1,200 kilometers (745 miles).

Travelers are defined as people who have left their home and their town. So long as they are traveling, the above-mentioned Prayers can be shortened. If they reach a place and intend to stay there for less than fifteen days, they are considered to be travelers and are therefore allowed to shorten their Prayers as outlined above. If they are still there on the fifteenth day for reasons beyond their control, although they originally intended to stay for less than fifteen days, they are still considered travelers and can shorten the appropriate prayers. Most scholars opine that travelers may offer the *sunna* and supererogatory Prayers without shortening them.

The main reason for shortening the above-mentioned Prayers is traveling, not the hardship of travel. Thus, these Prayers are shortened even if no difficulty is encountered while traveling. The cause for establishing a rule differs from its expected wisdom and benefit. Wisdom or benefit is the reason for its preference, while the cause requires its existence. So, traveling Muslims shorten their Prayers. The cause for this Divine dispensation is traveling, and the underlying wisdom is the hardship of traveling. Thus, Prayers are shortened even if no hardship is encountered, for the cause exists. Muslims who encounter hardship while at home cannot shorten their Prayers, for the wisdom or benefit cannot be the cause for this dispensation.

Those who are traveling must pray whether they are on a ship or a train or a plane, if the Prayer will be missed before reaching a place where one can offer it.

The *Sunna* Prayers

There are *Sunna* Prayers—the Prayers which were legislated by God's Messenger based on the Revelation which is not included in the Qur'an, to be performed before or after the obligatory ones. Some of them are *mu'akkad* (those whose importance was emphasized by God's Messenger), while the others are of a lesser degree of importance. As reported by 'A'isha and Umm Habiba, Mothers of the Believers, God's Messenger said, "If any Muslim servant (of God) prays for the sake of God twelve *rak'a*s every day, before and after the obligatory ones, God will build for him a house in Paradise."[75] According to both of our mothers, these are two *rak'a*s before the dawn Prayer, four *rak'a*s before and two *rak'a*s after the noon Prayer, and two *rak'a*s after the evening and night Prayers.[76]

- Praying two *rak'as* before the dawn or early morning Prayer was highly recommended and stressed by God's Messenger, who never abandoned it.[77] They are performed just as in the dawn Prayer, except that one recites shorter Qur'anic passages after *al-Fatiha*.
- Praying four *rak'as* before the noon Prayer was highly advised and stressed by God's Messenger. They are performed just as in the noon Prayer, except that one recites Qur'anic passages after *al-Fatiha* in all *rak'as*. God's Messenger also prayed another two or four *rak'as*[78] after the noon Prayer, and Muslims are urged to follow his example.
- Praying two *rak'as* after the evening and late evening Prayers is also recommended highly, as stated above.
- Praying four *rak'as* before the afternoon and night Prayers is also recommended, though not stressed so strongly as the twelve *rak'as* of the *Sunna* Prayers mentioned above. They are performed just as the four *rak'as* before the obligatory noon Prayer, except that one recites the supplications for God's blessings, peace, and gifts upon our master Muhammad and his Family after the *tashahhud* during the first sitting,[79] and the supplication before *al-Fatiha* in the third *rak'a*, which one recites while beginning the Prayer after the opening *takbir*.

Tahajjud and Witr Prayers

The *tahajjud* Prayer has a very important place among the highly advisable, stressed Sunna Prayers. It was obligatory for the most noble Messenger, upon him be peace and blessings, from the very beginning of his mission, as decreed in the verses below:

> O you enwrapped one, (under the heavy responsibility of Messengership)! Rise to keep vigil at night, except a little: Half of it, or lessen it a little—or add to it (a little). And pray and recite the Qur'an calmly and distinctly (with your mind and heart concentrated on it). (73:1–4)

> And in some part of the night, rise from sleep and observe vigil therein (through Prayer and recital of the Qur'an) as additional worship for you; your Lord may well raise you to a glorious, praised station (of nearness to Him.) (17:79)

The believers in the company of God's Messenger, upon him be peace and blessings, were also very careful of observing the *tahajjud* Prayer, as stated in the following verses:

> Surely your Lord knows that you (O Messenger) rise and keep vigil sometimes nearly two-thirds of the night or (other times) a half of it or a third of it, and so do some of those who are in your company as believers. (73:20)

> Their sides forsake their beds at night, calling out to their Lord in fear (of His punishment) and hope (for His forgiveness, grace, and good pleasure).... (32:16)

> And (those true servants of the All-Merciful are they) who spend (some of) the night (in worship) prostrating before their Lord and standing.... (25:64)

> They used to sleep but little by night (almost never missing the *tahajjud* Prayer). (51:17)

Interrupting sleep for God's sake and turning to Him with devotion and pure feelings during the night is a great support and source of nourishment for the human spirit. While ordering the Messenger to pray this prayer, God Almighty says, *We will surely charge you with a weighty Word (and with applying it in your daily life, and conveying it to others). Rising and praying at night impresses (mind and heart) most strongly and (makes) recitation more certain and upright. For by day you have extensive preoccupations* (73:5–7).

Since every good Muslim is a devoted servant of God and dedicated to His cause, the *tahajjud* Prayer's importance is clear. God's Messenger, who declared that the *tahajjud* Prayer is the most virtuous after the obligatory Prayers,[80] never abandoned it.[81] His *tahajjud* Prayers were so long that the soles of his feet swelled. When asked why he tired himself so much, he answered, "Shall I not be a thankful servant of God?"[82] He also said concerning the merit of the *tahajjud* Prayer:

> God "descends" every night to the lowest heaven when one-third of the first part of the night is over and says, "I am the Lord; I am the Lord: who is there to supplicate to Me so that I answer him? Who is there to beg of Me so that I grant to him? Who is there to beg forgiveness from Me so that I forgive him?" He continues like this till the day breaks.[83]

According to most acceptable reports from the Messenger, together with the *witr* Prayer, which is three *rak'as*, the *tahajjud* Prayer consists of eleven *rak'as* and is performed in cycles of two, just like the early morning Prayer.[84] Although the *witr* Prayer can be performed after the night Prayer before going to bed, so that one will not miss it because of sleep, its preferable time is after *tahajjud*.[85] *Witr* consists of three *rak'as* and is performed like the evening Prayer, but with the following exceptions:

In the third *rak'a*, a Qur'anic passage and the *qunut* prayers are recited after *al-Fatiha*. Before praying *qunut*, say *takbir* (*Allahu akbar*), raising the hands as when beginning the Prayer. The Messenger's reported *qunut* prayers are: *Allahumma inna nasta'inuka wa nastaghfiruka wa nastahdika wa nu'minu bika wa natubu ilayk; wa natawwakkalu 'alayka wa nuthni 'alayka'l-khayra kullahu nashkuruka wa la nakfuruk. Wa nakhla'u wa natruku man yafjuruk. Allahumma iyyaka na'budu wa laka nusalli wa nasjudu wa ilayka nas'a wa nahfidu; narju rahmataka wa nakhsa 'adhabaka inna 'adhabaka bi'l-kuffari mulhiq* (O God! We ask You for help, forgiveness, and guidance. We believe in You and turn to You in repentance for our sins, and place our trust in You. We praise You by attributing all good to You, and thank You, and never feel ingratitude to You. We reject and cut our relations with those who are in constant rebellion against You. O God, You alone do we worship, and we pray and prostrate for You alone. We endeavor in Your cause to obtain Your good pleasure and approval. We hope and expect Your mercy and fear Your chastisement, for Your chastisement is to surround the unbelievers).

Tarawih

The specific Prayer during Ramadan, which is known as *tarawih*, is *sunna* for both men and women and is to be performed after the prescribed late evening Prayer and before *witr*. As generally accepted, it consists of twenty *rak'a*s and is performed preferably in cycles of two *rak'a*s.[86]

Tarawih prayers can be performed in congregation or alone. The majority of scholars, however, prefer to pray them in congregation. The Messenger, upon him be peace and blessings, prayed it in congregation but then stopped doing so, fearing that it would be made obligatory.[87] 'Umar established the practice of praying *tarawih* behind an imam.[88]

Specific *Sunna* Prayers

The Prayer to Ask for What Is Good (Salatu 'l-Istikhara)

The Messenger strongly advised all Muslims to follow his practice when confronted with a choice between permissible alternatives: pray two non-obligatory *rak'a*s and then say the specific prayer to ask God to enable one to choose what is good or better.

Jabir ibn 'Abdullah narrates:

> The Prophet, upon him be peace and blessings, taught us the way of doing *istikhara* (to ask God to guide one to the right sort of action concerning any deed) in all matters as he taught us the *sura*s of the Qur'an. He said, "If anyone of you is thinking of doing any deed, he should offer a Prayer of two *rak'a*s other than the obligatory ones and say (after the Prayer):
>
> 'My God! I seek guidance through Your Knowledge, and power through Your Power, and I ask from Your tremendous favoring. You are capable to do whatever You will, but I am not. You know but I do not, and You are the Knower of the Unseen. My God! If, according to Your Knowledge, this affair is good for me concerning my religion and my life and my end, with respect to its immediate and later consequences, then ordain it for me

> and make it easy for me to get, and then favor me with Your blessings through it. If, acording to Your Knowledge, this affair is evil for me concerning my religion and my life and my end, with respect to its immediate and later consequences, then keep it away from me and let me be away from it. Ordain for me whatever is good for me, and make me pleased with it.'"

The Prophet added that the person should mention his need after the prayer.[89]

The Prayer of Glorification (Salatu't-Tasbih)

Ibn 'Abbas reports that God's Messenger said to 'Abbas ibn 'Abd al-Muttalib:

> O 'Abbas, O uncle, shall I not give you, present to you, donate to you, tell you of ten things which, if you do them, God will forgive your first and last sins, past and present sins, intentional and unintentional sins, private and public sins? The ten actions are: pray four *rak'as*, reciting in every *rak'a al-Fatiha* and a *sura*. When you finish the Qur'anic recitation of the first *rak'a*, say, while standing: *Subhana'llah, al-hamdu li'llah, wa la ilaha illa'llahu wa'llahu akbar* (All-Glorious is God, all praise is for God, there is no deity save God, and God is the All-Great) fifteen times. Then do *ruku'*, and while in *ruku'*, say the same phrases ten times. Then stand and say the same ten times. Then go down and do *sajda*, and while you are in *sajda*, say the same phrases ten times. Then sit after *sajda* and say the same phrases ten times. Then do *sajda* and say the same phrases ten times. Then sit after the second *sajda*, and say the same phrases another ten times. That is seventy-five (repetitions of the phrases) in each *rak'a*. Do that in each of the four *rak'as*. If you can pray it once a day, do so. If you cannot, then once every Friday. If you cannot do that, then once a year. And if you cannot do that, then once during your life.[90]

According to another report preferred by the Hanafis,[91] the phrases to be recited seventy-five times during one *rak'a* are recited fifteen times before *al-Fatiha*. They are recited ten times following the Qur'anic recitation and before doing the *ruku'*, and are not recited after the second *sajda* between the first and second, and the third and fourth *rak'as*.

After saying the phrases ten times following the second *sajda* in the second *rak'a*, recite the *tashahhud* and calls for God's blessings and peace upon the Messenger and his Family, and then end the first two *rak'as* by giving the salutation. Pray the second two *rak'as* in the same way.

The Prayer in Times of Need (Salatu'l-Haja)

Take the proper ablution, pray two *rak'as*, and say the prayer reported from the Messenger concerning this. It is as follows:

> There is no deity but God, the All-Clement, the All-Munificent. All-Glorious is God, the Lord of the Supreme Throne. All praise is for God, the Lord of the worlds. We ask You for the requirements of Your mercy, and Your definite forgiveness, and a share in everything good, and freedom from every offense. Do not leave any sin of mine unforgiven, any pain unremoved, and any need approvable by You unfulfilled, O the Most Compassionate of the compassionate.[92]

If God's overall Wisdom requires it to be met, God will grant whatever is asked, either sooner or later.

The Prayer of Repentance (Salatu't-Tawba)

Take the appropriate minor or major ablution, offer a Prayer of two *rak'as*, and ask for His forgiveness. Hopefully, God will grant it. Having strongly advised this Prayer, God's Messenger, upon him be peace and blessings, recited this verse: *They are also the ones who, when they have committed a shameful deed or wronged themselves (through any kind of sinful act), immediately remember God and implore Him to forgive their sins—for who will forgive sins save God?—and do not persist knowingly in whatever (evil) they have committed* (3:135).[93]

The Prayer during a Solar or Lunar Eclipse (Salatu 'l-Kusuf and al-Khusuf)

Scholars agree that this is a *sunna mu'akkada*, a stressed or confirmed one, which is to be performed by both men and women. It is best, but not absolutely necessary, to pray it in congregation. It consists of two *rak'as* and is performed like the *Sunna* Prayers before the dawn or after the evening Prayers. Its time is from the eclipse's beginning until its end. It is also advised to say *takbir*, supplicate, give charity, and ask God for forgiveness during the eclipse. It should be noted that this has nothing to do with asking for the eclipse to end, for its beginning and end are clear. An eclipse is only an occasion for such a Prayer.[94]

The Prayer for Rain (Salatu 'l-Istisqa')

This Prayer is performed to entreat God for rain during a drought. While God's Messenger, upon him be peace and blessings, was giving the sermon on a Friday, a man came and complained to him about drought. The Messenger prayed, "My God! Give us water, give us water!" While previously there were no signs of rain, clouds now appeared in the sky, and it rained heavily. Another man came the next Friday, and asked God's Messenger to pray for the cessation of rain, saying, "O Messenger of God! Our animals have died, and the roads been closed off." The Messenger, upon him be peace and blessings, prayed, "My God! Send rain not upon us but upon our environment. My God, send it upon mountains, fields, and forests, and into valleys!"[95]

The Prayer for rain is performed in congregation like the dawn Prayer. After the Prayer, the imam gives a sermon while standing. If rain is late, people wear their worn-out clothes and go out to the country together with some of their cattle, and children, and perform the Prayer there. It is advisable to continue the Prayer until rain comes. The supplication reported from God's Messenger to be recited after the Prayer is as follows:

> My God! Give us water, useful, plentiful, and within a short time, and not late! My God! Give water to Your servants and animals, and spread Your mercy, and revive Your dead land.[96]

Supererogatory Prayers

Supererogatory (*nafila*) Prayers are important in that they make up for any deficiencies in performing the prescribed Prayers and bring us closer to God, Who declares:

> My servant cannot get near to Me through anything else more lovable to Me than doing the obligatory religious duties. However, by doing supererogatory duties he gets nearer to Me, and when he becomes near to Me, I become his eyes to see with, his ears to hear with, his hands to grasp with, and his legs to walk with.[97]

Supererogatory Prayers are offered in cycles of two *rak'as*. Praying two to eight *rak'as* in broad daylight in the time before the sun reaches its zenith (*duha*), and four *rak'as* between the evening and late evening Prayers (*awwabin*) are the most advisable of the supererogatory Prayers.

Such supererogatory Prayers are important, for God's Messenger, upon him be peace and blessings, said the following about the *duha* (broad daylight) Prayer:

> Charity is required from every part of your body daily. Every saying of "All-Glorious is God" is charity. Every saying of "All praise is for God" is charity. Every saying of "There is no deity but God" is charity. Every saying of "God is the All-Great" is charity. Ordering good is charity. Forbidding evil is charity. And what suffices for all these (as charity) are the two rak'as of the duha (broad daylight) Prayer.[98]

Praying two *rak'as* on entering a mosque before sitting down is also advised by God's Messenger, upon him be peace and blessings.[99] This Prayer is called the Prayer of greeting the mosque (*Salatu tahiyyati'l-masjid*).

Offering Supererogatory Prayers at Home

Ahmad ibn Hanbal and Muslim relate from Jabir that the Messenger of God said, "If one of you offers his Prayers in the mosque, then he should offer a portion of his Prayers at home, as God has made saying Prayers in one's home a means of betterment (for him)."[100] Ahmad records from 'Umar that the Messenger of God said, "The supererogatory Prayers prayed by a person at home are a light. Whoever wishes should light up his house."

Reciting Long Passages

It is preferred to prolong one's recitation during supererogatory Prayers. God's Messenger would stand and pray until his feet swelled. When he was asked about it, he said, "Should I not be a thankful servant?"[101]

The *Jumu'a* (Friday) Congregational Prayer

The Friday congregational Prayer is obligatory and a significant Islamic symbol. It is ordered in the Qur'an specifically:

> O you who believe! When the call is made for the Prayer on Friday, then move promptly to the remembrance of God (by listening to the sermon and doing the Prayer), and leave off business (and whatever else you may be preoccupied with). This is better for you, if you but knew. (62:9)

God's Messenger declared that God seals the heart of one who misses *Jumu'a* congregational Prayer three consecutive times without a valid excuse.[102] He also said that *Jumu'a* (Friday) is the best of the days.[103] The *Jumu'a* congregational Prayer also has aspects concerning the Muslim community's political freedom and condition, and cannot be offered alone.

When and Who

It is offered at the time of the noon Prayer on Friday. Every free, adult, sane, resident, male Muslim who can attend must attend, unless he has a valid reason not to do so. It is not obligatory upon women, children, those with valid excuses (e.g., illness, lack of security, extreme cold), and travelers.[104]

Preparations

Increase prayers, supplications, and calling God's blessings and peace upon the Messenger and his Family on Friday, especially before the Friday Prayer. Perform the major ablution (*ghusl*) and put on your best clothes. Men should use the best allowable perfume. According to some scholars, based on a Prophetic Tradition, taking the major ablution is necessary. It is also recommended to follow the Messenger's example of reciting ten verses from the beginning and end of *Surat al-Kahf*. Also, men should go to the mosque early.[105]

Conditions for Its Validity

The Friday congregational Prayer has aspects concerning the Muslim community's political freedom, as follows:

- It is offered in a city (*misr*) that contains a government (local or national), or in a village having thirty, forty, or more houses—which looks like a city in its outward form.[106]
- It is preferably offered in a large, central mosque and led by the district or city governor or imam (Prayer leader) who is able to lead it and has been appointed by the governor to do so. In the capital city, it is preferably offered by the president or a capable imam appointed by him.[107]
- There must be at least three people to form a congregation behind the imam. Although according to Imam as-Shafi'i and Ahmad ibn Hanbal there must be at least forty people, Imam Malik argues that while God's Messenger was giving the sermon during a Friday Prayer, a long-expected caravan came to Madina from Syria during a famine, and most of the congregation left the mosque. There were only twelve people left in the mosque, and the Messenger performed the Prayer with them.[108]

The Adhan

A second call to the Prayer (*adhan*), other than the usual one, is made before the Friday sermon in the mosque.

The Sermon

A sermon must be given before the Friday Prayer. The imam gives it from a pulpit while standing.[109] He begins it by praising God and calling God's blessings and peace upon His Messenger and his Family. Next, he gives a sermon in which he exhorts Muslims to good deeds, discourages them from evil, advises them, and seeks to enlighten them mentally and spiritually and to guide them. He should not give a lengthy sermon. After this part of the sermon, he sits for a short while and then, standing up, praises God, calls God's blessings and peace upon God's Messenger and his Family, and prays for all Muslims.[110] The congregation must listen carefully and silently.[111]

Sunna Prayers before and after the Friday Prayer

The Friday Prayer consists of two *rak'as*. It is *sunna* to offer four *rak'as* before it, just like the four *rak'as* offered before the noon Prayer. After the Prayer, another supererogatory Prayer of four *rak'as* is recommended.[112]

Scholars have had some doubts about the Friday Prayer's validity for centuries, due the Muslim community's condition. Therefore, to be sure about the performance of the prescribed noon Prayer, they have ruled that another Prayer of four *rak'as* (*Salatu'z-Zuhr*), just like the noon prescribed Prayer and with the intention of offering a later noon Prayer, should be offered after the four-*rak'a* supererogatory Prayer.[113] They also advise following this with another supererogatory Prayer of two *rak'ats* with the intention of offering the *sunna* Prayer for that time.

'Iyd (Religious Festive Days) Prayers (*Salat al-'Iydayn*)

The two *'Iyd* Prayers are considered necessary (*wajib*) and are to be offered on the two annual religious festive days: *'Iydu'l-Fitr* (marking the end of Ramadan) and *'Iydu'l-Adha* (on the tenth day of Dhu'l-Hijja, the Day of Sacrifice). The former continues for three days, and the latter for four days.

The Religious Festive Days

On these days, Muslims visit, congratulate and offer gifts to one another, and display greater generosity by honoring elders and pleasing the needy and children especially. They amuse themselves within religious and moral bounds, occupy themselves with reciting the Qur'an, mentioning God's Names, and supplicating. It is advisable to perform *ghusl* (major ablution) and wear the best clothes and religiously allowed perfume. On the Day of Sacrifice, they offer cattle or sheep or goats to God as a sacrifice, as will be explained below.

The Prayer

The *'Iyd* Prayers can be offered from when the sun is three spears above the horizon (approximately three quarters of an hour after sunrise) until it reaches its zenith. During the Age of Happiness, the *'Iyd* Prayers used to be performed on an area of open land. God's Messenger, upon him be peace and blessings, wanted all men, women (regardless of marital status, age, or if they are menstruating), and children to go out to the place of Prayer. Menstruating women did not participate in the Prayer; they witnessed the Prayer and supplications of the Muslims. All the women wore loose, outer garments.[114] There is no *adhan* or *iqama*, unlike the Friday Prayer.[115]

Offering the 'Iyd Prayer

The *'Iyd* Prayer consists of two *rak'as* and is offered like the Friday Prayer, except for extra *takbirs* (*Allahu akbar* [God is the All-Great]). Like other Prayers, the imam and the congregation make the intention and say the opening *takbir*, and then recite the supplication silently. After the supplication and before reciting *al-Fatiha*, the imam leads the congregation in three extra *takbirs* by raising his hands while saying the opening *takbir*. After the first two *takbirs*, they leave their arms down, and after the third, they hold their hands under the navel and the imam begins to recite *al-Fatiha*. After completing the first *rak'a* and reciting *al-Fatiha* and another Qur'anic passage in the second *rak'a*, the imam leads the congregation in extra *takbirs* again. This time they say four *takbirs* and, leaving their arms down after the first three, bow after the fourth one. Then they complete the Prayer.

The Sermon

After the Prayer, the imam gives a sermon just as he does at the Friday congregational Prayer.

Takbirs during the 'Iyds

Muslims must exalt God on the Festive Days of Sacrifice by pronouncing, *Allahu akbar, Allahu akbar; la ilaha illa'llahu wa'llahu akbar; Allahu akbar wa li'llahi'l-hamd* (God is the All-Great, God is the All-Great. There is no deity but God, and God is the All-Great. God is the All-Great and His is all praise). It is pronounced after every prescribed Prayer after the dawn Prayer on the day before the Festive Day, and ends after the afternoon Prayer on the fourth day of *'Iyd*.

Religious Festivals

Almost every nation has religious festivals to commemorate important events in its history or to celebrate special occasions. There are two religious festivals in Islam: *'Iydu'l-Fitr* (marking the end of Ramadan's month-long, dawn-to-sunset fast) and *'Iydu'l-Adha* (the festival of sacrifice), which falls on the tenth day of Dhu'l-Hijja, the last month of the Islamic year in which the pilgrimage is performed. Both festivals enjoy a special place in the life of Muslims, and leave indelible impressions upon their cultures.

Religious festivals are times of deepened Islamic thoughts and occasions of paradoxical feelings—pangs of separation and hopes of reunion, regrets and expectations, and joys and sorrows.

Muslims enjoy the pleasure of reunion and universal fellowship on festive days. They smile at each other lovingly, greet each other respectfully, and visit each other. Members of families divided by modern, industrialized life and forced to live in different towns come together and enjoy the delight of eating and living together once again, if only for a few days.

Religious festivals are occasions for spiritual revival through seeking God's forgiveness and through praising and glorifying Him. Muslims are enraptured by special supplications, odes, and eulogies for the Prophet, upon him be peace and blessings. Especially in traditional circles where traces of the past are still alive, people experience the festival's meaning in a more vivid, colorful fashion, on cushions or sofas, or around stoves in their humble houses, or under the trees among their gardens' flowers, or in the spacious halls of their homes. They feel its meaning in each morsel they eat, in each sip they drink, and in each word they speak about their traditional and religious values.

Religious festivals have a much greater significance for children. They feel a special joy and pleasure in the warm, embracing climate of the festivals, which they have been preparing to welcome for several days. Like nightingales singing on the branches of trees, they cause us to experience the festivals more deeply through their play, songs, smiles, and cheerfulness.

Religious festivals provide the most practical means for improving human relationships. People experience a deep inward pleasure, and meet and exchange good wishes in a blessed atmosphere of spiritual harmony. When the festival permeates hearts with Prayer and supplications performed consciously, souls are elevated to the realm of eternity. They then feel the urge to abandon the clutches of worldly attachments and live in the depths of their spiritual being. In the atmosphere overflowing with love and mercy, new hope is injected with life.

Believing souls welcome the religious festivals with wonder and expectations of otherworldly pleasures. Indeed, it is difficult to understand fully what believing souls feel in their hearts during these religious festivals. To perceive the feelings thus aroused in pure souls who lead their life in ecstasies of otherworldly pleasures, we must experience such pleasures to the same degree. Having reached the day of the festival after fulfilling their prescribed duty of praying and responsibility, these souls display such a dignity and serenity, and such a grace and spiritual perfection, that those who see them think that they have all received a perfect religious and spiritual education. Some of them are so sincere and devoted to God Almighty that each seems to be the embodiment of centuries-old universal values. One may experience through their conduct and manners that taste of the fruits of Paradise, the peaceful atmosphere on its slopes, and the delight of being near to God.[116]

The Funeral Prayer

God's Messenger, upon him be peace and blessings, exhorts us to remember death much, for it destroys pleasures.[117] He also exhorts us to remember the decay of our bodies under the earth, and reminds us that one who desires the afterlife abandons the ornaments of the worldly life.[118] This does not mean that death is something to fear. For a believer, death is a discharge from this worldly life's duties, a change of residence, a transferal of the body, an invitation to and the beginning of an everlasting life. Life or coming to the world is through the judgment and creation of God, and departure from the world is also through His judgment and creation, as well as through His wisdom and rule. For, the dying of plants, the simplest level of life, is a work of Divine artistry, as is their living—but more perfect and better designed. This is so because when a fruit seed dies, it seems to decompose and rot away into the soil. But in reality, it undergoes a perfect chemical process, passes through predetermined states of re-formation, and grows again into an elaborate new tree. Thus the seed's "death" is a new tree's beginning, and death, which is something created like life, is as perfect as life. Since like life, death is something created (Qur'an, 67:2) and whatever God creates is beautiful (32:7), death is also beautiful.

As the death of fruits and animal flesh in people's stomachs raises them to the degree of human life, this death can be regarded as more perfect than their lives. Since a plant's death is so perfect and serves so great a purpose, each person's death must be much more perfect and serve a still greater purpose, for humanity is life's highest level. After "going underground," each of us will be brought into eternal life.

Death is a blessing for many reasons. Let me[119] briefly set down four:

First: It discharges us from life's hardships, which gradually become harder through old age. It also allows us to meet again the ninety-nine percent of our friends who have already died.

Second: It releases us from worldly life, which is a turbulent, suffocating, narrow dungeon, and admits us to the wide circle of the Eternally Beloved One's Mercy, where we enjoy a pleasant and everlasting life without any suffering.

Third: It frees us from our suffering on account of our beloved ones. For example, if your old parents and grandparents were living in misery in front of your eyes, you would see death as a great blessing and life as an unendurable pain. Besides, to cite another example, the autumnal death of insects (lovers of lovely flowers) shows how death is a mercy for them, for they do not have to live through winter's harshness and severity.

Fourth: Sleep is a time of repose and relief, and thus a mercy, especially for the sick and afflicted. Similarly, death (the "brother" of sleep) is a blessing and mercy especially for those afflicted with such misfortune that they might contemplate suicide. As for the misguided, both life and death are torment within torment and pain after pain.

The Rights of a Living and a Dead Muslim upon Living Muslims

Bara ibn 'Azib says:

> God's Messenger ordered us to follow the funeral procession, to visit the sick, to accept invitations, to help the oppressed, to help others to fulfill their oaths, to return the greeting, and to reply to one who sneezes (saying, "May God have mercy on you," provided the sneezer says, "All praise is for God.").[120]

A dead Muslim has four rights over living Muslims: The right to be washed, shrouded, prayed over, and buried. However, Muslims are not obliged to do so for those who die as apostates or while fighting against them.

Visiting a Sick Person

Sickness causes the forgiveness of a Muslim's sins, so long as he or she shows becoming patience. God's Messenger declared, "No Muslim is afflicted with harm because of sickness or some other inconvenience, but that God will remove his sins for him as a tree sheds its leaves."[121] It is a highly recommended and meritorious act to visit a sick person and pray for them.[122] Muslims suggest to the dying that they should declare God's Oneness: *La ilaha illa'llah, Muhammadun Rasulu'llah* (There is no deity but God, and Muhammad is His Messenger) or the profession of faith: *Ashhadu an la ilaha illa'llah wa ashhadu anna Muhammadan 'abduhu wa rasuluh* (I bear witness that there is no deity but God, and I also bear witness that Muhammad is His servant and Messenger.).[123] The Messenger advises the suffering not to wish for death but to pray, "My God! Make me live so long as living is good for me, and make me die when dying is good for me."[124]

Washing a Corpse

When a Muslim dies, the corpse should be turned in the direction of the Ka'ba, and washed by one knowledgeable in the way the major ablution (*ghusl*) is taken. Before the washing, he or she is given minor ablution. Women wash deceased women, and men wash deceased men. However, a woman can wash her deceased husband. The corpse should be scented with camphor, musk, and similar scents.

Offering the Funeral Prayer

After the washing, the deceased Muslim is wrapped in a shroud and put in a coffin. This holds true for everyone except martyrs, who are buried in the clothes in which they were martyred. The corpse is placed upon a raised platform or a smooth stone so that its right side faces the *qibla*. The congregation then stands to pray with the corpse lying before them. While this Prayer is obligatory upon all Muslims and must be prayed in congregation, when only some of them offer it, the others do not have to. Women also can attend. As many Muslims as possible should participate in the Prayer, and say good things for or testify in favor of the deceased Muslim, for their testimony will be taken into consideration about the deceased one.[125]

The imam makes the intention to pray for the deceased (the deceased's gender should be specified) for God's sake and good pleasure. The congregation makes the same intention and then adds the intention to pray behind the imam. Then, following the imam, they begin the Prayer with the opening *takbir* (as in all other Prayers) and supplicate while, according to the Hanafi School, keeping the hands under the navel (or on the chest in the case of women). Then, they say *takbir* again while keeping the hands under the navel (or on the chest for women) and call God's blessings and peace upon His

Messenger and his Family (as in the final sittings of other Prayers). They repeat *takbir* while keeping the hands under the navel (or on the chest for women), pray for the deceased and all other Muslims (both alive or dead). They say *takbir* for the fourth time, and give salutations to the right and left.[126]

Burying the Deceased

While a deceased person is being taken to the grave, those happening to be on the sides of the road should stand up if they are sitting. When God's Messenger did so once, those present said, "That one is a Jew." The Messenger replied, "Is that one not a human being?"[127]

Muslims place the deceased in the grave while saying, *Bi'smi'llahi 'ala millat-i Rasuli'llah* (In God's Name and according to the religion and way of God's Messenger). The deceased is laid on his or her right side facing the *qibla*, and the shroud is then untied. A stone or something similar is placed in the grave diagonally and in a slanting position so that the corpse should not be covered with soil. Soil is placed on the stone and then is used to cover the grave. After reciting some Qur'anic passages and praying to God for the deceased one, the people leave. However, it is considered good that a Muslim stays behind and suggests to the buried one the pillars of faith.

Congregational Prayer

Reciting *al-Fatiha* in Prayers is obligatory. Even if we pray individually, we address our Lord in *al-Fatiha*, saying, "You alone do *we* worship, and from You alone do *we* seek help." This demonstrates that praying in congregation is, at least, better and preferable. So, although according to the majority of scholars performing the Prayers in congregation is a *sunna mu'akkada* (a *sunna* emphasized by the Messenger), many scholars consider it necessary (*wajib*).

While describing *Salatu'l-Khawf* (the Prayer performed during times of fear or danger), God Almighty says, *When you are among the believers and stand to lead the Prayer for them, let a party of them stand in Prayer with you and retain their arms with them (while the other party maintain their positions against the enemy). When the first party have done the prostrations (finished the rak'a), let them go to the rear of your company (and there, hold positions against the enemy), and let the other party who have not prayed come forward and pray with you, being fully prepared against danger and retaining their arms* (4:102). That is to say, even in times of fear and danger during war, God mentions congregational Prayer. This shows the importance of peforming Prayers in congregation in times of security. Concerning congregational Prayer, God's Messenger, upon him be peace and blessings, says:

> The Prayer in congregation is twenty-seven times superior to the Prayer performed alone.[128]
>
> Whoever performs ablution and does it perfectly, and then goes out to the mosque with the sole intention of praying, then for each step he takes towards the mosque God raises him a degree in reward and forgives one sin till he enters the mosque. So long as he is busy in Prayer after having entered the mosque, the angels keep on asking for God's forgiveness for him and they keep on saying, "O God! Have mercy on him; O God! forgive him!"[129]
>
> If the people knew what excellence there is in the adhan and in the first row (in congregational Prayers) and found no other way to get that except by drawing lots, they would draw lots; and if they knew what excellence lies in joining the Prayer in the first (opening) takbir, they would vie with one another for it. And if they knew what excellence lies in 'isha' and fajr (early morning) Prayers in congregation, they would come to offer them even if they had to crawl.[130]

Women. As mentioned before, God's Messenger, upon him be peace and blessings, asked women to attend particularly the *'Iyd* Prayers. Even the menstruating women went out for the *'Iyd Prayers* but did not perform the Prayer. They stood away from the place of the Prayer. All of them wore loose, outer garments. However, it has been considered better for women to pray in their houses than to attend congregational Prayers.[131] But if women go to the mosque to attend the congregational Prayer, they must avoid flaunting their charms as women used to do in the former Times of Ignorance (Qur'an, 33:33), wearing attractive clothing and using any tempting perfume.[132]

Conditions to be Met by the Muadhdhin (the Caller to the Prayer). The Messenger praised *muadhdhin* and gave them good tidings of great reward.[133] However, in order to deserve this praise and reward, they have to meet certain conditions, as follows:

- Make the call when it is time to pray.[134]
- Make the call to the Prayer for God's sake, not for wages. God's Messenger advised Uthman Ibn Abi'l-'As, whom he appointed as the imam of his people, to have a *muadhdhin* who would not demand payment for calling to the Prayer.[135] However, this does not mean that no payment should be made to the *muadhdhin* by people or authorities.
- Be clean from major or minor impurities.[136]
- Stand and face the *qibla*. Turn his head, neck, and chest to the right upon saying, *Hayya 'ala's-salah*, and to the left upon saying, *Hayya 'ala'l-falah*. Insert his index fingers into his ears so that his voice may be louder.[137]
- Raise his voice for the call, even if he is alone in the desert. So, a *muadhdhin* should be one with a beautiful, clear, and loud voice, and adorn the *adhan* with his beautiful voice and tone.[138]
- Pause between each phrase of the *adhan*.[139]
- The call to the Prayer should be made in its own, original language—Arabic.

  The *adhan* is one of the important, collective symbols or marks of Islam. In addition, it is a declaration of Islam's basic principles.

- Those who hear the *adhan* should listen to it silently. They repeat its phrases except *hayya 'ala's-salah* and *hayya 'ala'l-falah*. When these two phrases are called, they say, *La hawla wa la quwwata illa bi'llah* (There is no might and strength save with God).[140]

Whoever Gives the Adhan Gives the Iqama. It is highly recommended and preferable that whoever gives the *adhan* gives the *iqama*. A man who prays alone is encouraged to give the *adhan*, if he did not listen to its public recitation, and should give the *iqama*.[141]

The Adhan and Iqama for Women. The majority of scholars state that there is no *adhan* or *iqama* for women. However, some maintain that women can form a congregation and pray, and that one of them can serve as the imam. She must stand in the middle of the first row. This is reported from the Prophet by 'Ali ibn Abi Talib.[142]

The Imam. The imam must meet several conditions, as follows:

- If the congregation includes men and women, the imam must be a Muslim, adult man of sound reason.
- He must be well-versed in Qur'anic recitation and knowledgeable of the Prayer's obligatory, necessary, and *sunna* acts.
- He should be of good character and reputation.
- He should be the most knowledgeable (of those present) of Islamic jurisprudence and Qur'anic recitation, have excellent qualities and character.[143]
- He should not have a health problem that causes him to continually lose his ablution, unless all others in the congregation have the same or a similar problem.[144]
- Being older in age is another reason of preference for imamate.[145]
- If a congregation is formed in a house to pray, the householder who has the necessary qualities for imamate should lead the Prayer.
- According to scholars, any adult male whose Prayer is valid for himself is valid for others if he serves as the imam. However, Muslims do not like to pray behind an evildoer or an innovator.

Where the Imam and the Congregation Stand. The imam stands before the congregation. Preferably, one person stands to the imam's right. If there are two or more people, they stand behind the imam. The Messenger placed the men in front of the young boys and the women behind the young boys.[146]

Straightening the Rows and Filling the Gaps. The imam should tell the members of the congregation to straighten the rows and fill in any gaps before starting the Prayer. Even if the imam does not tell them to do so, the congregation must do that.[147]

The Imam's and Congregation's Recitation. It is enough for the imam to recite *al-Fatiha* and another Qur'anic passage, and for the congregation to keep silent. The congregation makes all other recitations, including *takbirs*, the supplication before *al-Fatiha*, the words of glorification in *ruku'* and *sujud*, and *tashahhud* and calls for God's blessings and peace upon God's Messenger and his Family.

Correcting the Imam's Mistake. If the imam forgets a verse, recites incorrectly, or makes a mistake in praying, someone in the congregation should correct him, and anyone who is known to be able to correct him is preferred to stand just behind the imam.[148]

Following the Imam. Every member of the congregation must follow the imam without delay, and must not to precede him in any action during the Prayer.

Putting a Partition in front of Oneself while Praying. Anything that one sets in front of oneself while praying qualifies as a partition, even if it is only the bed's end. The Messenger said, "When one of you prays, he should make a partition for his Prayer, even if it is an arrow." This is done so that others cannot pass in front of one who is praying. It is forbidden to pass in front of one who is praying (i.e., between the person and his or her partition). If there is no such probability, making a partition is not necessary. The partition should be close enough that there is only room enough to prostrate.

A person can make a gesture to stop someone from passing in front of him or her; however, this must not be of the kind that will invalidate one's Prayer, like speaking. The Prayer is not invalidated if a person or an animal passes in front of the one who is praying.[149]

The Earth as a Mosque. A Muslim can pray anywhere, as long as the place does not have enough dirt to invalidate the Prayer, has not been usurped, and does not belong to one who will not allow the Prayer therein. This is a special blessing of God for the Muslim community. Given this, the whole earth can serve as a mosque.[150]

Three Most Excellent Mosques. One can pray in any mosque. However, three mosques have a particular sacredness and provide those praying within them with far more merit than others one may pray in. In order of merit and sacredness, they are the Sacred Mosque in Makka, the Prophet's Mosque in Madina, and the Masjid al-Aqsa in Quds (Jerusalem).[151]

Joining the Congregation

Whoever joins a congregation which has already started praying must say the opening *takbir* while standing and then move directly to the act that the congregation is performing. For instance, if the congregation is prostrating one should perform the opening *takbir* and then prostrate.

- God Almighty orders bowing together with those who bow (2:43). This shows that *ruku'* is the symbol of the *rak'a*. If one joins the congregation during the *ruku'* following the standing position (*qiyam*), one is considered to have performed that *rak'a*. If it belongs to the first *rak'a*, one who joins the congregation during it and completes the Prayer after the imam is considered to have performed the whole Prayer.
- If one joins after the *ruku'*, one is considered to have missed the *rak'a* or *rak'as* preceding it. If one joins during the second *rak'a*, no matter in which Prayer it occurs, after the imam gives the first salutation (to his right), one stands up and performs the first missed *rak'a*, reciting *al-Fatiha* and a Qur'anic passage, performs the *ruku'*, *sujud*, and the final sitting, and ends the Prayer with salutations.
- If one joins after the *ruku'* of the second *rak'a* in the dawn Prayer, one stands up after the imam gives the first salutation and performs the Prayer completely, without, however, saying

the opening *takbir*. If one joins the evening Prayer, one follows the imam until he gives the first salutation, and then stands up, recites *al-Fatiha* and a Qur'anic passage, performs the *ruku'* and *sujud*, and sits. This is one's second *rak'a*. After reciting the *tashahhud*, one stands up and recites *al-Fatiha* and a Qur'anic passage, does the *ruku'* and *sujud*, performs the final sitting, and ends the Prayer with salutations. If one joins the noon, afternoon, or late evening Prayers, one follows the imam until he gives the first salutation and then stands up. One completes the Prayer by performing the two first *rak'as* missed as if performing a Prayer of two *rak'as*.

- If one joins the congregation in the fourth *rak'a* or after the *ruku'* following the third *rak'a*, one follows the imam until he gives the first salutation and then stands up. One performs the first *rak'a* missed by reciting *al-Fatiha* and a Qur'anic passage, doing the *ruku'* and *sujud* and sits. After reciting the *tashahhud*, one stands up, recites *al-Fatiha* and a Qur'anic passage, does the *ruku'* and *sujud*, and stands up. Then one recites only *al-Fatiha*, does the *ruku'* and *sujud*, and sits to recite *tashahhud*, calls for God's blessings and peace upon the Messenger and his Family, and ends the Prayer by giving salutations.
- If one joins the congregation after the *ruku'* of the last *rak'a* of any Prayer, one has missed that Prayer and, standing when the imam gives the salutation to the right, offers the Prayer completely without, however, saying the opening *takbir*.
- If one is offering the dawn or evening Prayer alone and people form a congregation behind an imam in the place where one is praying, and if one has not yet prostrated after the second *rak'a*, one must leave the Prayer by giving salutations and join the congregation. If one is offering a Prayer of four *rak'as* and is offering the first *rak'a*, one also joins the congregation, having left the Prayer one was performing. If one is offering the second *rak'a*, one completes the first two *rak'as*, as if perform-

ing a Prayer of two *rak'as*, and joins the congregation. If one is offering the third *rak'a*, one joins the congregation. If one is offering the fourth *rak'a*, one completes the Prayer without joining the congregation.

Making up Missed Prayers

The Prayer is the most important kind of worship. It is the support of the Religion, and therefore can never be omitted. So, scholars agree that all Prayers that have been missed for whatever reason must be made up. One can perform the missed Prayer at any time, except when praying is prohibited. The Muslim army missed the early morning Prayer during its return from the conquest of Khaybar due to tiredness and sleep. After the sun rose to some height they took ablution, Bilal al-Habashi made the call to the Prayer, they made up the *Sunna* Prayer, Bilal gave the *iqama* and they performed the two *rak'as* of the obligatory Prayer in congregation.[152] One day, during the Battle of the Trench, the Muslims could not perform the noon, afternoon, and evening Prayers. At some time during the night, God's Messenger ordered Bilal to make the call to Prayer. Bilal made the call and the *iqama*, and the Messenger led the noon Prayer which had been missed. Then he led the other missed Prayers before each of which Bilal made the *iqama*.[153]

If a person has missed less than six Prayers, he or she should first perform the missed Prayer or Prayers before performing a new Prayer whose time it is. Doing so shows that one is a person of order, and making up missed Prayers reinforces this. However, if one has missed more than six Prayers, one can make them up in all times when praying is permissible.

Chapter 4

Sawm ar-Ramadan
(Fasting the Month of Ramadan)

SAWM AR-RAMADAN

(FASTING THE MONTH OF RAMADAN)

The fourth pillar of Islam is the Ramadan fast, during which Muslims abstain from eating, drinking, and sexual relations or satisfaction from dawn until sunset. Concerning the order to fast, the Qur'an declares:

> The month of Ramadan, in which the Qur'an was sent down as guidance for people, and as clear signs of Guidance and the Criterion (between truth and falsehood). Therefore whoever of you is present this month must fast it, and whoever is so ill that he cannot fast or is on a journey (must fast the same) number of other days. God wills ease for you, and He does not will hardship for you, so that you can complete the number of the days required, and exalt God for He has guided you, and so it may be that you will give thanks (due to Him). (2:185)

Mu'adh ibn Jabal narrates:

> We were together with God's Messenger on an expedition. I happened to be beside him and went on together. I said to him, "O Messenger of God! Please tell me a deed which will keep me away from Hell and cause me to enter Paradise." He said, "You asked about an important matter. It is easy for one whom God favors with its easy fulfillment. You will worship God, without associating any partners with Him. You will perform the Prayer, pay the Prescribed Alms, fast Ramadan, and do pilgrimage to God's House (the Ka'ba)." He added, "Shall I show you to the doors of good?" "Yes, please O Messenger of God!" I replied. He said, "Fasting is a veil to Hell; charity wipes away faults, just as water extinguishes fire. The Prayer performed at night (*tahajjud*) is the mark of the righteous." Then he recited the verse: *Their sides forsake their beds at night, calling out to their Lord in fear (of His punishment) and hope (for His forgiveness, grace,*

> *and good pleasure), and out of what We have provided for them (of wealth, knowledge, power, etc.), they spend (to provide sustenance for the needy and in God's cause, purely for the good pleasure of God and without placing others under obligation).* (32:16)[1]

God's Méssenger declared:

> "Every (good) deed of the Adam's children would be multiplied, a good deed receiving a tenfold to seven hundredfold reward," God, the All-Exalted and Majestic, said, "except fasting. It is meant for Me, and I will give the reward for it." Fasting is a shield (against the fire and from committing sins.) When one of you is fasting, he should avoid sexual relations with his wife and quarreling, and if somebody should fight or quarrel with him, he should say, "I am fasting." By Him in Whose Hands my soul is, the smell coming out from the mouth of a fasting person is better in God's sight than the smell of musk. The one who fasts has two (occasions) of joy, one when he breaks his fast, and the other when he will meet his Lord—when he will be pleased because of his fasting.[2]

The Holy Month of Ramadan[3]

> The month of Ramadan, in which the Qur'an (began to be) sent down as guidance for people, and as clear signs of Guidance and the Criterion (between truth and falsehood) (2:102).

First point. Fasting Ramadan is one of Islam's foremost pillars and greatest symbols. Many of its purposes relate to God's Lordship and giving thanks for His bounties, as well as to humanity's individual and collective life, self-training, and self-discipline.

One purpose connected with His Lordship is that God displays His Lordship's perfection and His being the All-Merciful and All-Compassionate upon the earth's surface, which He designed as a table to hold His bounties in a way beyond human imagination. Nevertheless, people cannot perfectly discern this situation's reality due to heedlessness and causality's blinding veil. But during Ramadan, like an army waiting for its marching orders, believers display an attitude of worship towards the end of the day as if they expect to be told to help themselves to the banquet prepared by the Eternal Monarch. Thus they respond to that magnificent and universal manifestation of Divine Mercifulness with a comprehensive and harmonious act of collective worship. I wonder if those who do not worship or share in the honor of being so favored deserve to be called human.

Second point. From the viewpoint of its being related to gratitude to God, one of the instances of wisdom in fasting during Ramadan is this: As stated by Said Nursi in "The First Word" in "The Words" collection, there is a price for the food brought by a servant from the king's kitchen. Obviously, it would be an incredible folly to tip the servant and not recognize the king, [for this would show] a clear disrespect for that gift. In the same way, God Almighty spreads His countless bounties on the earth and bestows them for a price: thanksgiving.

The apparent causes of those bounties or those who bring them to us are like the servant in the above example. We pay servants, feel indebted to and thank them, even though they are only causes or means. We sometimes show them a degree of respect they do not merit. The true Giver of Bounties is infinitely more deserving of thanks for these bounties. Such thanksgiving assumes the form of acknowledging one's need for the bounties, appreciating them fully, and ascribing them directly to Him.

Fasting Ramadan is the key to a true, sincere, comprehensive, and universal thanksgiving. Many people cannot appreciate most of the bounties they enjoy, for they do not experience hunger. For example, a piece of dry bread means nothing to those who are full, especially if they are rich. However, the believers' sense of taste testifies at the time of breaking the fast that it is indeed a very valuable bounty of God. During Ramadan, everyone is favored with heartfelt thanksgiving by understanding the value of Divine bounties.

While fasting, believers think, "These bounties do not originally belong to me, and so I cannot regard them as mere food or drink. Since the One Who owns them grants them to me, I should wait for His permission to eat them." By thus acknowledging food and drink as Divine gifts, believers tacitly thank God. This is why fasting is a key to thanksgiving, which is a fundamental human duty.

Third point. Fasting is related to humanity's collective life, for humans have been created differently in regard to livelihood. So God invites the rich to help the poor. Without fasting, many rich and self-indulgent people cannot perceive the pain of hunger and poverty or to what extent the poor need care. Care for one's fellow beings is a foundation of true thanksgiving. There is always someone poorer, so everyone must help such people. If people do not experience hunger, it is nearly impossible for them to do good or to help others. Even if they do, they can do so only imperfectly because they do not feel the hungry one's condition to the same extent.

Fourth point. Fasting Ramadan contains many Divine purposes related to self-training and self-discipline, such as: The carnal self desires—and considers itself—to be free and unrestricted. It even wishes, by its very nature, for an imagined lordship and free, arbitrary action. Not liking to think that it is being trained and tested through God's countless bounties, it swallows up such bounties like an animal and in the manner of a thief or robber, especially if its wealth and power are accompanied by heedlessness.

During Ramadan, everyone's selfhood understands that it is owned by One Other, not by itself; that it is a servant, not a free agent. Unless ordered or permitted, it cannot do even the most common things, like eating and drinking. This inability shatters its illusory lordship and enables it to admit its servanthood and perform its real duty of thanksgiving.

Fifth point. Fasting Ramadan prevents the carnal self from rebelling and adorns it with good morals. A person's carnal self forgets itself through heedlessness. It neither sees nor wants to see its inherent, infinite impotence, poverty, and defect. It does not reflect upon how it is exposed to misfortune and subject to decay, and that it consists of flesh and bones that disintegrate and decompose rapidly. It rushes upon the world with a violent greed and attachment, as if it had a steel body and would live forever, and clings to whatever is profitable and pleasurable. In this state it forgets its Creator, Who trains it with perfect care. Being immersed in the swamp of immorality, it does not think about the consequences of its life here or its afterlife.

But fasting the month of Ramadan causes even the most heedless and stubborn to feel their weakness and innate poverty. Hunger becomes an important consideration and reminds them of how fragile their bodies really are. They perceive their need for compassion and care and, giving up haughtiness, want to take refuge in the Divine Court in perfect helplessness and destitution, rising to knock at the door of Mercy with the hand of tacit thanksgiving— provided, of course, that heedlessness has not yet corrupted them completely.

Sixth point. God revealed the Qur'an during Ramadan. This has many implications, such as: In order to welcome the month when the Qur'an, that Divine Address, was revealed, believers should try to be like angels by abandoning eating and drinking. They also should seek to divest themselves of the carnal self's vain preoccupations and gross needs. During Ramadan, they should recite or listen to the Qur'an as if it were being revealed for the first time. If possible, they should listen to it as if they were hearing Prophet Muhammad recite it, or Archangel Gabriel reciting it to Muhammad, upon him be peace and blessings, or God revealing it to Muhammad through Gabriel. They should respect the Qur'an in their daily actions and, by conveying its message to others, demonstrate the Divine purpose for its revelation.

Ramadan transforms the Muslim world into a huge mosque in which millions recite the Qur'an to the earth's inhabitants. Displaying the reality of *The month of Ramadan, in which the Qur'an (began to be) sent down* (2:185), Ramadan proves itself to be the month of the Qur'an. While some in the vast congregation in the great mosque of the Muslim world listen to its recitation with solemn reverence, others recite it. It is most disagreeable to forsake that heavenly spiritual state by obeying the carnal self, and thus eating and drinking in the sacred "mosque," for this provokes the whole congregation's hatred. It is also most disagreeable, and must provoke the Muslim world's dislike and contempt, to counter and defy those Muslims who fast Ramadan.

Seventh point. Fasting Ramadan has many purposes related to a person's spiritual rewards, as everyone is sent here to sow this world with the seeds of the next life. The following paragraphs explain one such purpose, as follows:

The rewards for good deeds done during Ramadan are multiplied by a thousand. One Tradition states that ten rewards are given for each letter of the Qur'an. Reciting one letter means ten good deeds and brings forth ten fruits of Paradise. But during Ramadan, this reward is multiplied by a thousand and even more for such verses as the "Verse of the Throne."[4] The reward is even greater on Ramadan's Friday nights. Furthermore, each letter is multiplied thirty thousand times if recited during the Night of Power and Destiny.

During Ramadan the Qur'an, each letter of which yields thirty thousand permanent fruits of Paradise, becomes like a huge, blessed tree producing millions of permanent fruits of Paradise. Consider how holy and profitable this trade is, and how great a loss for those who do not appreciate the Qur'an's letters.

So Ramadan is the most proper time for such a profitable trade in the afterlife's name. It is like a most fertile field to cultivate for the afterlife's harvest. Its multiplication of rewards for good deeds makes it like April in spring. It is a sacred and illustrious festival for the parade of those who worship His Lordship's Sovereignty.

This is why fasting Ramadan is obligatory, why believers are not allowed to gratify the carnal self's animal appetites and indulge in its useless fancies. Since they become like angels while fasting or engaging in such a trade, each believer is a mirror reflecting God's Self-Sufficiency. They move towards becoming a pure spirit manifested in corporeal dress by abandoning the world for a fixed period. In fact, Ramadan contains and causes believers to gain, through fasting, a permanent life after a short period in this world.

One Ramadan may enable believers to gain eighty years' worth of reward, for the Qur'an declares the Night of Power and Destiny to be more profitable than eighty years having no such night (97:3). A king may announce a few holidays to mark a special occasion, like his enthronement, and then honor his faithful subjects on those days with special favors. Likewise, the Eternal and Majestic Sovereign revealed the Qur'an, His exalted decree, during Ramadan. Thus wisdom requires that Ramadan be a special Divine festival during which God's Lordship pours out bounties and spirit beings come together. Given that Ramadan is a Divinely ordained festival, fasting is commanded so that people withdraw from their bodily preoccupations to some extent.

Fasting also enables people to abandon sins committed by their bodily senses or members and use them in the acts of worship particular to each. For example, those who fast should stop their tongue from lying, backbiting, and swearing by busying it with reciting the Qur'an, glorifying God, seeking His forgiveness, and calling His blessing upon Prophet Muhammad, upon him be peace and blessings. They should prevent their eyes from looking at, and their ears from listening to, forbidden things; rather, they should look at things that give a spiritual lesson or moral warning and listen to the Qur'an and truths. When the factory-like stomach is stopped from working, other members (small workshops) can be made to follow it easily.

Eighth point. One purpose of fasting is to put people on a physical and spiritual diet. If the carnal self acts, eats, and drinks as it wishes, people's physical health is harmed. But, and more importantly, their spiritual life is harmed because they do not discriminate between the allowed and the forbidden. Such a carnal self finds it very difficult to obey the heart and spirit. Recognizing no principles, it takes the person's reins and drives him or her as it pleases.

However, fasting Ramadan accustoms it to dieting, and self-discipline trains it to obey. The stomach is not harmed by overeating before the previous meal has been digested properly and, learning to forsake what is allowed, it can follow the decree of reason and the Religion to refrain from what is forbidden. Thus the carnal self tries not to corrupt its owner's spiritual life.

Also, most people suffer hunger to various degrees. To endure long-lasting hunger patiently, people should train themselves in self-discipline and austerity. Fasting Ramadan provides this patience-based training by causing people to feel hungry for fifteen hours, or even for twenty-four hours if the predawn meal is missed. Thus, fasting cures impatience and the lack of endurance, which double humanity's misfortune.

Many bodily members somehow serve the stomach. If that "factory" does not stop its daytime routines during a certain month, it keeps those members busy with itself and forgetful of their own worship and sublime duties. This is why saints always prefer austerity as a way to spiritual and human perfection. Fasting Ramadan reminds us that our bodily members were created for more than just serving the stomach. During Ramadan, many bodily members take and experience angelic and spiritual—as opposed to material —pleasures. As a result, fasting believers receive degrees of spiritual pleasure and enlightenment according to their level of spiritual perfection. Fasting Ramadan refines a person's heart, spirit, reason, and innermost senses. Even if the stomach complains, these senses rejoice.

Ninth Point. Observing the fast of Ramadan breaks the carnal self's illusory lordship and, reminding it that it is innately helpless, convinces it that it is a servant. As the carnal self does not like to recognize its Lord, it obstinately claims lordship even while suffering. Only hunger alters such a temperament.

God's Messenger relates that God Almighty asked the carnal self, "Who am I, and who are you?" It replied, "You are Yourself, and I am myself." However much God punished it and repeated His question, He received the same answer. But when He subjected it to hunger, it replied, "You are my All-Compassionate Lord; I am Your helpless servant."

> O God, grant peace and blessings to our master Muhammad in a way to please You and to give him his due, to the number of

> the rewards for reciting the Qur'an's letters during Ramadan, and to his Family and Companions. All-Glorified is your Lord, the Lord of honor and power; exalted above what they falsely ascribe to Him. Peace be upon the Messengers, and all praise be to God, Lord of the worlds. Amen.

Types of Fasting

There are two types of fasting: obligatory and voluntary. Obligatory fasts can be further subdivided into the fast of Ramadan, the fast of expiation, and the fast of fulfilling a vow. Here we will examine the Ramadan and voluntary fasts.

When Does Ramadan Begin and End?

Ramadan is the ninth month of the Islamic lunar calendar. A lunar month is approximately 29.5 days, which is the time it takes for the moon to orbit the earth. Since a lunar month is, on average, one day shorter than a solar month, a lunar year is ten to twelve days shorter than a solar year. Therefore, according to the solar calendar, Ramadan comes ten to twelve days earlier each year and so moves through the seasons, providing equal conditions for people living in different lands over the years.

A new lunar month begins when, during the moon's orbit around the earth, the moon is in conjunction with the sun and the sun's light hits the side of the moon that is turned away from the earth. In this position, the moon is said to be a "new moon," with its dark side turned toward the earth. By definition, a new moon is not visible from the earth, as the sun's light shines only on the side facing the earth.

As the moon continues to orbit around the earth, it starts to form a crescent. This will be minutes after the new moon forms, even though the crescent will not be visible for several hours. In some traditional Islamic countries, Muslims do not start fasting until they see the actual crescent. This event is confirmed by sighting the moon, even if it is seen by only one person, or by the passage of thirty days in the immediately preceding month of Sha'ban. God's Messenger decreed, "When you see the crescent (of Ramadan), start fasting, and when you see the crescent (of Shawwal), stop fasting; and if the sky is overcast (and you can't see it) then regard Sha'ban (for the beginning of Ramadan, and Ramadan for its end) as of thirty days."[5] Some modern scholars maintain that God Almighty has given us scientific knowledge to determine exactly when a lunar month will begin and end. Therefore, according to those scholars, any observatory or other astronomy-related center should have this information for the area in which we live. However, at the present, the criteria used for the establishment of the beginning of the month may vary in Muslim countries.

Fasting starts at the first dawn of the new month. During the few hours between the new moon and the following dawn, Muslims can eat and drink, and then start fasting when the first thread of light is observed in the sky.

Different Locations

Most scholars say that it does not matter if the beginning of Ramadan has been established elsewhere. In other words, after it has been established anywhere in the world, all Muslims must begin fasting.

The End of Ramadan

The Ramadan fast ends when the beginning of the month of Shawwal has been established. Most jurists state that the beginning of Shawwal must have been established by moonsighting and reported by at least two trustworthy witnesses.

The Hours Decreed for Fasting

According to the Qur'an, the fasting hours are as follows: *You can eat and drink until you can discern the white streak (of dawn) against the black streak (of night); then complete the fast until night sets in* (2:187). Thus, the fast should start at the first thread of light at dawn (between one and a half to two hours before sunrise, depending on the time of year), and maintained until sunset (the beginning of night).

Who Must Fast?

The Qur'an declares:

> (Fasting is for) a fixed number of days. If any of you is so ill that he cannot fast, or on a journey, he must fast the same number of other days. But for those who can no longer manage to fast, there is a redemption (penance) by feeding a person in destitution (for each day missed, or giving him the same amount in money). Yet better it is for him who volunteers greater good (by either giving more, or fasting in case of recovery), and that you should fast (when you are able to) is better for you, if you but knew (the worth of fasting). (2:184)

Fasting is obligatory upon every sane, adult, healthy Muslim male who is not traveling or fighting on a battlefield at that time.[6] As for women, those who are menstruating or having post-childbirth bleeding cannot fast. In addition, the following groups of people do not have to fast: those who are insane, minors, or travelers; pregnant women who fear that their unborn child might be harmed[7]; the old and sick who think that fasting might harm them[8]; and, as the verse above has established as a general decree, those who are absolutely unable to fast due to some reason such as working in harsh circumstances or suffering such hunger or thirst that they fear fasting might result in death.

Making up the Missed Days

People who are (not chronically) ill and travelers can break their fast during Ramadan, but must make up the missed days. If travelers make the intention to fast during the night, they can still break their fast during the day. If they have already made the intention to fast while resident but then decided to travel during the day, most scholars maintain that they must fast.[9]

Those who have broken their fast because of harsh circumstances also must make up the missed days. The scholars agree that menstruating women, women with post-childbirth bleeding, and pregnant and breast-feeding women who fear that fasting might harm them or the baby, must make up the missed days.

Paying a Recompense

Those who are too old to fast, as well as the chronically ill, are permitted to break their fast, for fasting would place too much hardship on them. However, as decreed in verse 2:184, they must feed one poor person daily for each day that they did not fast. If those who were traveling or had another excuse die before making up the missed days, no recompense has to be paid. If they requested their heirs to pay such a recompense, however, the money should be taken out of the deceased's estate. Those who die without making up the missed days, even though they had enough time to do so, must request their heirs to pay the necessary recompense.[10]

Days When Fasting Is Forbidden

All scholars, based on relevant *hadiths*,[11] agree that fasting on the two 'Iyds ('Iydu'l-Fitr and 'Iydu'l-Adha) is forbidden. It does not matter if the fast is obligatory or voluntary. Fasting voluntarily on Friday exclusively is disliked. If one fasts on the day before or after it, if it is a day on which one customarily fasts (e.g., the thirteenth, fourteenth, or fifteenth day of the month), or if it is the day of 'Ashura (Muharram 10), then it is not disliked to fast on such a Friday.[12] The same rule applies to Saturday.[13] Fasting on the "day of doubt," when one is not sure if it is the last day of Sha'ban or the first day of Ramadan, is also disliked,[14] as is fasting on consecutive days without eating at all (*al-wisal*)[15]; and meeting Ramadan by fasting on the last days of

Sha'ban (just before Ramadan)[16]; and fasting on the eve of 'Iydu'l-Adha if one is doing the major pilgrimage.[17]

Voluntary or Supererogatory Fasts

God's Messenger, upon him be peace and blessings, exhorted Muslims to fast on the following days: six days of Shawwal[18]; Muharram 10 ('Ashura) and the days immediately preceding and following it[19]; the first nine days of Dhu'l-Hijja (the month when the major pilgrimage is performed)[20]; most of Sha'ban (the month preceding Ramadan)[21]; every Thursday, Friday, and Saturday during the months in which fighting is forbidden (Dhu'l-Qa'da, Dhu'l-Hijja, Muharram, Rajab); every Monday and Thursday[22]; and the thirteenth, fourteenth, and fifteenth days of each lunar month.[23] He also permitted those who can fast every other day, which is called *Sawm* Dawud (the fast of Prophet David), to do so.[24]

The Pre-Dawn Meal and Breaking the Fast

Having a pre-dawn meal between the middle of the night and dawn is *sunna* (recommended). It is considered best to delay it so that it will be eaten as close to dawn as possible.[25] Those who are fasting should hasten to break the fast when the sun has set and, just before eating, make the following supplication (highly recommended): "O God, I have fasted for You, believed in You, placed my trust in You, and break my fast with Your provisions."[26]

The Essential Elements of Fasting

Making the proper intention to fast the month of Ramadan is required. Preferably, this intention should be made before dawn and during every night of Ramadan. However, it is valid if made during any part of the night and can even be made as late as when the sun is at its zenith if one forgot to make it before dawn and did nothing to invalidate one's fasting. Intention after noon sets in is not valid for any kind of fast. Intention does not have to be spoken out loud, for it is in reality an act of the heart that does not involve the tongue. In addition, it is fulfilled by one's intention to fast out of obedience to God and to seek His good pleasure. According to the overwhelming majority of jurists, the intention for a voluntary fast can in any wise be made until noon. Intention for make-up, expiation, and vow fasts must be made until break of dawn.[27]

During the fasting hours, one cannot eat, drink, or engage in sexual relations. The Qur'an allowed sexual intercourse between married couples during the nights of Ramadan:

> It is made lawful for you to go in to your wives on the night of the Fast. They are a garment for you (enfolding you to protect you against illicit relations and beautifying you) and you are a garment for them. God knows that (you felt that) you were betraying yourselves (by doing what you supposed was prohibited), and has turned to you in leniency (and protected you from possible sins by not legislating such a prohibition). So now, associate in intimacy with them and seek what God has ordained for you. (2:187)

Avoiding Unbefitting Actions

Fasting is a type of worship which serves to draw us closer to God and purify the soul and train it in good deeds. Those who are fasting must guard against any act that might cancel the benefits of their fast. In this way, their fast will increase their personal God-consciousness and piety. Fasting is more than not eating and drinking; it also means to avoid everything else that God has forbidden. We should especially save our tongue from lying, backbiting and similar other acts. The Messenger warned, "Whoever does not give up false statements (i.e. telling lies), and evil deeds, and speaking bad words to others, God has no need for his leaving his food and drink (fasting)."[28] He also warned and advised, saying, "Fasting is not (abstaining) from eating and drinking only, but also from vain speech and foul language. If one of you is being cursed or annoyed, he should say, 'I am fasting, I am fasting.'"[29]

Being Generous and Doing Other Meritorious Acts

Being generous, studying the Qur'an, and supplicating to God are recommended at all times, but are especially stressed during Ramadan. During the last ten days of Ramadan, God's Messenger would wake his wives during the night and then, remaining apart from them, engage in acts of worship. He would exert himself in worshipping his Lord during this time more than he would at any other time.[30]

The Acts That Do Not Invalidate the Fast

Some acts do not invalidate the fast but demand care in order not to break it. They are as follows:

- Pouring water over oneself and submerging oneself in water.
- Applying kohl, eye-drops, or anything else to the eyes.[31]
- Kissing, touching, and stroking one's spouse, provided that one has self-control and no ejaculation occurs, as well as any sexual activity that does not result in ejaculation. Ejaculation that is the result of looking and thinking only does not invalidate the fast.[32]
- Rinsing the mouth and nose with abundant water, without swallowing any water.
- Tasting a liquid, food, or something else that one wants to buy. Anything edible must not be swallowed.
- Chewing gum (unlike something that has no sweetness or fragrance) is disliked but does not invalidate the fast.
- Those who are fasting can use a tooth stick or a brush to clean their teeth. It does not matter if this is done at the beginning or at the end of the day. However, they must be careful in order not to swallow anything sweet.
- Smelling perfumes.
- Swallowing anything smaller than a chickpea remaining in the mouth after rinsing which is wet with saliva.

- Swallowing only a few drops of tears and sweat, the taste of which one does not feel.
- Eating anything edible remaining between the teeth and which is smaller than a chickpea.
- Anything that is inedible and enters the mouth without intention (e.g., smoke, dust, and the taste of medicine put on teeth) does not invalidate the fast.
- Bloodletting[33] and unintentional vomit which is not so much as it fills the mouth, whether it is swallowed back or not.[34]

There are some other acts that some may feel doubt whether they invalidate the fast but they do not. They are as follows:

- Eating, drinking, or having sexual intercourse during the night until dawn.
- If one eats due to forgetfulness, the day does not have to be made up later or expiated because it does not invalidate the fast.[35]
- Performing *ghusl* before dawn due to a wet dream or sexual intercourse or ejaculation in any way is not required, but it is advisable to be pure when beginning the fast.
- If a woman's menstrual or post-childbirth bleeding stops during the night, she can delay *ghusl* until the morning and still fast. However, she must perform *ghusl* before the dawn Prayer.
- Having a wet dream during the day or any unintentional ejaculation of seminal fluid.[36]
- Swallowing anything like dust and smoke which enters the mouth and does not have any nutritious quality. Also, unintentionally swallowing a fly which enters the mouth does not invalidate the fast.

Forbidden Acts Requiring a Make-up Day

- Eating, drinking, or having intercourse due to a mistake or coercion, or thinking that the sun has set or that *fajr* has not occurred.

- Swallowing blood which is more than the saliva with which it is mixed and the taste of which one feels.
- Swallowing more than a few drops of tears and sweat the taste of which one feels.
- Removing from the mouth anything edible that remains between the teeth and which is greater than a chickpea, and then eating it.
- Vomiting a mouthful. Anything less and which goes back into the stomach does not invalidate the fast. However, if one intentionally takes it back, the fast is broken.
- Ejaculation that occurs with pleasure by kissing, touching, and masturbation.
- Menses and post-childbirth bleeding, even if either begins just before sunset.
- Any injections, whether for feeding or for medicinal purposes. It does not matter if the injection was intravenous or underneath the skin, or whether what was injected reaches the stomach.
- Any drink or medicine that passes through throat or nose. However, water that passes through the ears is allowed.
- Any fluid going into the body through the rectum.

One who does any of the acts which invalidate the fast must make it up, whether the fast intended is an obligatory Ramadan fast or a voluntary or supererogatory one. God Almighty declares:

> (Fasting is for) a fixed number of days. If any of you is so ill that he cannot fast, or on a journey, he must fast the same number of other days.

One who does not fast any of the Ramadan days without a valid excuse becomes sinful. Even if they make it up later, this will not not substitute for it.[37] However, they must sincerely repent and ask for God's forgiveness for the day they have not fasted, and make it up.

Acts That Invalidate the Fast and Require Both a Make-up Day and Expiation

Intentional eating, drinking, and having sexual intercourse during the day which one has intended to fast during Ramadan require making up the day and an expiation. Expiation is defined as freeing a slave if one can do so; if the person has no slaves or cannot free one for a valid reason, he or she must fast for sixty consecutive days; if he or she cannot do so, he or she must feed a poor person for sixty days or sixty poor people for one day with meals that are similar to what one would eat at home.

As reported by Abu Hurayra, may God be pleased with him, a man came to the Prophet and said, "I have been ruined for I had sexual relations with my wife in Ramadan (while I was fasting)." The Prophet, upon him be peace and blessings, said, "Emancipate a slave!" The man said, "I cannot afford that." The Prophet said, "Then fast for two successive months without interruption!" The man said, "I cannot do that." The Prophet said, "Then feed sixty poor persons." The man said, "I have nothing (to feed them with)." The Prophet asked the man to sit down. Then a big basket full of dates was brought to the Prophet, who asked, "Where is the questioner?" The man said, "Here I am!" The Prophet said (to him), "Take this basket (full of dates), and go and give this in charity." The man said, "(Shall I give this in charity) to a poorer person than me? By God, there is no family in between these two mountains (of Madina) that is poorer than us." The Prophet smiled, and said, "Then (feed) your family (with it)."[38]

Most scholars say that both men and women have to perform acts of expiation if they intentionally have sexual intercourse during the day they had intended to fast. If they engaged in it out of forgetfulness, coercion, or having no intention to fast, they do not have to perform any act of expiation. If the woman was raped or coerced by the man, only the man has to make an act of expiation.

If the expiatory fast, which must be performed for sixty days consecutively, is interrupted by menstruation or post-childbirth bleeding, it is not required that the days already fasted should be repeated.

All scholars agree that people who intentionally broke the fast and made expiation, and then broke it again in a way that requires another expiation, must perform another act of expiation. Similarly, they all agree that if people break the fast twice during a day, before performing the expiation for the first act, they need to perform only one act of expiation. If people break their fast and then repeat it during the same Ramadan without expiation, they only have to make expiation one time. The reason for this is that there is a punishment for acts that are repeated, and if the expiation or punishment is not carried out, all of these acts are combined into one.

Places with Very Long Days and Very Short Nights

Muslims who are in such areas (e.g., close to the polar regions) should follow the norms of the areas in which the Islamic legislation took place (e.g., Makka or Madina) or follow the schedule of the closest area that has "normal" days and nights.

The Virtue of the Night of Power and Destiny (*Laylatu'l-Qadr*)

This night is the year's most virtuous night. God says, *We have surely sent it (the Qur'an) down on the Night of Power and Destiny [Laylatu'l-Qadr]. What enables you to perceive what the Night of Power and Destiny is? The Night of Power and Destiny is better than a thousand months* (97:1–3). For example, any action therein (e.g., reciting the Qur'an, remembering God) brings as much reward as would doing the same action for thousand months that do not contain this night.

It is preferred to seek this night during the last ten nights of Ramadan, as the Prophet, upon him be peace, strove his best to seek it during that time. He said, "Whoever is in search of it should seek it in the last ten nights of Ramadan." He also said, "It is in the odd nights of the last ten nights (of Ramadan)."[39] He would stay up during the last ten nights, wake his wives, and then stay apart from them in order to worship.[40] He said, "Whoever prays during the night of *Qadr* out of sincere faith and hoping for its reward from God, then all his previous sins will be forgiven; and whoever fasts in the month of Ramadan out of sincere faith and hoping for its reward from God, then all his previous sins will be forgiven."[41]

The Meaning and Principles of *I'tikaf*

I'tikaf literally means to stick to something, whether good or bad, and to block out everything else. As an Islamic term, it denotes devoting oneself, especially during the last ten days of Ramadan, to praying in a mosque. The Qur'an refers to it, saying, *But do not associate in intimacy with them (your wives) during the period when you are in retreat in the mosques* (2:187). God's Messenger, upon him be peace and blessings, performed *i'tikaf* for ten days every Ramadan. In the year that he died, he performed it for twenty days.[42]

I'tikaf is not acceptable from an unbeliever, a non-discerning child, a person requiring major purification because of (sexual) defilement, a menstruating woman or a woman with post-childbirth bleeding.

I'tikaf will be fulfilled if a person stays in the mosque with the intention of becoming closer to God. If these conditions are not met, it is not *i'tikaf*. If an individual intends to perform a voluntary *i'tikaf* for ten days but ends it before the ten-day period has ended, he or she must make up the remaining days later.

Any voluntary *i'tikaf*, which is other than the *sunna i'tikaf* during Ramadan, can be fulfilled at any time for any term or period.

Oaths

Making an oath means to swear by God or any of His Attributes or Names that one will do or not do something. In Islam, one can swear only by God. People who make such an oath must do their best to fulfill it, and so should not make one carelessly.

People who make false statements by mistake or unknowingly, and then swear to them by God, are not held responsible for them and do not have make any expiation. However, consciously lying and then swearing by God or declaring God as a witness to the lie is an extremely grave sin that has often resulted in misfortune descending upon the liar. Such people must perform an act of expiation, earnestly seek God's forgiveness, and repair any damage caused by the lie. God decrees in the Qur'an:

> God does not take you to task for a slip (or blunder of speech) in your oaths, but He takes you to task for what you have concluded by solemn, deliberate oaths. The expiation (for breaking such oaths) is to feed ten destitute persons (or one person for ten days) with the average of the food you serve to your families, or to clothe them, or to set free a slave. If anyone does not find (the means to do that), let him fast for three days. That is the expiation for your oaths when you have sworn (and broken them). But be mindful of your oaths (do not make them lightly, and when you have sworn them, fulfill them). Thus God makes clear to you His Revelations (the lights of His way), that you may give thanks (from the heart and in speech, and in action by fulfilling His commandments). (5:89)

If people swear by God to do or not to do something in the future and then act contrarily, they must seek God's forgiveness and make an expiation. In this case, this involves emancipating a slave. If this is not possible, the oath-breaker must feed a poor person for ten days or ten persons for a day with meals that are similar to what his or her family eats. If this is not possible, he or she must fast for three consecutive days.

It may sometimes happen that breaking an oath will give a better result than fulfilling it. In this case, one who swears should break their oath and make an expiation for it. An oath which was made to do something unlawful or not to do something which is better to be done should also be broken. The Qur'an declares:

> Let not those among you who are favored with resources swear that they will no longer give to the kindred, the needy, and those who have emigrated in God's cause (even though those wealthy ones suffer harm at the hands of the latter). Rather, let them pardon and forbear. Do you not wish that God should forgive you? God is All-Forgiving, All-Compassionate. (24:22)

God's Messenger, upon him be peace and blessings, decreed, "When you take an oath to do something and later you find that something else is better than the former, then do the better one and make expiation for your oath."[43]

Vows

A vow is a solemn promise to do, in God's name, something that resembles an act of worship and make obligatory upon oneself that which is not obligatory. A vow is considered "Islamic" only if it is made in God's name and involves an obligatory or necessary act of worship (e.g., to fast or help the poor). For example, one can vow to perform two *rak'a*s of Prayer or fast, but cannot vow to make a prostration of recitation or perform ablution, for these latter two acts are not obligatory acts of worship in themselves but rather are the means to such acts. If a person vows to help the poor, this must be out of his or her own property. Also, vows can be made concerning only that which can be fulfilled. Also, one cannot vow to do something which involves disobedience to God or the Religion. God's Messenger decrees, "Whoever vows that he will be obedient to God, should remain obedient to Him; and whoever made a vow that he will disobey God, should not disobey Him."[44]

There are two kinds of vows: appointed and unappointed. An appointed vow can be, for example, vowing to fast on a certain day if one's desire for something religiously lawful is met. If the desired thing happens, the vow must be fulfilled preferably on the appointed day, but it can also be fulfilled any other day.

An unappointed vow can be, for example, a vow to fast for one day or to give charity to the poor if one's desire for something religiously lawful is met. If the desired thing happens, the vow must be fulfilled.

If one vows to do something resembling an act of worship if something does not occur, he or she must either fulfill the vow or make an expiation. For example, if one addicted to lying vows to fast for a week if he or she does not lie again, but then does so, he or she either has to fulfill the vow or make an expiation like that made for broken oaths.

The Qur'an wants us to fulfill our vows (22:29) and condemns those who say what they do and will not do, saying, *O you who believe! Why do you say what you do not do (as well as what you will not do)? Most odious it is in God's sight that you say what you do not (and will not) do* (61:2–3).

Chapter 5

az-Zakah
(The Prescribed Purifying Alms)

AZ-ZAKAH

(THE PRESCRIBED PURIFYING ALMS)

Another basic, important duty of servanthood is the *Zakah*, which the Qur'an usually mentions together with the *Salah*. While, in the words of God's Messenger, the Prayer is Islam's pillar or support, the *Zakah* is its bridge, for the *Zakah* not only brings the social strata closer to each other and fills in the gaps already formed between them and their members, but also stops such gaps from forming.

The *Zakah* means purity and growth. Since it purifies wealth and people's attachment to it, and causes both it and Muslims to grow in purity and sincerity, the Qur'an calls it *Zakah* (or the Prescribed Purifying Alms):

> (O Messenger,) take alms (prescribed or voluntary) out of their wealth so that you may cleanse them thereby and cause them to grow in purity and sincerity, and pray for them. Indeed your prayer is a source of comfort for them. God is All-Hearing, All-Knowing. (9:103)

Taking into account its very nature, the *Zakah* constitutes one of Islam's five pillars. It is associated with the Prayer (*Salah*) in eighty-two Qur'anic verses. God, the All-Exalted, prescribed it in His Book (the Qur'an), His Messenger corroborated it by his *Sunna*, and the Muslim community by consensus upheld it. Ibn 'Abbas reported that when the Prophet sent Mu'adh ibn Jabal to Yemen (as its governor), he said to him:

> You are going to a people who are People of the Book. Invite them to accept the *Shahada*: that there is no deity but God and I am His Messenger. If they accept and affirm this, tell them

> that God, the All-Glorious One, has enjoined five Prayers upon them during the day and night. If they accept that, tell them also that He has enjoined *sadaqa* (meaning *Zakah*) upon their assets, which will be taken from the rich of the (Muslim) community and distributed to the poor. If they accept that, refrain from laying hands upon the best of their goods and fear the cry of the oppressed, for there is no barrier between God and it.[1]

Many verses exhort Muslims to pay the *Zakah* and forbid hoarding wealth, for example:

> The believers, both men and women, they are guardians, confidants and helpers of one another. They enjoin and promote what is right and good and forbid and try to prevent the evil. They establish the Prayer in conformity with its conditions, and pay the *Zakah* (Prescribed Purifying Alms) fully. They always obey God and His Messenger. Those are the distinguished ones whom God will treat with mercy. Assuredly, God is All-Glorious with irresistible might, All-Wise. (9:71)

and:

> Those who hoard gold and silver and do not spend it in God's cause (to exalt His Word and help the poor and needy: O Messenger,) give them the glad tidings of a painful punishment. (9:34)

The amount in the property of the rich to be paid as *Zakah* essentially belongs to those in need of it. For, God has created it in the property of the rich so that the rich, who are expected to be thankful to God, the All-Munificent, and show mercy to the poor, may, by paying *Zakah*, thank God, gain great reward, and purify themselves of attachment to the world and worldly things, and purify their property of the right of others, and not provoke the grudge of the poor, and so that the poor may not feel any grudge against the rich and may feel respect for them. God never wants property or riches to be a fortune circulating among the rich (59:7). The *Zakah* prevents riches from circulating only among the rich, and secures its circulation among all members of society. The following considerations of Bediüzzaman Said Nursi, which he wrote before the Second World War, are worthy of mention:

> Revolutions, social corruption, and moral failings arise from two basic attitudes. One is that "I don't care if others die of hunger so long as my own stomach is full," and the other is: "You must work so that I can eat." The first attitude is cured through the Zakah; the second by prohibiting usury and interest. Qur'anic justice stands at the door of humanity and turns away usury and interest, proclaiming, "You have no right to enter!" Yet humanity ignored this prohibition and received a great blow.[2] It must heed it now to avoid receiving a greater one.[3]

Who must pay?

Zakah must be paid by every free Muslim, man or woman, who has a *nisab* (the required amount of wealth). As for the insane and children who have a *nisab*, if their wealth is under disposal or in market or in circulation, their guardians pay it on their behalf. If a person dies before paying it, it must be taken from the estate before paying off any debts, if there are any, and before the heirs share the inheritance.

Conditions for Nisab and the Zakah

- *Nisab* is the amount of wealth remaining after meeting all yearly expenses for such vital necessities as food, clothes, housing, and a mount. Thus, a person does not have to pay *Zakah* on what he or she needs to make a living, such as tools or machines related to carpentry, farming, tailoring, or working as a doctor, or motor vehicles by which they earn their living, essential household appliances, and the books needed by a scientist or an academic. All debts are subtracted from one's wealth. If one has enough secured credit to pay off the debt, it is added to one's wealth, and if the resultant wealth reaches the *nisab*, one must pay *Zakah*.The Qur'an orders us to give out of what is left over after we have spent on our own and our dependents' needs

(2:219). The same was also emphatically stated by the Prophet, upon him be peace and blessings.[4]

- For many items subject to *Zakah* (e.g., money, gold, silver, and cattle), a full year of the Islamic calendar should pass, starting from the day of the *nisab*'s possession.[5] If the wealth possessed decreases during the year but is still possessed one year later, *Zakah* must be paid. What matters is the availability of *nisab* at the beginning and end of the year. However, this condition does not apply to plantations and fruits, for their *Zakah* should be paid, or at least calculated, on the harvest day and include what has been consumed before the harvest. The Qur'an orders:

> He it is Who produces gardens (and vineyards, and orchards) trellised and untrellised, and date palms, and crops varying in taste, and olives, and pomegranates, resembling one another and yet so different. Eat of their fruits when they come to fruition, and give (to the poor and the needy) the due thereof on harvest day. (6:141)

In short, there are two types of *Zakah*: one grows by itself (e.g., crops and fruits), and the other is used for growing and production (e.g., money, merchandise, and cattle). In the former case, *Zakah* should be paid at harvest time; in the latter, at the end of the year.

- The wealth subject to the *Zakah* should be actively or potentially increasing, growing, or productive. Increase or multiplication through birth, breeding, and production (as in crops and animals) is active growth; while increase through commerce or having potential of increase (as in banknotes and gold or silver used in transactions or business) is potential growth.
- One must have private, indisputable ownership or possession and the right and possibility of disposal of the wealth liable to the *Zakah*. Goods that were lost and whose restoration is not expected, and goods that are impossible to use although privately owned are not liable to the *Zakah*.[6]

Intention

Since paying *Zakah* is an act of worship, its validity depends upon one's sincere intention to pay it for God's sake.[7] If one pays it without making the intention, one can still intend while the wealth expended as *Zakah* has not yet been consumed.

Paying Zakah at Its Due Time

Zakah must be paid immediately at its due time. Deferring it is prohibited, unless there is a valid reason to do so.

Holdings Subject to Zakah and their Nisab

Islam enjoins *Zakah* on currencies and similar things, such as shares, bonds and checks, gold and silver, crops, fruit, livestock, merchandise, minerals, and treasure.

The Standard of Richness or the Level of Wealth

Islam does not criticize earning; rather, it encourages working and earning one's livelihood, and condemns begging. God's Messenger, upon him be peace and blessings, warns, "A man who keeps on begging from others comes on the Day of Resurrection without any piece of flesh on his face."[8] He also says, "By Him in Whose Hand my life is, it is better for anyone of you to take a rope and cut wood and carry it over his back and sell it (as a means of earning his living) rather than to beg, whether that person (begged from) may give him or not."[9] However, Islam does not approve of earning for luxury and a luxurious life, and urges Muslims to work and make their own and dependents' earning, and to live with the other life as their goal. It encourages mutual helping in society and spending in God's cause and for the needy, and has not established a fixed standard of living. It regards having a house, a mount, two suits and other articles of clothing, and one month's worth of livelihood (some say that one can keep a year of livelihood at the most) as the necessary commodities or wealth upon which one does not have to pay *Zakah*. Bediüzzaman Said Nursi expresses a standard that can be valid for all times, as follows: While most Muslims live at below the average standard of living, a Muslim cannot live a luxurious, comfortable life.[10]

The *sunna* has established approximately ninety grams of gold or about six hundred grams of silver or forty sheep or thirty heads of cattle or five camels as the standard. Shah Waliyullah Dahlawi (d., 1792) writes that each of these amounts was equal to the yearly expenses for a standard family (formed of four persons) during the time of God's Messenger.[11] If, according to the place or the general standard of living of the people in a particular place, one has banknotes, merchandise, or other kinds of increasing income or capital whose value is equal to any of the standard values given, he or she must pay the *Zakah*. However, in establishing the *nisab*, the minimum amount or value, which favors the poor, is considered.

The Kinds of Possessions Liable to the *Zakah* and their *Nisab*

The Nisab and Zakah for Gold, Silver, and Other Jewelry

The *nisab* for gold is twenty *dinars* (approximately ninety grams) and for silver is two hundred *dirhams* (approximately six hundred grams), both being owned for one year. God's Messenger, upon him be peace and blessings, decreed, "Nothing is incumbent on you, that is, on gold, till it reaches twenty *dinars*. When you possess twenty *dinars* and one year passes on them, half a *dinar* is payable. Whatever exceeds, that will be reckoned properly."[12] He also decreed, "Pay a fortieth (out of silver). A *dirham* is payable on every forty, but you are not liable for payment until you have accumulated two hundred *dirhams*. When you have two hundred *dir-*

hams, five *dirhams* are payable, and that proportion is applicable to larger amounts."[13]

The due on them is one-fortieth of their value. Any additional amount is to be calculated in this manner. Gold and silver are combined. Thus, if one has gold and silver whose value is equal to two hundred *dirhams* of silver, *Zakah* must be paid. Likewise, gold, silver, banknotes and the like, and commercial merchandise are also combined. Things made of gold and silver are treated like gold and silver. In other words, if the weight of gold and silver they contain amounts to the *nisab*, their *Zakah* is paid.

God's Messenger, upon him be peace and blessings, ordered, "O women! Give *Zakah* from your ornaments!"[14] Although according to some scholars Zakah must be paid from ornaments, most of the scholars, who interpret this *hadith* as being concerned with ornaments made of gold and silver, opine that unless they are used for trade or kept for later use, no *Zakah* has to be paid on diamonds, pearls, sapphires, rubies, corals, or other precious stones that women wear as ornaments. One should not buy such precious stones in order to avoid paying *Zakah*. It is also advised as piety and a measure to be saved from the obligation of *Zakah*, which is both God's and people's right on rich people, to make some payment due to them.The ornaments made of gold and silver like bracelets are liable to *Zakah*.[15] The ornaments worn by men, whatever precious stone they are made of, are also liable to *Zakah*.

Banknotes, Checks, and Bonds

As these are documents with guaranteed credits, banknotes, checks, and bonds are subject to *Zakah* at the rate of one-fortieth of their value, when they are owned for one year and attain the minimum of *nisab* (being equal in value to two hundred *dirhams* of silver or about ninety grams of gold). A person may change them into currency immediately. They are combined with currencies, gold and silver, and commercial merchandise.

Commercial Merchandise

The Qur'an orders:

> O you who believe! Spend (in God's cause and for the needy) out of the pure, wholesome things you have earned and of what We have produced for you from the earth, and do not seek after the bad things to spend thereof when you would not take it save with disdain; and know that God is All-Wealthy and Self-Sufficient (absolutely independent of the charity of people), All-Praiseworthy (as your Lord, Who provides for you and all other beings and meets all your needs). (2:267)

Any commercial merchandise that is religiously lawful to use, consume, buy, and sell (e.g., clothes, grain, iron, copper, cattle, sheep, houses, shops, and cars) is subject to *Zakah* one year after its value reaches the *nisab*. Even if the minimum amount of *nisab* decreases any time during the year, so long as one owns that amount at the beginning and end of the year, their *Zakah* must be paid. Their due is one-fortieth. Due to gold's stable value, jurists maintain that it should be the basis upon which the *nisab* of commercial merchandise is determined.

Buildings and Vehicles of Transportation That Are Sources of Income

One who rents out a house, a shop, tools, vehicles, or land, or who has vehicles working in transportation, must pay the *Zakah* on the rent and income received. If their annual revenue is equal to *nisab*, after the money spent on them is deducted, the owner pays their *Zakah* every month. Since they are compared with land and land produce, their *Zakah* rate is one-tenth.

Industrial Investments and Means of Production

These items are currently among the greatest sources of income. Although people's private houses, tools, and machines by which they earn their living are not subject to *Zakah*, industrial investments and means of production (e.g., factories) are, for they are growing and sources of revenue. Some jurists compare them to land and land produce, and say that their *Zakah* rate is one-tenth. Others compare them to commercial activities and merchandise, and say that their *Zakah* rate is one-fortieth of the value remaining after debts, expenses on necessary material, workmanship, production, marketing, and financing have been subtracted.

Wages, Salaries, and Independent Businesses

Since wages, salaries, and earnings from independent businesses are steady and continuous and potentially growing, they are subject to *Zakah* if the amount remaining after the yearly average expenditure on livelihood reaches *nisab*. The rate is one-fortieth. Although there are diverse standards of living, Muslims do not think of living a comfortable life when the majority of Muslims and humanity are living a below-average life. If one has other kinds of wealth subject to *Zakah* such as gold, silver, checks, and bonds, they are added to wages and salaries in calculating the among of the *Zakah*. Most jurists say that this type of *Zakah* should be paid after one year.

Credit

There are two kinds of credit: one is that which is acknowledged by the debtor with the willingness to pay it off; and the other is that which is not acknowledged either because the borrower is insolvent or its payment is deferred, or due to the nature of the debt. Inheritance, the goods left in one's will, and the bridal-due promised are of this second kind of credit.

The creditor should pay the *Zakah* on the first kind of credit retroactively when he or she has received at least one-fifth of the *nisab* from the debtor. Since one is responsible for the *Zakah* on the wealth one has possessed for one year at least, the duration for the credit is calculated from the beginning of being a creditor or the time when one lent. The *Zakah* on the second kind of credit is paid when one year passes after it is restored.

Cattle, Sheep, and Goats

Cattle, camels, sheep, and goats are subject to *Zakah*. They must be commercial or grazing, and have been in one's possession for a year. The *nisab* of each is as follows:

- When one has five grazing camels for one year, their due is one sheep, which is also the due for five to nine camels. The due for ten to fourteen camels is two sheep, for fifteen to nineteen camels is three sheep, and for twenty to twenty-four camels is four sheep. The due for twenty-five to thirty-five camels is a two-year-old she-camel, for thirty-six to forty-five it is a three-year-old she-camel, for forty-six to sixty it is a four-year-old she-camel, for sixty-one to seventy-five a five-year-old she-camel, for seventy-six to ninety, it is two three-year-old she-camels, and for ninety-one to 120 it is two five-year-old she-camels.
- When one has forty sheep or goats, their due is one sheep or goat. For forty to a hundred and twenty it is the same, for a hundred and twenty to 200 it is two sheep, for 200 to 399 it is three sheep, and for 400 to 500 it is four sheep.[16]
- The *nisab* for cattle is thirty. For thirty to forty head of cattle, a two-and-a-half-year-old male or female weaned calf; for forty to sixty, a three-year-old weaned calf; for sixty, two one-year-old calves. When there are more than sixty head of cattle, the rate is one calf for every thirty head and one weaned calf for every forty head.[17]

Farm Produce

The *Zakah* on farm produce from one's privately owned field is paid when it is harvested (6:141). One must calculate it in advance if one wants to use or benefit from it. Another verse ordering *Zakah* on this warns: .... *do not seek after the bad things to spend thereof when you would not take it save with disdain; and know that God is All-Wealthy and Self-Sufficient (absolutely independent of the charity of people), All-Praiseworthy (as your Lord, Who provides for you and all other beings and meets all your needs)* (2:267).

Most scholars maintain that its *nisab* is about fifty quarters (650 kg), that is, if one has that amount of farm produce, one must pay its *Zakah*. The due for farm produce naturally irrigated (with rain) is one-tenth; if it is irrigated by the owner, who must pay the related expenses, the due is one-twentieth.[18]

Minerals, Ores, and Buried Treasure

Most of these items have been considered to be like spoils or gains of war, about which God Almighty decrees, *Know that whatever you take as gains of war, to God belongs one fifth of it, and to the Messenger, and the near kinsfolk, and orphans, and the destitute, and the wayfarer (one devoid of sufficient means of journeying)* (8:41). God's Messenger says, "A one-fifth amount is compulsory for buried treasures."[19]

Ores and minerals are of three kinds. One kind is hard, such as gold, silver, lead, and iron that are able to be melted and moulded. The *Zakah* on such items is one-fifth. The second kind consists of the hard ores or minerals unable to be melted and moulded, such as diamond, marble, and limestone. The third kind consists of fluid sources or minerals, such as crude oil and mercury. The last two kinds become subject to *Zakah* of one-fortieth when they are worked and offered for sale as commercial merchandise.

If buried treasure is found in land whose owner is unknown or which belongs to the state, one-fifth of it is given as *Zakah* and the rest belongs to the finder. If it is found in land whose owner is known, one-fifth is given to the owner. Scholars have ruled that there is no *nisab* for such items. However, some maintain that when these items are worth about six hundred *dirhams* of silver or ninety grams of gold, *Zakah* must be paid.

Fish and Farm Animals

Fish and animals such as poultry that are bred on farms either for their meat or milk or eggs are considered among commercial merchandise and become subject to *Zakah* of one-fortieth one year after their value reaches the *nisab*. Even if the minimum amount of *nisab* decreases at any time during the year, so long as one owns that amount at the beginning and end of the year, their *Zakah* must be paid. Due to gold's stable value, jurists maintain that it should be the basis upon which the *nisab* of commercial merchandise is determined.

Recipients

Scholars have divided property into two categories: hidden (kept at home, such as money, gold, and silver) and property kept in the open (e.g., animals and farm produce). During the Prophet's lifetime and that of the caliphs, *Zakah* was collected by officials appointed for that purpose. There was even a special *Zakah* fund in the state budget. In later times, the state began to collect *Zakah* on property in the open and let the owners of hidden property be responsible for it by themselves.

Muslims or Muslim communities must find a good, preferable way to collect *Zakah* in the absence of an Islamic authority and distribute it properly, as mentioned in the Qur'an, 9:60. Suitable recipients and purposes of *Zakah* are:

- Poor people who do not earn enough to keep themselves and their families alive.
- The destitute who cannot meet their basic needs.
- *Zakah* collectors.
- Those whose hearts, due to their weak Islam, need to be reconciled or strengthened for Islam; those whose hearts can be swayed towards Islam; or those whose evil against Islam and the Muslims could be prevented in this way.

- To free Muslim prisoners of war and emancipate slaves.
- To help those who are overburdened with debt.
- To support those who exalt God's Word, strive or fight for God's cause (*mujahidun*), and provide for students and pilgrims.
- Travelers, either at home or abroad.

The recipients of *Zakah* are mentioned in the following verse:

> The Prescribed Purifying Alms are meant only for the poor and those in destitution (although, out of self-respect, they do not give the impression that they deserve help); those in charge of collecting and administering them; those whose hearts or friendship and support are to be won over for God's cause, (including those whose hostilities might be prevented thereby); to free those in the bondage of slavery and captivity; to help those overburdened with debt; and in God's cause (to exalt God's Word, to provide for students and help pilgrims); and for the wayfarer (in need of help). This is an ordinance from God. God has full knowledge of everything, All-Wise. (9:60)

Zakah is distributed among the recipients according to their need and priority, assigned to those in greater need, or according to circumstances. But *Zakah* is not voluntary charity given to please the poor; rather, it is spent to eradicate poverty, provide capital for the needy in order to save them from their need, to fill the gaps between classes, or to prevent such gaps from appearing in society.

A person cannot give *Zakah* (1) to his or her kindred for whose livelihood he or she is responsible or with whom he or she has a relationship of inheritance, such as parents, grandparents, children, grandchildren, and wife; nor (2) to unbelievers except with the hope and intention of winning their hearts in favor of Islam or neutralizing their hostility; nor (3) to those who are wealthy enough to support themselves and their dependents. The *Zakah* to be paid for those who are mentally ill or younger than seven years of age is submitted to their guardians.

Sadaqatu'l-Fitr (The Charity of Existence and Fast-Breaking)

Sadaqatu'l-fitr is the kind of charity which must be paid by every free Muslim whose wealth meets his or her basic needs and who has extra wealth equal to six hundred grams of silver. A Muslim must pay it for himself, his wife, children, and servants at the end of Ramadan before the *'Iyd* Prayer.[20] One who forgets to pay it, or cannot pay it at this time due to some valid excuse, must pay it when he or she remembers it or no longer has an excuse.

As reported from 'Abdullah ibn 'Abbas, God's Messenger enjoined *sadaqatu'l-fitr* on the one who fasts to shield the self from any indecent act or speech and for the purpose of providing food for the needy. It is accepted as *Zakah* for the person who pays it before the *'Iyd* Prayer, and it is *sadaqa* (charity) for the one who pays it after the Prayer.[21] Traditionally, *sadaqatu'l-fitr* has been calculated on the basis of, and paid as, wheat, barley, dates, and dried grapes. However, the amount to be paid must be sufficient to meet an average person's daily food intake. It can be paid either in kind, as mentioned above, or in its monetary equivalent.

Infaq (Spending for God's Sake and for the Needy)

Islam views wealth realistically—as an essential aspect of life and the main means of individual and group subsistence. God Almighty says, *Do not give to those devoid of good judgment and sanity your property, which God has put in your charge as means of support for you (and the needy)* (4:5). This amounts to saying that wealth is to be distributed to meet basic needs (e.g., food, clothing, lodging, and other indispensables), and that no one is to be lost, forgotten, or left without support. The best way to distribute wealth so that everyone's basic needs are met is through the *Zakah*, for it places no burden upon the wealthy, meets the basic needs of the poor, and relieves them of life's hardships and deprivation's pain.

The *Zakah* is not a favor of the wealthy to the poor; rather, it is a due that God entrusted to the rich so that they might deliver it to the poor and distribute it among the deserving. This establishes the following truth: Wealth is not exclusively for the rich, but for the rich and the poor. This is what is meant by God's saying, *so that this (wealth) should not be a fortune circulating solely among the rich among you* (59:7). *Zakah* must be paid by those who can pay it, and must be given to the poor and the needy so that they can meet their basic needs, not go hungry, and acquire a sense of security and general well-being. If there is not enough *Zakah* to meet such needs, the rich can be subjected to further taxation. How much should be taken is not specified, for that depends upon the needs of the poor.

The Qur'an urges the wealthy to spend in God's cause and for the needy. For example, in praising the believers, it declares:

> They spend in God's cause (of whatever God has bestowed upon them) both in ease and hardship, restrain their rage (even though they are able to retaliate and avenge), and pardon people their offenses. God loves (such) people devoted to doing good, conscious that God always sees them. (3:134)

> They establish the (prescribed) Prayer (in awe and veneration of God and in conformity with its conditions), and spend as subsistence out of whatever We provide for them (of wealth, knowledge, power, and so on to those really in need purely for His good pleasure and without placing others under obligation). (8:3)

The Qur'an tells us to give from what we love and not to place people under obligation because of what we spend in God's cause or give to them:

> Those who spend their wealth in God's cause and then do not follow up what they have spent with placing under obligation and taunting, their reward is with their Lord, and they will have no fear, nor will they grieve. A kind word and forgiving (people's faults) are better than almsgiving followed by taunting. God is All-Wealthy and Self-Sufficient, (absolutely independent

> of people's charity), All-Clement (Who shows no haste in punishing). (2:262–63)

> You will never be able to attain godliness and virtue until you spend of what you love (in God's cause or to provide for the needy). Whatever you spend, God has full knowledge of it. (3:92)

> Spend in God's cause (out of whatever you have), and do not ruin yourselves with your own hands (by refraining from spending. Whatever you do), do it in the best way, in the awareness that God sees it. God loves those who are devoted to doing good, aware that God is seeing them. (2:195)

God promises great reward to those who spend their wealth in His cause, and warns against being miserly and spending only to attract people's attention:

> The parable of those who spend their wealth in God's cause is like that of a grain that sprouts seven ears, and in every ear there are a hundred grains. Thus God multiplies for whomever He wills. God is All-Embracing (with His Mercy), All-Knowing. (2:261)

> Those who act meanly (in spending of what God has granted them) and urge others to be mean, and conceal the things God has granted them out of His bounty (such as wealth and certain truths in their Book), We have prepared for (such) unbelievers a shameful, humiliating punishment. And (likewise) those who spend their wealth (in charity or for another good cause) to make a show of it to people (so as to be praised by them) when they believe neither in God nor in the Last Day: whoever has Satan for a comrade, how evil a comrade he is! (4:37–38)

Another point to stress here is that generalizing certain matters sometimes has caused great misunderstanding and wrong applications, as in the cases of condemning the world and asceticism. Humanity is God's vicegerent on the earth, meaning that people have the right to interfere with things to improve the earth within the bounds established by God, and rule it in God's name and according to His laws. This duty falls first of all upon believers, because denying God in any way severs the link between God and humanity and makes people beings who shed blood and cause unrest upon the earth.

Since maintaining human existence depends upon belief and the existence of a formidable group of believers with the potential to bear the Divine Trust, the earth's Divine bounties belong, first of all, to believers. In return, they are obliged to administer them and distribute them justly among people. Thus, they are to use the earth's bounties in accordance with God's Will, and to thank Him in return. However, they are forbidden to go beyond the lawful limits in benefiting from them and make eating, drinking and consuming resources the goal of their lives.

In addition to engendering competitive clashes over such items, overconsumption also leads to accumulated energy that, if not controlled, causes such destructive sins as adultery and prostitution. So, to avoid such destruction, individuals can adopt, and are even advised to embrace, asceticism. But the Muslim community cannot leave earthly bounties, as well as their administration and distribution, to others in the name of asceticism. As Bediüzzaman Said Nursi puts it, believers must not set their hearts on the world but must work and earn to maintain themselves, uphold God's Word, and spend in His cause.

Some Glimpses of Islam's Economic System[22]

Islam guides its followers in all phases and activities of life, material as well as spiritual. Its basic teaching on economics is mentioned in several Qur'anic passages. We find it stated clearly in several verses, as in some of those mentioned above, that God has offered everything on the earth, in the seas, and the heavens for humanity's benefit, meaning that everything submits to Him and can be used by humanity, which is tasked with knowing and profiting from the creation in a rational way and by paying due regard to the Creator.

Islam's economic policy is explained in unequivocal terms: *so that this (wealth) should not become a fortune circulating solely among the rich among you* (59:7). Nevertheless, equality of all people in wealth and comfort does not promise to be an unmixed blessing. For example, since people do not have equal natural talents, even if complete equality were achieved, spendthrifts would soon fall into difficulties and begin envying and coveting other people's good fortune. Furthermore, on philosophical and psychological grounds, it is in humanity's interest that there be differences in wealth.

Human livelihood is, in general terms, in the direction of developing toward more complex forms and processes, for humanity continues to dominate and exploit one thing after the other in God's creation, whereas animals have changed nothing in their livelihood since God created their species. One cause of this difference is the simultaneous existence in a society of cooperation and liberty of competition among the people who live in that society. Perhaps the most developed social cooperation is found among bees, ants, and termites, all of which live collectively and with complete equality in livelihood. But there is no competition among its members, and so any bee which is more intelligent or industrious cannot live more comfortably than others. Thus none of these species evolves, changes, or makes any progress in the sense of those terms.

Human history shows that every advance and discovery of how to become more comfortable has come into existence through competition and the desire for improvement, as well as through the existence of grades of wealth or poverty. Yet absolute liberty would lead devilish people to exploit and oppress the needy. So each progressive civilization and healthy culture had to impose certain duties (e.g., paying taxes, forbidding oppression and cheating), and to recommend certain supererogatory acts (e.g., charity and spending for God's sake), while nevertheless allowing a great deal of liberty of thought and action to its members, so that each person benefits his or her self, family, friends, and society at large. This is the exigency of Islam.

Islam has based its economic system on this fundamental principle. If it tolerates richness, it imposes certain obligations on the rich. For example, they have to pay taxes to help the poor, and cannot engage in immoral economic practices (e.g., exploitation, hoarding, and wealth accumulation). To achieve this goal, it makes various laws, as well as some recommendations (e.g., charity and sacrifice), with the promise of a spiritual (otherworldly) reward. Furthermore, the law distinguishes between the necessary minimum and the desirable plenitude, and there is a further distinction between those laws that are accompanied by material sanctions and those that are not by persuading and educating.

We will describe this moral aspect first through several illustrations. Islam has used very emphatic terms to show that begging charity from others is abominable and a source of shame. Yet at the same time, it highly praises those who help others, calling the "people of upper hand" those who sacrifice and prefer others to themselves. Similarly, avarice and waste are prohibited.

One day, the Prophet, upon him be peace and blessings, needed considerable funds for a public cause. One of his friends (Abu Bakr) offered a certain amount and, when asked by the Prophet, replied, "I have left nothing at home but the love of God and of His Messenger."[23] This person received the warmest praise from the Prophet. But on another occasion, another Companion, Sa'd ibn Abi Waqqas, who was seriously ill, told him when he came to inquire about his health, "O Messenger of God, I am a rich man and want to bequeath all that I possess for the welfare of the poor." The Prophet replied, "No, it is better to leave your relatives with an independent means of livelihood so that they will not be dependent upon others and have to beg." When the man decreased the bequest to two-thirds and then one half, the Prophet still refused, saying that it was too much. When the man finally proposed one-third of his property in charity, the Prophet said, "Well, even one-third is a large amount."[24]

One day the Prophet saw a Companion in miserable attire. When asked why, he replied, "O Messenger of God, I am not at all poor, but I prefer to spend my wealth on the poor rather than on myself." The Prophet remarked, "No. God likes to see on His servant traces of the bounty that He has accorded him."[25]

There is no contradiction in these accounts, for each has its own context and relates to distinct individual cases. Muslims are allowed to determine how much charity they will give after their wealth has exceeded the obligatory minimum.

Inheritance

Both the individual right to control one's wealth and the right of the collectivity with regard to each person's wealth, inasmuch as one is a member of society, have to be satisfied simultaneously. Individual temperaments differ enormously, and sickness or other accidents may affect a person out of all proportion to the norm. Therefore, a certain discipline is imposed upon the individual in the interest of the collectivity.

Thus Islam has taken two steps: distributing a deceased person's goods among his or her close relatives according to a method that cannot be challenged, and restricting the freedom of bequest through wills and testaments. The legal heirs require no testamentary disposition and inherit the property in the proportions determined by law. A testament is required only for those who have no prior right to inherit.[26]

Parents and grandparents inherit, and one cannot award to one son (elder or younger) more than to another, regardless of age. Before the property is distributed, however, the burial expenses have to be paid, and then the creditors, as paying debts has priority over the inheritors' rights. After this, all bequests are executed in such a way that this does not exceed one-third of the remaining property. Only after satisfying these obligations are the heirs considered. The surviving spouse, parents, and descendants (sons and daughters) are the first beneficiaries and inherit in all cases. Brothers, sisters, and more remote relatives (e.g., uncles, aunts, cousins, nephews, and others) only inherit if there are no nearer relatives. While the inheritance is distributed, those present and the poor are also considered, as ordered by the Qur'an:

> If some from among other relatives (who do not have a legally defined share), and orphans and the destitute, are present at the division (of the inheritance), give them something thereof (for their provision), and speak to them kindly and pleasing words. (4:8)

Wills

Wills are operative only for one-third of property and favor persons other than creditors and heirs.[27] The goal of this rule seems to be twofold: to permit a person to adjust things, in extraordinary cases, when the normal rule causes hardship (one-third of the property is enough for fulfilling such moral duties) and to prevent the accumulation of wealth among a few people. This could happen if a person willed all of his or her property to only one person. Islam desires that wealth circulate as widely as possible, taking into account the family's interest.

Public Goods

One also has obligations as a member of a larger family (i.e., society and the state of residence). In the economic sphere, one pays taxes that the government then redistributes in the collectivity's interest. Tax rates differ according to the sources of income. Interestingly, the Qur'an, which gives precise directions about the expenditure of the *Zakah*, contains no rules or rates of the income for the state. While scrupulously respecting the practice of the Prophet and his immediate successors, this silence may be interpreted as allowing the government to adopt new rules for income according to circumstances and in the people's interest.

Social "Insurance"

This consists of measures taken to counter the risks of heavy financial penalties incurred because of damage to the objects of insurance, and differs according to the times and social conditions. Among the Arabs of the Prophet's time, the cost of medical care was practically nothing. The average man built his house and paid for almost none of the material. Thus it is easy to understand why one did not need fire, health, and other types of insurance. However, measures against captivity and assassination were a real need. The Prophet's contemporaries were aware of this and so desired certain flexible arrangements that could be modified and adapted to different circumstances when necessary.

For example, in the Constitution of Madina, which was formulated during the first year of the Islamic era, these measures are called *ma'aqil* and worked as follows. If someone became a prisoner of war, paying a ransom could procure his freedom. Similarly, all bodily torts or culpable homicides required the payment of damages or blood money. The person concerned often could not afford the sum demanded. Thus, the Prophet organized a system of mutual assistance. A tribe's members could count on the tribe's central treasury, to which everybody contributed according to their means. If the treasury proved inadequate, other related or neighboring tribes had to help. Thus a hierarchy was established for organizing the units into a complete whole. At Madina, the Ansar tribes were well known. The Prophet ordered the Makkan refugees in Madina to form their own "tribe," even though they belonged to different Makkan or regional tribes, or were Abyssinians, in order to provide social solidarity.

Under Caliph 'Umar, the branches of "insurance" or social solidarity were organized according to which professional, civil, or military administration one belonged (or even which region). Whenever needed, the central or provincial government helped those branches, as we described above when speaking of state expenditure.

Insurance signifies the spreading of one individual's burden among as many people as possible in order to lighten each person's burden. Unlike modern capitalistic insurance companies, in Islam insurance was organized on the basis of mutuality and cooperation, aided by a pyramidal gradation of the branches that culminated in the central government.

Such a branch can engage in commerce with the help of the unutilized funds at its disposal, so that the capital will be augmented. A time might come when a branch's members can be exempted from paying further contributions or may even receive some of the profits of commerce. Such elements of mutual aid can insure against risk (e.g., traffic accidents, fire, and loss in transit). Also, the insurance industry can be nationalized in order to deal with certain risks.

Without entering into technical details, Islamic jurisprudence does not tolerate the capitalist version of insurance, for the insured person does not participate in the company's benefits in proportion to his or her contributions, which makes it resemble a game of chance.

Prohibition of Games of Chance

The Qur'an prohibits all games of chance and characterizes them as the "work of Satan" for cogent reasons such as provoking enmity and hatred among people and barring believers from God's remembrance and the Prayer (5:90). There are, of course, many other evils which games of chance cause, some of which may be included in "provoking enmity and hatred among people. For example, a great many social evils emanate from an inequitable distribution of the national wealth. As a result, the rich can exploit the poor. In games of chance and lotteries, there is great temptation for quick and easy gain and for shirking working and producing, although such easy gain is often bad for society and even for individuals themselves. If people spend three million dollars every week on horse races, public or private lotteries, and other games of chance, as is the case in certain countries, over the course of only ten years, 1.56 billion dollars would be collected from a large number of people and distributed among a ridiculously small number of people. Less than one percent of the people thrive at the expense of the remaining ninety-nine percent. In other words, ninety-nine percent of the people are impoverished in order to enrich one percent.

Whether games of chance and lotteries are private or nationalized, the evil of a few people accumulating wealth at the expense of a the vast majority works with full force. This is why Islam prohibits such activities. As is the case with capitalistic insurance, games of chance bear one-sided risks.

Prohibition of Interest

Probably every religion has prohibited usury or interest. However, in Islam there are remedies to undermine the causes leading to this evil institution. Nobody willingly pays interest on borrowed money. He or she pays interest because the money is needed and there is no other choice.

God has made a very clear distinction between commercial gain and interest on money-lending: *God permits trading and forbids interest* (2:275) and:

> If you do not give up (interest), be warned of war from God and His Messenger. If you repent, you will have your principal, (without interest); neither you wrong nor be wronged. (2:279)

One basis of this prohibition is also unilateral risk, for one who borrows money at interest earns money for the rich. Circumstances may be propitious enough for the borrower to earn enough money to pay back the promised interest, and the lender assumes none of the risk involved.

People may not desire to deprive themselves of their money in order to make interest-free loans to others. In addition to exhorting the rich to help the poor by lending them interest-free loans in return for gaining God's good pleasure and great otherworldly reward,[28] Islam, as decreed in the Qur'an (57:18; 64:17) encourages helping those who are in financial difficulty. Interest-free loans can be organized in addition to, and to supplement, the loans offered by charitable people or organizations to help the poor and the needy. The principle here is mutual aid and cooperation.

In the case of commercial loans, there is the system of *mudaraba*, in which one lends money and participates equally in any potential gain or risk. For example, if two people form a company, each one furnishing half of the capital and labor, the resulting profit distribution is quite easy. However, if the capital comes from one party and the labor from the other, if both furnish the capital though only one of them works, or their shares are not equal in proportion, in such cases a reasonable remuneration for labor, based upon previously agreed conditions is given before distributing any gains and profit. Although all precautions are taken to prevent risk, Islamic jurisprudence demands that both contracting parties to any contractual negotiation must share the profit as well as the loss.

To sum up, the principle of mutual participation in profits and risks must be observed in all commercial contracts.

Statistics

When planning, one needs to have an idea about the available resources. The Messenger, upon him be peace and blessings, organized a census of the Muslim population, as al-Bukhari informs us.[29] During 'Umar's caliphate, a census of animals, fruit trees, and other goods was organized, and cultivable lands were measured in the newly acquired provinces. With a large spirit and full of concern for the public's well-being, 'Umar would invite representatives of the people of different provinces, after taxes were collected, to find out if they had any complaints about the collector's behavior during the year.

Prohibition of Dealings with Intoxicants

Having discussed gambling, which causes the vast majority of its participants to spend money for years without gaining anything in return, we now turn to a discussion of alcohol. Alcohol has a very interesting quality: drinking only a little of it weakens any resolution to stop drinking. While drunk, people lose control over their actions. For example, they may squander money without being aware of what they are doing. In addition, various negative effects of alcohol are transmitted to a drinker's children and future generations. The Qur'an (2:219) speaks about such matters in the following terms: *They ask you about intoxicating drinks and games of chance. Say: "In both there is great evil, though some use for people, but their evil is greater than their usefulness."*

The Qur'an does not deny that alcohol brings people some profit—such as gains from its trade, but declares it a sin against society, the individual, and the Legislator. In 5:90, alcohol is relegated to the same level as idolatry and declared to be the handiwork of Satan. It adds that if one wants to be happy in both worlds, one should avoid alcohol and not involve by any means in its production, sale, or consumption.

Fulfilling Agreements

All financial and other dealings are based on some expressed or implicit agreements. Honoring these agreements is the key to happy and smooth relationships among members of a community or a society. Therefore, the Qur'an stresses this principle and, in several places, actually lists it as being among a believer's most important characteristics.

> (Believers are those) who are faithful to their trusts and to their commitments. (23:8)
>
> Those who fulfill their covenant when they have engaged in a covenant. (2:177)
>
> O you who believe, fulfill the bonds (you have entered into with God and people). (5:1)
>
> Fulfill the covenant. One is responsible for one's covenant and will be called to account for it (on the Day of Judgment). (17:34)

God's Messenger, upon him be peace and blessings, strongly warns against unfaithfulness to agreements and covenants, saying, "Whoever has the following four (characteristics) is a pure hypocrite, and whoever has one of the following four characteristics will have one characteristic of hypocrisy unless he gives it up. When he is entrusted, he betrays. When he speaks, he tells lies. When he makes a covenant, he proves treacherous. When he quarrels and shows hostility, he deviates from the truth."[30]

The failure to honor agreements is a primary cause of difficulty in dealings among people, especially financial dealings. If we analyze broken business partnerships or other difficulties in financial dealings, we will always find their root in the failure of one or more parties to fulfill one or more of the agreements related to those dealings.

Writing and Witnessing a Deal

To avoid such problems due to forgetfulness or other reasons, and to reduce any chance of misunderstanding and bad faith, the Qur'an orders that all financial deals be committed to paper and witnessed, as we read in the following passage:

> O you who believe! When you contract a debt between you for a fixed term, record it in writing. Let a scribe write it down between you justly, and let no scribe refuse to write it down: as God has taught him (through the Qur'an and His Messenger), so let him write. And let the debtor dictate, and let him avoid disobeying God, his Lord, and curtail no part of it. If the debtor be weak of mind or body, or incapable of dictating, let his guardian dictate justly. And call upon two (Muslim) men among you as witnesses. If two men are not there, then let there be one man and two women from among those of whom you approve as witnesses, that if either of the two women errs (through forgetfulness), the other may remind her. Let the witnesses not refuse when they are summoned (to give evidence). And (you, O scribes) be not loath to write down (the contract), whether it be small or great, with the term of the contract. Your doing so (O you who believe), is more equitable in the sight of God, more upright for testimony, and more likely that you will

> not be in doubt. If it be a matter of buying and selling concluded on the spot, then there will be no blame on you if you do not write it down; but do take witnesses when you settle commercial transactions with one another, and let no harm be done to either scribe or witness (nor let either of them act in a way to injure the parties). If you act (in a way to harm either party, or the scribe and witnesses), indeed it will be transgression on your part. (Always) act in due reverence for God and try to attain piety. God teaches you (whatever you need in life, and the way you must follow in every matter); God has full knowledge of everything. If you are (in circumstances like being) on a journey and cannot find a scribe, then a pledge in hand will suffice. But if you trust one another, let him (the debtor) who is trusted fulfill his trust, and let him act in piety and keep from disobedience to God, his Lord (by fulfilling the conditions of the contract). And do not conceal the testimony; he who conceals it, surely his heart (which is the center of faith) is contaminated with sin. God has full knowledge of what you do. (2:282–283)

In these verses, the Qur'an distinguishes between financial transactions that involve credit for a definite period and those that are carried out on the spot. Examples of the first type include loans for a definite period and the purchase or sale of goods with either the payment or delivery promised for some fixed, future date. An example of the second type includes buying something in a shop on a cash-and-carry basis.

Some people might be surprised that the Qur'an recommends that even on-the-spot transactions (e.g., sale of goods on cash-and-carry basis) should have some proof in writing or through witnesses. Perhaps because at first sight it looks unnecessary, this recommendation has been almost completely ignored in the Muslim world. However, as business became more organized, the wisdom behind this recommendation has been independently discovered in modern times. These days, whenever we make any purchase, no matter how small, we receive a receipt. This receipt serves many purposes, such as enabling the customer to return defective items with little or no argument, prosecuting merchants who overcharge or cheat the customer in some way, catching and prosecuting shoplifters, and making it easier for buyers and sellers to keep accounts.

After briefly discussing the usefulness and relevance of the Qur'anic orders to write and/or witness financial deals, we now consider just how obligatory they are.

Avoiding Bad Faith

Writing a clear, detailed agreement and having it duly signed and/or witnessed can prevent two problems: forgetfulness and misunderstanding. In addition, it can reduce the chance of any involved party being tempted to take advantage of the other party or parties by lying, cheating, or other crooked ways resulting from bad faith. But to avoid bad faith, more than just recording the deal in writing is needed. What is needed here is piety, on which such emphasis is laid in Islam, defined as the respect for moral values that comes through fear and consciousness of God and belief in the Hereafter.

Enforcing Agreements

Nevertheless, there will always be people who do not give much importance to piety and thus will break an agreement whenever it suits them. To counter such people, there must be a legal apparatus to enforce any deals that they may willingly sign.

Justice as the Basis of Economic Life

Justice (*'adl*) means to divide two things equally or keep the balance. The Qur'an uses it for justice in all matters, and Islam teaches the believers to be fair in their dealings, as we read in:

> God commands you to deliver trusts (including all public and professional duties of service) to those entitled to them, and when you judge between people, to judge with justice. How excellent is what God exhorts you to do. Assuredly, God is All-Hearing, All-Seeing. (4:58)

God commands the believers to be just among themselves and exhorts them to be fully just even to their enemies:

> O you who believe, be upholders and standard-bearers of right for God's sake, being witnesses for (the establishment of) absolute justice, and by no means let your detestation for a people (or their detestation for you) move you to (commit the sin of) deviating from justice. Be just: this is nearer and more suited to righteousness and piety. Seek righteousness and piety, and always act in reverence for God. Surely God is fully aware of all that you do. (5:8)

Justice and righteousness are the cornerstone of the Islamic way of life. God's Messenger was known for this justice even before he declared his Prophethood. Throughout his life, he exhorted his followers to be truthful and just. Moreover, he set a perfect example of justice even to the followers of other religions and his enemies.

In accordance with the Divine law, the concept of social justice lays down certain conditions to treat people as individuals having liberty and equality as their birthright. This concept provides them with equal opportunities for personal development so that they are better able to fill the position to which they are entitled, to give each person his or her due, and to regulate his or her relations with society in terms of value and welfare.

Duties to Society

This concept of social justice is achieved by giving people a better understanding of their individual duties in society and the reward thereof. This understanding is provided in the Qur'an and the *Sunna* of the Prophet. The Messenger made education, being the measure and touchstone in this context, obligatory upon every Muslim, male and female. More specifically, he said and knew that knowledge enabled one to distinguish right from wrong.

Society depends upon the interaction between the individual and society, for this establishes and maintains a balance in human affairs. Humanity should always keep in mind that God created the universe for a particular purpose and that humanity has been asked to strive for its fulfillment.

Equality and Freedom

Broadly speaking, human rights center on equality and freedom. Caliph 'Umar reprimanded the governor of Egypt, whose son had struck a Copt (an Egyptian Christian), with the following instructive words: "How long have you enslaved men who were born free by their mothers?"[31] Again, the caliph's obedience to God's command to establish equality among people demonstrates the best egalitarian features: highly placed people cannot take advantage of their position, and the weak are not made to despair of their condition.

All people are God's servants. The only permissible characteristic by which one can claim superiority, distinction, and pre-eminence over others is the virtue of piety. No worldly status can be a cause of superiority. This is fully manifested in the congregational Prayers, where there is no room for rank and special privilege. All are equal in God's sight, whether one happens to be a caliph or a slave. The Messenger declared that all people were equal, like the teeth of a comb.[32]

The Qur'an declares:

> O humankind! Surely We created you from a single (pair) of a male and female, and made you into nations and tribes that you may know (and help) each other. Surely the noblest, most honored of you in God's sight is the one best in piety, righteousness, and reverence for God (taqwa). Surely God is All-Knowing, All-Aware. (49:13)

Balance in Society

Islam avoids extremes in order to maintain social balance and order. Therefore, monopoly and cut-throat competition are disapproved. Islam's essence is justice for all, which enables people to lead a good and happy life while, at the same time, strengthening the bonds of human fellowship and the social fabric.

The social framework prevalent today in most Muslim countries is not Islamic. Many places are characterized by monstrous and oppressive conditions for the poor, rampant corruption, poverty, and need. A few people have acquired substantial wealth and thus enjoy the numerous amenities and luxuries of life, whereas the majority do not even receive two square meals a day. An Islamic social order stresses simple and austere efforts that are free from ostentation. The Messenger strove to bridge the gap between the rich and the poor, the high and the low. He advocated a society in which one sector would not exploit another, for Islam seeks a balanced life that represents the equilibrium of social forces.

The fullest development of humanity's potential can be achieved through the implementation of Islamic principles. The optimum level of civilization, which embodies the maximum well-being, can never be possible without spiritual and moral development. All basic Islamic principles, which descend from Divinity, are perfect. The Islamic approach is therefore just, natural, humane, and perfectly balanced and rational.

Abu'l-Fazl Ezzati outlines the Islamic economic system as follows:

- Islam represents a complete way of life. There is no compartmentalization of human activity in Islam. Its economic policy is, therefore, an integral part of the Religion of Islam.
- An Islamic economic system is based on equality, justice, moderation, and collective self-sufficiency.
- Humanity's spiritual development is fundamental but their physical welfare is instrumental.
- Islam is based on faith in God, Who has given human beings the ability to choose between good and evil, and assume full responsibility for their conduct. *A person has only that for which he[she] makes effort, and this effort will be seen*. (53:39–40)
- Islam is a universal system embodying eternal values which safeguard a person's rights while constantly reminding him or her of his or her obligation to himself or herself and society.

- Islam forbids exploitation and monopoly in all forms and strictly prohibits unearned interest such as usury, gambling, and so on.
- Islam honors labor and contracts, enjoins work and toil, encourages human beings to earn their own living by honest means and to spread their earnings.
- Islam encourages mutual helping and never likes "wealth to circulate among the rich only" (59:7). Every member of the Muslim community feels obliged to help his or her poor brother or sister while he or she is equally entitled to live a private life and to own property.[33]

Chapter 6

al-Hajj (Pilgrimage to Makka)

AL-HAJJ (PILGRIMAGE TO MAKKA)

Hajj, one of the five pillars of Islam, is a rehearsal of life in both this world and the next, a theater of all Islamic life based upon deep devotion to God and perception of one's servanthood and God's Divinity and Lordship. It consists of love, action, humility, God-consciousness, sacrifice, and dominion over the carnal self.

It has two pillars: staying at 'Arafat for a certain length of time on the ninth day of Dhu'l-Hijja (the last day of the Islamic lunar calendar) and circumambulating 'Arafat any day after staying at 'Arafat. *Ihram* is also essential to both the major (*Hajj*) and minor (*'Umra*) pilgrimage. *Ihram* is the intention to perform either *Hajj* or *'Umra*, or both, and marks the beginning of *Hajj* or *'Umra*, or both if they are performed together. It also signifies making some things forbidden. Men wear special attire while in *ihram*, and this is why some people call this attire *ihram*.

THE VIRTUE OF *HAJJ*

Hajj mabrur (a faultless *Hajj* that is free of sin and graced with Divine acceptance and good pleasure) is one of the best, most virtuous deeds in Islam.

Concerning the importance of the *Hajj*, the Qur'an declares:

> Behold, the first House (of Prayer) established for humankind is the one at Bakkah (Makkah), a blessed place and a (center or focus of) guidance for all peoples. In it, there are clear signs (demonstrating that it is a blessed sanctuary, chosen by God as the center of guidance), and the Station of Abraham. Whoever enters it is in security (against attack and fear). Pilgrimage to the House is a duty owed to God by all who can afford a way

> to it. And whoever refuses (the obligation of the Pilgrimage), or is ungrateful to God (by not fulfilling this command), God is absolutely independent of all creatures. (3:96–97)

God's Messenger says, "He who performs the *Hajj* for God's good pleasure and avoids all lewdness and sin will return after the *Hajj* as free from all sins as he was the day his mother gave birth to him."[1] and, "Pilgrims and those performing *'Umra* are God's guests. Their prayers are answered and their supplications for forgiveness are granted. The reward of *Hajj mabrur* is Paradise."[2]

Among many excellencies of the *Hajj*, such as being a means for the purification of sins and strengthening spirituality and devotion to God Almighty, there are many benefits for Muslims individually and collectively. It reinforces Islamic fellowship, solidarity, and mutual assistance. It also has benefits for economic and social cooperation among Muslims and Muslim communities. But unfortunately, it is difficult to say that at the present Muslims can derive these benefits from it. The Qur'an declares:

> Remember when We assigned to Abraham the site of the House ('Arafat) as a place of worship (directing him), "Do not associate any partners with Me in any way, and keep My House pure (from any material and spiritual filth) for those who will go round it in devotion, and those who will stand in Prayer before it, and those who will bow down and prostrate themselves in worship." Publicly proclaim the (duty of) Pilgrimage for all humankind, that they come to you on foot and on lean camels, coming from every faraway point, so that they may witness all the (spiritual, social, and economic) benefits in store for them, and offer during the known, appointed days the sacrificial cattle that He has provided for them by pronouncing God's Name over them. Eat of their meat and feed the distressed, the poor. Thereafter, let them tidy themselves up (by having their hair cut, removing their *ihram* [*Hajj* attire], taking a bath, and clipping their nails, etc.), and fulfill the vows (if they have made any, and complete other acts of the Pilgrimage), and go round the Most Ancient, Honorable House in devotion. (22:26–29)

Some Facts

Hajj is obligatory only once. All Muslim scholars agree that *Hajj* is obligatory only once during a Muslim's lifetime, unless someone vows to perform an extra *Hajj*, in which case the vow must be fulfilled. Whatever is done over and above is supererogatory or optional.[3]

When Hajj must be performed. Although some scholars opine that *Hajj* may be performed at any time during one's life, and that one who must perform it can postpone it, it is preferred that *Hajj* be performed as soon as one is physically and financially able to do so. God's Messenger says, "He who intends to perform *Hajj* should hasten to do so, for no one among you knows when death will come to him."[4] This is because if the person dies before performing the obligatory *Hajj* or a vowed one, his or her heir must carry out this duty. Even if the deceased did not specify this in his or her will, if one-third of the estate is enough for an heir to make *Hajj*, an heir should perform it for the deceased. All ensuing *Hajj* expenses, as well as any debts, must be paid from the deceased's property. However, the heir who wants to do this must obtain all of the other heirs' agreement, or at least acquiescence, before departing. If such an agreement is not reached, the heir must pay all expenses out of his or her own property.

Hajj on behalf of others. If people can perform *Hajj* but do not do so, and then are overtaken by sickness, old age, or death, they must arrange for someone else who preferably has already performed his or her duty of *Hajj*,[5] to perform it on their behalf, for they might never have another chance to do it.[6] If sick people recover after having sent someone in their place, some scholars say that their duty to make *Hajj* has been fulfilled and that they do not have to "repeat" it. However, most scholars opine that the recovered people still must perform *Hajj*, for a "substitutory" *Hajj* is not enough.

Doing Business. Pilgrims can pursue trade and business or economic benefits during *Hajj* or *'Umra*, provided that they are making *Hajj* solely to fulfill their responsibility for God's sake. The Qur'an declares:

> Publicly proclaim the (duty of) Pilgrimage for all humankind, that they come to you on foot and on lean camels, coming from every faraway point, so that they may witness all the (spiritual, social, and economic) benefits in store for them, and offer during the known, appointed days the sacrificial cattle that He has provided for them by pronouncing God's Name over them. Eat of their meat and feed the distressed, the poor. (22:27–28)

> There is no blame on you that you should seek of the bounty of your Lord. (2:198)

Prerequisites

All jurists agree upon the following prerequisites for *Hajj*:

- Being an adult, free Muslim of sound mind. Children can do *Hajj* along with their parents, but they have to perform it again after reaching the age of responsibility (puberty). A mentally ill person performs it after recovery.[7]
- Being physically fit and healthy enough to perform it.
- Finding a safe way to reach Makka, so that the pilgrim's life and possessions are not in danger.
- Having the necessary provisions, meaning that they must be able to take care of themselves while performing *Hajj*, meet their family's needs back home, and be able to make the trip in an Islamically acceptable way. All of the money spent to perform *Hajj* must have been earned in an Islamically acceptable way.

  The last three prerequisites are included in the concept of "having capacity" or "can afford" in verse 3:97: *Pilgrimage to the House is a duty owed to God by all who can afford a way to it*.[8]
- *Hajj* must be performed during the correct months for it: *The Hajj is in the well-known months appointed for it* (2:197). The months of the *Hajj* are Shawwal, Dhu'l-Qa'da and the first ten days of Dhu'l-Hijja.[9] Nothing concerning the *Hajj* can be per-

formed in a month other than these ones. God's Messenger performed the *Hajj* during Dhu'l-Hijja and decreed, "Learn from me the rites and ceremonies of the *Hajj*."[10] One of the two pillars of the *Hajj* is staying for some time on Mount 'Arafat. This is done on the ninth day of Dhu'l-Hijja, the eve of *'Iydu'l-Adha* (the religious festival of the day of sacrifice). The time of performing the other pillar, which is the Circumambulation of *Ifada*—the obligatory going round 'Arafat seven times— begins on the first of the three days of *'Iydu'l-Adha*.

- A woman who performs *Hajj* from such a distance that she will be considered a traveler by Islamic jurisprudence[11] must be accompanied by her husband, or a male relative who cannot legally marry her, or one or more reliable women.[12]

Ihram

Ihram is the intention to perform *Hajj* or *'Umra*, either singly or together, and marks the beginning of either one or both if they are performed together. It also signifies making some things forbidden, because of which the special *Hajj* attire is called *ihram*, meaning making some things forbidden (*haram*). Men wear special attire of two white, unstitched, cloth sheets. One of these is wrapped around the body's upper part (except the head), and the other (*izar*) is wrapped around the body's lower part. There is no special *Hajj* attire for women.

Fixed Time

This refers to the specific time during which the rites of the *Hajj* have to be performed in order to be valid. The Qur'an states, *They ask you, (O Messenger,) about the new moons. Answer them, "They are signs for the people to determine the time and the period of the Pilgrimage"* (2:189), and, *The Pilgrimage is in the well-known months, appointed for it* (2:197). As stated before, these months are Shawwal, Dhu'l-Qa'da and the first ten days of Dhu'l-Hijja. Therefore, entering into the state of *ihram* with the intention of performing the *Hajj* is not valid outside these months, except for *'Umra*, which can be performed at any time of the year.

Fixed Places (Mawaqit) for Ihram

Mawaqit (plural of *miqat*) are the specific places where pilgrims or people intending to perform *Hajj* or *'Umra* must declare their intention to do so and enter the state of *ihram*. Men put on their special *Hajj* attire in these places. It is permissible to make the intention and enter the state of *ihram* before reaching these places but anyone intending to perform *Hajj* or *'Umra* must not pass beyond them without *ihram*.

God's Messenger, upon him be peace and blessings, specified these places as follows:

- For the people of Madina and those coming through Madina, the *miqat* is Dhu'l-Hulayfa, 450 kilometers north of Makka.
- For those coming from Syria, Jordan, Palestine, and Lebanon, the *miqat* is al-Juhfa, 187 kilometers northwest of Makka, and close to Rabigh, 204 kilometers from Makka. Rabigh became the *miqat* for people coming from Syria and Egypt after the settlement of al-Juhfa disappeared completely.
- The *miqat* for the people of Najd is Qarnu'l-Manazil, a mountain 94 kilometers east of Makka, overlooking 'Arafat.
- Yalamlam, a mountain 54 kilometers south of Makka, is the *miqat* for those coming from Yemen.
- For the people of Iraq, the *miqat* is Dhat 'Irq, 94 kilometers northeast of Makka.
- For those living in Makka who intend to perform *Hajj*, the *miqat* is the place where they are staying in Makka. However, if they intend to perform *'Umra*, they should go to al-Khol or at-Tan'im, for that is the proper *miqat* for *'Umra* for the residents of Makka.

- Those who live between a *miqat* and Makka can make their *ihram* from their house.[13]
- Those whose way does not pass through any of these places must enter the state of *ihram* in that place which shares the same line (latitude) as one of the places listed.[14]

Etiquette of Ihram

This involves clipping the fingernails, shaving the hair under the armpits, shaving the pubic hair, making *wudu'* or (preferably) performing *ghusl*, and combing their hair and beard and trimming the moustache, (the last two for men only). Men can put perfume on their body and *Hajj* attire when they put it on, even if it continues to smell afterwards.[15] After cleansing oneself in accord with these rules, one should pray two *rak'as*, intend to assume the state of *ihram*, and perform either *Hajj* or *'Umra*, or both if one intends to perform them together.[16]

Restrictions during *Ihram*

These are as follows:

- Sexual intercourse and all matters leading to it (e.g., kissing, touching, or talking to one's spouse about intercourse or related matters).
- Committing sins that cause deviation from the path of obeying God.
- Disputing, arguing, or fighting with companions, servants, and other people. God declares:

> The *Hajj* is in the well-known months appointed for it. Whoever undertakes the duty of *Hajj* in them, there is no sensual indulgence, nor wicked conduct, nor disputing during the *Hajj*. Whatever good you do (all that you are commanded and more than that, especially to help others), God knows it. Take your provisions for the *Hajj* (and do not be a burden upon others). In truth, the best provision is righ-

> teousness and piety, so be provided with righteousness and piety to guard against My punishment, O people of discernment! (2:197)

- Wearing any sewn clothes (e.g., a shirt, hooded robes, cloak, underpants), wrapping anything around the head (e.g., a cap or a fez), wearing shoes or sewn slippers (for men), wearing clothes dyed with a nice fragrant dye. Women should uncover their faces.[17]
- Killing any animal or game or showing it to someone else so that he or she may kill it, or cutting any green grass or trees (whether within or outside the sacred precincts of Makka).[18]
- Shaving oneself (whether beard, moustache, head, armpit, or pubic area); clipping the fingernails, trimming the moustache, and dressing the hair, beard, or moustache with fragrance.[19]
- Marrying. Even though the Hanafi School, based on the narrations that God's Messenger made the marriage contract with Maymuna while he was in the state of *ihram*,[20] permits marrying, to have sexual relations in *ihram* is absolutely forbidden.

KINDS OF *IHRAM* OR *HAJJ*

These are divided into three categories, each of which all scholars say are legitimate: *Qiran* (combining *ʿUmra* and *Hajj* in one state of *ihram*), *Tamattuʿ* (combining *Hajj* and *ʿUmra* with a break in between), and *Ifrad* (*Hajj* only).

Qiran

Here, pilgrims declare their intention to perform both *Hajj* and *ʿUmra* together, and say when doing *talbiya*, "O God, I answer your call to perform *Hajj* and *ʿUmra*." [*Talbiya* is: *Labbayk, Allahumma labbayk; labbayk la sharika laka; inna'l-hamda wa'l-minnata laka wa'l-mulk, la sharika lak*. ("Here I am, my God. Here I am at Your service. Here I am at Your service. You have no partner. Assuredly, all praise and gratitude are for You, and all dominion. You have no partner.")][21] Such pilgrims must remain in the state of *ihram* until they have performed all the rites of *'Umra* and *Hajj*.

Tamattu'

In this case, pilgrims perform *'Umra* during the *Hajj* season and then perform *Hajj*. It is called *tamattu'* (enjoyment) because these pilgrims have the added advantage of performing *Hajj* and *'Umra* together without having to go back home, and also because after performing *'Umra* they can wear their usual clothes, apply perfume, and do other things until they have to put on their attire for *Hajj*.

Anyone intending to do *tamattu'* should, on approaching the *miqat*, make the intention for *'Umra*. While uttering *talbiya*, they should say, *Labbayk bi'l-'Umra* (O God, I answer Your call to perform *'Umra*). They should wear their *Hajj* attire (women have no special *Hajj* attire) until they have circumambulated the Ka'ba, walked between Safa and Marwa to perform *sa'y*, and then cut off a little of their hair (women) or shaved it off altogether or had it shorter (men only). After that, they may wear their usual clothes and do all that is normally permissible but that is prohibited while in the state of *ihram*. On the eighth of Dhu'l-Hijja, they must declare their intention to perform *Hajj*, re-enter the state of *ihram*, and put on their special attire from Makka.

Ifrad

Ifrad means that pilgrims intending to perform *Hajj* only should only make the intention for *Hajj* while at the *miqat*. While saying *talbiya*, they should say: *Labbayk bi'l-Hajj* (O God, I answer your call to perform *Hajj*) and wear their *Hajj* attire until all the rites of *Hajj* are completed. After that, they can make *'Umra* if they so desire.[22]

The Obligatory Acts or Pillars of *Hajj*

The obligatory acts of *Hajj* consist of staying for some time in 'Arafat after noon on the eve of *'Iydu'l-Adha* (the ninth of Dhu'l-Hijja), and performing the obligatory circumambulation (*tawaf*) of visiting. *Ihram* is also essential for *Hajj*.

The Necessary Acts (*Wajib*) of *Hajj*

The necessary acts for *Hajj* are as follows:

- Entering the state of *ihram* in any of the *miqats*.
- Doing nothing forbidden while in *ihram*.
- Staying in 'Arafat until sunset on the ninth of Dhu'l-Hijja, the eve of *'Iydu'l-Adha*.
- As ordered in the Qur'an (2:198), staying at al-Muzdalifa during the night of *'Iydu'l-Adha* for at least one hour. However, the aged and the weak, especially those among the women, should hasten from al-Muzdalifa to Mina at the later part of the night before the people move in multitude. According to the Hanafis, one can fulfill this necessary act by staying there just after the dawnbreak. Al-Muzdalifa is located about 20 kilometers from Makka and 10 kilometers from 'Arafat. The evening and late Prayers are combined at al-Muzdalifa during the time of night Prayer, and the dawn Prayer is also performed there just at the break of dawn.[23]
- Performing the last three turns of the obligatory circumambulation (*tawafu'l-ifada* or *ziyara*) around the Ka'ba. (The first four turns are obligatory.)
- Doing the obligatory circumambulation of visiting during the first three days of *'Iydu'l-Adha*, during which sacrifice is offered.
- Performing the farewell circumambulation. (This is necessary for pilgrims coming from outside of Makka.)
- Performing the circumambulation in the state of ritual purity and covering all parts of the body that must be covered.
- Beginning the circumambulation from a point in line with the Black Stone and with the Ka'ba on one's left.
- Offering two *rak'as* of Prayer after every circumambulation.

- While performing the circumambulation, turning outside and around Hijr Isma'il, a place to the north of Ka'ba and surrounded by a semicircular wall.
- Performing *sa'y* (slightly running seven times between the hills of Safa and Marwa, going from Safa to Marwa four times, and the other way three times). The Qur'an mentions this also (2:158).
- Throwing seven pebbles at each of three stone columns (*jamarat*) standing in Mina with some distance between them. These are called *Jamratu'l-Ula*, *Jamratu'l-Wusta*, and *Jamratu'l-'Aqaba*. On the first day of *'Iydu'l-Adha*, one throws pebbles at *Jamratu'l-'Aqaba*, and at all of them on the following two days. Jabir ibn Abdullah narrates that he saw God's Messenger throwing pebbles at the *jamarat* on the *'Iyd* days and that he said, "Learn from me the rites and ceremonies of *Hajj*. I do not know whether I will be able to do *Hajj* after this year."[24]
- Those coming from outside of Makka and performing *Hajj al-Tamattu'* or *Hajj al-Qiran* should sacrifice a sheep or a goat any time within three days after throwing pebbles on the first day of *'Iydu'l-Adha*, and shave or cut some of their hair within Makka's sacred precincts. Women only clip a little of their hair.[25]

If one of these necessary acts is omitted, a sacrifice must be offered.

Sunna Acts

- Performing *wudu'* or *ghusl* before putting on the *Hajj* attire to enter the state of *ihram*.[26]
- Before donning the *Hajj* attire, putting on permitted perfume.[27]
- Offering two *rak'as* of Prayer as a *sunna* act of *ihram*, and reciting *Surat al-Kafirun* and *Surat al-Ikhlas* in each *rak'a* after *Surat al-Fatiha*.[28]
- Uttering *talbiya* loudly as soon as one enters the state of *ihram*, and doing so whenever one climbs a hill, descends into a valley,

meets one or more people, early in the morning, and after every prescribed Prayer until throwing stones at *Jamratu'l-'Aqaba* on the first day of *'Iydu'l-Adha*. (Women do not raise their voices while uttering *talbiya*.)[29]

- Calling God's blessings and peace upon our Prophet Muhammad, upon him be peace and blessings, and upon his Family many times after each *talbiya*; and saying prayers afterwards.
- Performing *ghusl* before entering Makka, praying upon seeing the Ka'ba, and exalting and glorifying God and declaring His Oneness in front of the Sacred Mosque.[30]
- Those coming from outside of Makka perform the arrival circumambulation.
- Making voluntary circumambulations while staying in Makka.[31]
- Walking fast, moving the shoulders vigorously, and taking small steps in order to give a sense of strength and energy during the first three turns of the obligatory *tawaf* of visiting.[32]
- Being quicker between the green markers while doing *sa'y* (between Safa and Marwa).[33]
- Leaving for Mina on the eighth of Dhu'l-Hijja after sunrise, and spending that day and night there.[34]
- Leaving for 'Arafat on the ninth of Dhu'l-Hijja after sunrise.
- It is also a *sunna* act that two sermons are given before the noon and afternoon Prayers to be combined at 'Arafat on the ninth of Dhu'l-Hijja, and another sermon at Mina on the *'Iyd* day.[35]
- Departing for al-Muzdalifa from 'Arafat after sunset and spending that night there, and proceeding to al-Mash'aru'l-Haram (near the hill of Quzah at al-Muzdalifa) and Mina at dawn after the Dawn Prayer.[36]
- As decreed in the Qur'an (2:198–200), praying to and mentioning God, and asking for His forgiveness sincerely and in utmost humility in 'Arafat, al-Muzdalifa, and Mina.

- Staying in Mina on the second, third (and fourth) days of *'Iydu'l-Adha*.[37]
- While throwing pebbles at the *jamarat*, standing so that Mina will be on one's right and Makka on one's left, and throwing in turn beginning with *Jamratu'l-Ula* and proceeding to *Jamratu'l-Wusta* and *Jamratu'l-'Aqaba*.[38]
- Throwing the pebbles between sunrise and noon on the first day of throwing, and between noon and sunset on the other days.[39]
- Going quickly from Mina to Makka. If one leaves Mina on the twelfth of Dhu'l-Hijja or the fourth day of *'Iydu'l-Adha*, one should leave before sunset.
- While going to Makka, staying in Muhassab or al-Abtah for a short time.[40]
- Kissing and touching or rubbing one's hand on the Black Stone and touching the two Yamani corners—the corner in which the Black Stone is embedded and the portion near it—while circumambulating.[41]
- Drinking Zamzam water to one's fill after making the farewell circumambulation and offering two *rak'a*s of Prayer.[42]
- Rubbing one's face and chest against Multazam, a part of the Ka'ba between the Black Stone and its gate.
- Holding onto the curtain covering the Ka'ba and praying without bothering and troubling anyone.
- Visiting the tomb of God's Messenger in Madina. God's Messenger, upon him be peace and blessings, declares that the place between his room (now his grave) and his pulpit is a garden from the gardens of Paradise, and that his pulpit is upon his *Hawd* (the watering place or Basin of the Prophet in the next world, whose drink will refresh those who have crossed the *Sirat* [the Bridge]before entering the eternal abode of happiness) in Paradise.[43]

Performing these *sunna* acts increases the reward for *Hajj*, and omitting any of them incurs no penalty.

The Sacred Precincts of Makka (*Haram* Makka)

God's Messenger, upon him be peace and blessings, declared on the day of the conquest of Makka:

> God made this town sacred, so it is sacred by the sacredness conferred on it by God until the Day of Resurrection. Fighting in it was not lawful to anyone before me, and it was made lawful for me only for an hour on one day. Its thorns are not to be cut, its game is not to be molested, and the things dropped are to be picked up only by one who makes a public announcement of it, and its fresh herbage is not to be cut.[44]

The sacred precincts of Makka include the area around Makka, which are marked by stones a meter high, on all roads leading to or from the city. On the northern side, *Haram* Makka extends to Tan'im, 6 kilometers from the Sacred Mosque; on the southern side to Adah, 12 kilometers from Makka; on the eastern side to al-Ji'rana, 16 kilometers away; on its northeastern side to the valley of Nakhla (14 kilometers away); and on the western side 15 kilometers away (al-Hudaybiya).

The Sacred Precincts of Madina (*Haram* Madina)

God's Messenger declared that Madina has the same sacredness or inviolability as Makka, and cursed anyone who would fabricate a religious innovation there.[45] In the sacred precincts of Madina, killing game animals and cutting down trees also are prohibited, with the exception that Madina's continuous residents can use trees and grass for their animals. The sacred precincts of Madina extend from Eer to Thawr. Eer is a mountain at the *miqat* for Madina, and Thawr is a mountain to the north near Uhud.

Penalty for Violating the Sanctity of *Ihram*

God Almighty decrees in the Qur'an:

> O you who believe! Do not kill game while you are in the state of pilgrim sanctity (*ihram*) or in the sacred precincts of

Makka. Whoever of you kills it, then its recompense is the like of what he has killed, from livestock, to be judged by two men among you of equity and probity, and to be brought to the Ka'ba as an offering; or (there shall be) an expiation by way of giving (as much) food to the destitute (as the value of the game killed), or fasting (a number of days) equivalent (to the number of the persons to be fed, or the shares assigned for them). (That is ordained) so that he may taste the evil consequences of his deed. God has pardoned what is past; but for one who re-offends, God will take retribution from him. And God is All-Glorious with irresistible might, Ever-Able to requite (wrong). (5:95)

The Violations Nullifying the Hajj or 'Umra and Requiring Make-up

- Having sexual intercourse while in the state of *ihram* before or while at 'Arafat nullifies *Hajj*. One who commits this sacrifices a sheep or goat, leaves the state of *ihram*, and must do a new *Hajj* in later years.[46] Committing the same "offense" before completing the fourth turning around the Ka'ba during *'Umra* nullifies it. One who commits it must do a new *'Umra*.

The Violations Requiring the Sacrifice of a Cow or an Ox or a Camel

- If one has sexual intercourse before shaving oneself or cutting some hair after staying in 'Arafat, or performs the obligatory circumambulation of visiting in the state of major ritual impurity or menstruation or post-childbirth bleeding, one must sacrifice a cow, an ox, or a camel. If, however, one repeats the circumambulation after being purified, the requirement for this sacrifice is cancelled.

The Violations to Be Paid for by Sacrificing a Sheep or a Goat

- If one has sexual intercourse after shaving oneself or cutting some hair, but before the obligatory circumambulation of visiting, one must sacrifice a sheep or a goat.[47]
- Putting perfume or similar things on any part of the body or henna on the head; wearing a stitched garment or covering one's head (for men) for a day or night; shaving at least one-fourth of one's head; clipping all of one's fingernails or those of one hand or foot. If all of the fingernails of one's hand or foot are clipped in different places or times, a different sacrifice is required for each place or time.
- Omitting one of the necessary things of *Hajj*—passing the *miqat* without *ihram*; omitting the whole or four runs of *sa'y*, or performing it without slightly running without a valid excuse; not performing the stay at al-Muzdalifa; not throwing the pebbles at the *jamarat* at all or more than half of the pebbles to be thrown during a day; not doing the one or the last three turns of the circumambulation of visiting; not performing the farewell circumambulation or four of its turns; not observing the condition of covering the parts of the body which must be covered while doing any of the obligatory or necessary circumambulations; doing the obligatory circumambulation without *wudu'*, and doing any of the necessary or *sunna* circumambulations while menstruating or being in a state of major impurity.

If one does such things while in the *ihram* for *qiran*, two sheep or goats must be sacrificed. If one does such things because of coercion or absolute necessity, one either sacrifices within Makka's sacred precincts or fasts for three days wherever he or she pleases, or gives charity in an amount equivalent to the *fitra* (that which provides a person with two average-sized meals) to a poor person.

The Violations That Require Giving a Fitra or a Lesser Amount of Charity

- If one wears perfume or something similar on some part of the body; wears a stitched garment or covers one's head for some part of the day (men only); shaves less than one-fourth of one's head (men only); clips only a fingernail or another person's fingernails; shaves someone else; or performs the arrival and farewell circumambulation without having performed *wudu'*, one must give a *fitra* amount of charity. Plucking a broken fingernail entails no penalty.
- If one kills a grasshopper, a louse, or a flea on one's own body or on that of somebody else, he or she must pay charity of less than a *fitra*. If one kills more than three of these vermin, one must pay a *fitra* amount of charity.

The Violations Requiring Compensation

- If one in the state of *ihram* kills an animal whose meat is not edible or a game animal, an estimate should be made and then one should make compensation. For an animal whose meat is not edible, this cannot be more than a sheep or a goat. If one has an animal of the equivalent value of the animal or game animal killed, one must sacrifice it and give its meat in charity. If one does not have such an animal, its value should be estimated by two just persons, and the person must give that amount of food to the poor. If one does not have enough money for this, one must fast according to how many poor people could be fed with that money. For example, if it is estimated that the amount of money could feed ten needy people, the person has to fast for ten days. The food given to the needy must be enough to satisfy their hunger.
- If one in the state of *ihram* cuts or plucks green grass or trees within Makka's sacred precincts, and these are not privately owned, their value is given away as charity. If they are privately owned, the compensation doubles, for the owner is compensated and its value is given to the poor as charity.[48]

PERFORMING *TAWAF* (CIRCUMAMBULATION)

One must begin *tawaf* (circumambulation) taking the Ka'ba on the left, and, while facing the Black Stone, kissing it (if possible), or touching it with one's hand, or pointing in its direction. Men keep their right shoulders uncovered during the *Tawafu'z-Ziyara* or *Ifada* (Obligatory *Tawaf* of Visiting). Jogging lightly through the first three circumambulations is encouraged.[49] One should walk fast, keep as close to the Ka'ba as possible, and take short steps. In the next four rounds, one should walk at a normal pace. Touching the Yemeni corner (ar-Ruknu'l-Yemeni) is encouraged, and so is kissing or touching the Black Stone in each of the seven rounds of *tawaf*, if possible. Remembering God and supplicating as much as possible is also encouraged.[50]

There are several kinds of *tawaf*, as follows:

- *Tawafu'l-Qudum* (Arrival Circumambulation). This is *sunna* for those coming from outside of Makka.
- *Tawafu'l-Ifada* or *Ziyara* (Obligatory Circumambulation of Visiting). This is one of the three pillars of *Hajj*, and should be done during the first three days of the *'Iydu'l-Adha*. If this is not possible, one can do it at any time during one's life, but must offer a sacrifice as penalty.
- *Tawafu'l-Wada'* (Farewell Circumambulation). This is necessary for all pilgrims coming from outside of Makka.
- *Tawafu't-Tatawwu'* (Supererogatory Circumambulation). Pilgrims can and are encouraged perform this as often as they want to during their stay in Makka.[51]

DOING *SA'Y* BETWEEN SAFA AND MARWA

Pilgrims, whether they are performing *Hajj* or *'Umra* perform *sa'y* as a necessary act[52] after *tawaf*. *Sa'y* means running from Safa to Marwa four times and the other way three times. The Qur'an stresses that each person meets that for whatever he or she strives or endeavors (53:39). *Sa'y* means endeavoring or making effort. For *Hajj*, this is held to commemorate Hagar's running between Safa and Marwa seven times in order to find water for her son, Ishmael. God told Abraham to leave Hagar and Ishmael, upon them be peace, in Makka, which was then an uninhabited barren valley (Qur'an, 2:126; 14:37). Both Abraham and Hagar submitted to God's order wholeheartedly. However, their submission did not prevent Hagar from trying to find water for her son, for both of them needed it.

Islam is the harmonious combination of submission and endeavor. Hagar did not wait for a miracle, but tried to find water in a desolate desert without losing hope. The water came miraculously from an unexpected place: under Ishmael's feet. That water, known as Zamzam, continues to meet the needs of millions of pilgrims every year, even after so many centuries. This miracle was the result of sincere belief, confidence in and submission to God, endeavor (humanity's duty), and never being desperate. People act, and God creates the result. This is why it has unanimously been said, "God is not found by looking for Him, but those who have found Him are those who have looked for Him."

Pilgrims begin *sa'y* from Safa and end in Marwa. They walk from Safa to Marwa four times, and the other way three times. They jog between the two green markers along the way. They supplicate and recite the Qur'an while walking and upon reaching either hill, and face the Ka'ba while supplicating.

'Umra (Minor Pilgrimage)

The word *'umra* is derived from *al-i'timar*, which means "to visit." In this context it means visiting the Ka'ba, performing *tawaf*, walking between Safa and Marwa seven times, and then shaving one's head or cutting one's hair short. It is a highly meritorious *sunna* act of worship. According to some Companions such as 'Abdullah ibn 'Umar, it is necessary for every Muslim having the required means to do *'Umra* at least once during their life. 'Abdullah ibn 'Abbas says that God mentions *'Umra* together with *Hajj* and orders to do both perfectly (2:196).[53] Those who do *Hajj Qiran* or *Tamattu'* do either kind of *Hajj* together with *'Umra*. It can also be done separately from *Hajj*. God's Messenger, upon him be peace and blessings, says that a perfectly performed *'Umra* serves as an atonement for the minor sins committed until another *'Umra*.[54] He also gives the glad tidings that the *'Umra* done during Ramadan gains the reward of *Hajj*.[55]

THE TIME. Most scholars have ruled that *'Umra* may be performed any time during the year. Abu Hanifa, however, opines that it is disliked to perform *'Umra* on five days: the Day of 'Arafat (eve), the Day of *Nahr* (Dhu'l-Hijja 10, the first day of *'Iydu'l-Adha*), and the three days of *Tashriq* (eleventh, twelfth and thirteenth of Dhu'l-Hijja).

THE *MIQAT*. If people who are intending to perform *'Umra* are outside the *miqat* fixed for *Hajj*, they must not cross these *miqats* (places fixed for *ihram*) without declaring *ihram*. Those people who are already well within the *miqat* area, even within Makka's Sacred Precincts, must go out to the *miqat* and declare *ihram* there.

HAJJ AND *'UMRA* FROM BEGINNING TO END

- People who intend to perform *Hajj* should ensure that all of the money to be spent during *Hajj* was earned in Islamically lawful ways. Debts must be paid off, and everyone who has rights upon the intending pilgrim must be asked to suspend those rights. In addition, the intending pilgrims must seek forgiveness from those whom they have wronged and forgive any wrongs done to them. They seek God's forgiveness, and offer two *rak'as* of Prayer before leaving home. When they get on their mount (animal or motor vehicle), they should pray as God's Messenger prayed when he set out for any journey. He used to glorify God (uttering *Allahu akbar*) three times, and then say:

> *All-Glorified is He Who has subjugated this to our use. We were never capable (of accomplishing this) by ourselves. And, surely, to our Lord we are indeed bound to return* (43:13–14). O God, we seek virtue and piety from You in this journey of ours and the deed with which You will be pleased. O God, lighten this journey of ours, and make its distance easy for us. O God, You are (our) companion during the journey, and guardian of (our) family. O God, I seek refuge in You from hardships of the journey, dejection, and any evil changes in my property and family, and from worsening after goodness, and from the malediction of an oppressed one.[56]

- While journeying, they must occupy themselves with reflecting upon God's works, reciting the Qur'an, and supplicating, while avoiding sin, speaking in vain, or harming any living creature.
- On arriving at the *miqat* (the place fixed for entering the state of *ihram*), pilgrims should shave themselves, clip their fingernails, perform *ghusl* or *wudu'*, and wear some perfume (men only). Men don their special *Hajj* attire, which is also called *ihram*, as it is the beginning and symbol of entering the state of *ihram*. There is no special attire for women. Pilgrim candidates should offer a two-*rak'a* Prayer and declare their intention (to perform *Hajj*, *Hajj* and *'Umra* together, or *'Umra*). It is recommendable to perform *Hajj Tamattu'* (*Hajj* and *'Umra* together, with a break in between) for pilgrims who come from far away. If one performs *Hajj Tamattu'*, one makes the intention for *'Umra* at the *miqat*. Wearing *ihram* (the special *Hajj* attire) and declaring the intention for *Hajj* or *'Umra* is an essential part of both, and neither will be correct without *ihram* and intention.

As soon as they enter the state of *ihram*, they must begin to utter the *talbiya* loudly (women do not raise their voices) and continue saying it whenever climbing a hill, descending into a valley, meeting one or more people, early in the morning, and after every prescribed Prayer until they throw pebbles at the *Jamratu'l-'Aqaba* on the first day of *'Iydu'l-Adha*.[57]

While in the state of *ihram*, pilgrims must avoid sexual intercourse and whatever leads to it, wrangling and useless bickering, marriage or joining others in marriage, wearing any sewn clothes or shoes that cover the feet above the ankles (men), covering their heads (men) or faces (women), wearing perfume, cutting their hair or nails, engaging in hunting game animals, or cutting trees or grass within Makka's Sacred Precincts.

- When entering Makka, pilgrims perform *ghusl*; hasten to the Sacred Mosque, and, upon reaching it, say the *talbiya*; ask God for forgiveness and pray to Him; call His blessings and peace on our master Muhammad, upon him be peace and blessings, and his Family and Companions; and recite words of God's Oneness, glorification, praise, and exaltation. As soon as they see the Ka'ba, they should pray for themselves, their parents, relatives, and all Muslims. In addition, they must always be humble. After this, they should proceed directly to the Black Stone and kiss it quietly or touch it with their hand. If this is not possible or doing so will harm others, one may just point toward it in the sense of greeting it.
- After this, one should begin circumambulating the Ka'ba and repeating the supplications, particularly those reported from the Prophet, upon him be peace and blessings. In the first three turns, men should uncover their right shoulder and jog slowly. In the remaining rounds, they may walk at a normal pace. It is *sunna* to touch the Yemeni Corner and to kiss the Black Stone in every round if it is possible and will not harm other people. After completing this rite's seven rounds, the pilgrims should go to the Station of Abraham, for God said:

> Remember, again, that We made the House (the Ka'ba in Makka) a resort for people, and a refuge of safety (a sanctuary, that is, a sign of the truth). Stand in the Prayer (O believers, as you did in earlier times) in the Station of Abraham. And We imposed a duty on Abraham and Ishmael: "Purify My House for those who go around it as a

> rite of worship, and those who abide in devotion, and those who bow and prostrate (in the Prayer)." (2.125)

There, they should pray two *rak'a*s of *tawaf*, if possible. If not, they can pray anywhere in the Mosque.

- Then they should approach Safa to begin *sa'y* in compliance with God's words:

> (The hills of) as-Safa and Marwah are among the emblems God has appointed (to represent Islam and the Muslim community). Hence, whoever does the *Hajj* (the Major Pilgrimage) to the House (of God, the Ka'ba) or the *'Umra* (the Minor Pilgrimage), there is no blame on him to run between them (and let them run after they go round the Ka'ba as a necessary rite). (2:158)

They should climb Safa, look towards the Ka'ba, and supplicate. After this, they should climb down and start walking toward Marwa as the first of seven rounds between the two hills, while remembering God and supplicating. On approaching one of the two green markers between the two hills, pilgrims should jog to the second green marker and, after passing it, resume their normal walking speed toward Marwa. Upon reaching Marwa, one should climb it, turn toward the Ka'ba, and supplicate and glorify God. This marks one complete round. One should perform the remaining six rounds in the same manner, thereby completing all seven rounds.

- If pilgrims are performing *Hajj Tamattu'*, men should shave their head or cut their hair short, (it is enough for women to cut off only a little of their hair) for this ends all *ihram*-related restrictions. After this, all things that were forbidden are allowed, including sexual intercourse with one's spouse. Those who intend to perform *Hajj Ifrad* (*Hajj* only) or *Hajj Qiran* (*Hajj* and *'Umra* together without a break) must continue in the state of *ihram*.
- On the eighth of Dhu'l-Hijja, those intending to perform *Hajj Tamattu'* must resume *ihram*, make the intention to perform

Hajj from their residences, proceed to Mina with those who have remained in *ihram*, and spend the night there.

- At sunrise on the ninth of Dhu'l-Hijja, the pilgrims leave for 'Arafat. Staying at 'Arafat begins only after the sun has passed its zenith. During this time, they should stand preferably by its rocks (*Jabalu'r-Rahma*) or as close as possible, because this is where the Prophet used to stand. However, it is permissible to stay at any location of 'Arafat. Staying at 'Arafat is the *Hajj*'s principal rite. During it, pilgrims should face the *qibla*, glorify and remember God, and supplicate as much as possible until nightfall.

  It is a *sunna* act that two sermons are given while in 'Arafat.
- After nightfall, the pilgrims must leave for al-Muzdalifa. Upon arriving there, they must offer the *maghrib* and *'isha'* Prayers, combining them after and following an imam, and spend the night there.
- At dawn, the pilgrims stand by al-Mash'aru'l-Haram (al-Muzdalifa), and perform *waqfa* there. That is, they must stay there for some time and remember and glorify God until it is almost sunrise, as God declares:

> There is no blame on you that you should seek of the bounty of your Lord (by trading during the *Hajj*, but beware of preoccupation to the extent of neglecting any of the rites of the *Hajj*). When you press on in multitude from 'Arafat (after you have stayed there for some time), mention God at Mash'aru'l-Haram (al-Muzdalifa); mention Him, aware of how He has guided you, for formerly you were surely of those astray. Then (do not choose to remain at al-Muzdalifa without climbing 'Arafat, in order to refrain from mixing with other people because of vanity. Instead,) press on in multitude from where all the (other) people press on, and implore God's forgiveness (for your opposing Him in any way before now, and for the mistakes you may have made during the *Hajj*). Surely God is All-Forgiving, All-Compassionate. And when you have performed those rites, mention God, as you mentioned your fathers (with the merits you approve of in them), or yet more intensely. (2:198–200)

- Before sunrise, they should return to Mina after collecting pebbles which they will throw at the *jamarat*. After sunrise, the pilgrims must throw seven pebbles at *Jamratu'l-'Aqaba*. While throwing, they say *Allahu akbar*, and take care not to harm others.[58] Then they offer their sacrifice, have their hair cut, remove their *ihram*, and lead their normal life—with the exception of having sexual intercourse with their spouse. It is best for men to shave their heads completely, although it is permissible merely to have some of their hair cut, while women only have a little of their hair cut.[59]
- Then they go to Makka to perform the obligatory *tawaf* of visiting, an essential part of *Hajj*. Performing this *tawaf* on the first day of *'Iydu'l-Adha* is recommended, but one can perform it during the following two days.[60] After this *tawaf*, sexual intercourse with one's spouse becomes permissible. If the pilgrims are performing *Hajj Tamattu'*, they must perform a *sa'y* after this *tawaf*. Those who are performing *Hajj Qiran* or *Ifrad* do not have to make this second *sa'y* if they performed the Arrival *Tawaf* and *sa'y* upon their arrival in Makka.
- The pilgrims must now return to Mina and spend the remaining three days of *'Iydu'l-Adha* there. After midday on the second, third, and fourth day (eleventh, twelfth and thirteenth of Dhu'l-Hijja), they throw seven pebbles at each of three *jamarat*, beginning with *Jamratul-Ula* and then *Jamratu'l-Wusta* and *Jamrat al-'Aqaba*. However, those who are in haste can stay there only for two days and be content with throwing pebbles at the *jamarat* on the second and third days. They exalt God at each throwing and, after finishing their throwing at the first two *jamarat*, pray for themselves, their parents and relatives, and for all Muslims.[61] If they want to stay in Mina on the fourth day of *'Iydu'l-Adha*, they throw pebbles at the *jamarat* before noon.
- After returning to Makka, those pilgrims who will be returning to their native lands must perform the Farewell *Tawaf*. Afterwards, they should go to the Zamzam well and drink as much

of its water as possible. Then they go to *al-Multazam*, rub their face and chest against it, hold the curtain covering the Ka'ba, pray, and supplicate.

Those Prevented from Completing *Hajj* or *'Umra*

Concerning those prevented from completing *Hajj* or *'Umra*, the Qur'an decrees:

> Complete the Hajj (the Major Pilgrimage) and the 'Umra (the Minor Pilgrimage) for God, and if you are impeded (after you have already put on the Pilgrimage attire), then send (to Makka) a sacrificial offering you can afford. Do not shave your heads (to mark the end of the state of consecration for the Pilgrimage) until the offering has reached its destination and is sacrificed. However, if any of you is ill (so that he is obliged to leave the state of consecration) or has an ailment of the head, he must make redemption by fasting, or giving alms, or offering a sacrifice. When you are secure (when the Pilgrimage is not impeded, or the impediment is removed), then whoever takes advantage of the 'Umra before the Hajj must give a sacrificial offering he can afford. For whoever cannot afford the offering, a fast for three days during the Hajj, and for seven days when you return home, that is, ten days in all. This is for those whose families do not live in the environs of the Sacred Mosque. Act in due reverence for God and piety (avoiding disobedience to Him and obeying His ordinances), and know that God is severe in retribution (2:196).

- If the pilgrims intended to perform either *Hajj* or *'Umra* but were prevented from approaching the House of God, they must sacrifice whatever animal they can afford (e.g., a sheep or a larger animal) within Makka's sacred precincts. After this, they shave their heads and leave the state of *ihram*, removing their special *Hajj* attire.[62] If the one prevented from the *Hajj* had intended to perform *Hajj Qiran*, he or she must pay for two sacrificial animals. If the intended but impeded *Hajj* or *'Umra* is an obligatory or necessary one, it must be made up later.[63] (According to the Shafi'is, it is necessary for every Muslim having the required means to do *'Umra* at least once during their life. Also, completing or making up *'Umra* becomes obligatory for a pilgrim who has intended for *Hajj Qiran*.)

- Those prevented from staying in 'Arafat: if they made the intention for *Hajj Ifrad*, they perform *'Umra* and make up the *Hajj* in any of the following years; if they intended to make *Hajj Tamattu'* or *Qiran*, they perform a second *'Umra* but do not have to sacrifice. They must make up their *Hajj* later.
- If the reason they cannot complete this duty is removed before staying in 'Arafat, they must complete their *Hajj*. If they are prevented (from doing so) after staying in 'Arafat, they arc not regarded as being prevented from completing their *Hajj*, for they can perform the obligatory *tawaf* at any time in their life, provided that they offer a sacrifice.

Offering a Sacrifice

Offering a sacrifice (a sheep, a goat, and for seven people a camel, a cow, or an ox)[64] is incumbent (*wajib*) upon every adult Muslim who has the *nisab* amount of wealth. The difference between having to pay the *Zakah* and offering a sacrifice is that *Zakah* must be paid on wealth if the person has had it for one year, while a sacrifice must be offered if the person has had a sufficient amount of wealth for only one day. The sacrifice must be made on any of the first three days of *'Iydu'l-Adha*.

A sacrifice has the meaning of seeking nearness to God and is based on piety and righteousness (*taqwa*). The Qur'an narrates that two of Adam's sons made sacrifices to seek nearness to God and it was accepted from the one who was sincere in intention and pious (5:27). The verse stresses that God Almighty accepts only from the sincere and pious. Another verses declares that it is not the flesh and blood of sacrificed animals which reaches God; it is only sincerity and piety which reaches God from people (22:37). Concerning sacrifice, the Qur'an also declares as follows:

For every believing community, We have laid down sacrifice as an act of worship to be performed at a certain time and place. So they must pronounce God's Name over what We have provided for them of cattle (while offering it). And (bear in mind that) your God is the One and Only God, so to Him alone submit yourselves wholly. And give glad tidings to the deeply devoted, humble servants—those whose hearts tremble with awe whenever God is mentioned, who are always patient with whatever ill befalls them, who always establish the Prayer in conformity with its conditions, and who spend (in God's cause and for the needy) out of whatever We provide for them. And the cattle, (including especially the camels)—We have appointed their sacrifice as among the public symbols and rituals set up by God for you, in which there is much good for you. When they (the camels) are lined up in standing position for sacrifice, pronounce God's Name over them. When they fall down on their sides and fully die, ready to be eaten, eat of their meat and feed the poor such as (beg not but) live in contentment and such as beg with due humility. (It is for the purposes and benefits mentioned, and based on the principles mentioned that) We have put the sacrificial animals in your service, so that you may give thanks to God. (22:34–36)

Sacrifice during Hajj

Pilgrims performing *Hajj Qiran* and *Hajj Tamattu'* who miss any necessary act (e.g., throwing pebbles, putting on *ihram* from a *miqat*, or performing *sa'y*) or violate any *ihram* restriction or the sanctity of the *Haram* in Makka must offer a sacrifice.

Concerning sacrifice during *Hajj*, the Qur'an decrees:

God has made the Ka'ba, the Sacred House, a standard and maintenance for the people, and also the Sacred Months (during which fighting is forbidden), and the animals for sacrificial offering, and the (camels wearing the sacrificial) collars. That is so that you may know that God knows whatever is in the heavens and whatever is on the earth, and that God has full knowledge of everything. Know (also) that God is severe in punishment, and that God is All-Forgiving, All-Compassionate. (5:97–98)

Remember when We assigned to Abraham the site of the House (Ka'ba) as a place of worship (directing him), "Do not associate

> any partners with Me in any way, and keep My House pure (from any material and spiritual filth) for those who will go round it in devotion, and those who will stand in Prayer before it, and those who will bow down and prostrate themselves in worship." Publicly proclaim the (duty of) Pilgrimage for all humankind, that they come to you on foot and on lean camels, coming from every faraway point, so that they may witness all the (spiritual, social, and economic) benefits in store for them, and offer during the known, appointed days the sacrificial cattle that He has provided for them by pronouncing God's Name over them. Eat of their meat and feed the distressed, the poor. (22:26–28)

During the Prophet's time, pilgrims used to garland or mark the animals they appointed for sacrifice during *Hajj*.[65] The Qur'an mentions this among the public symbols or emblems set up by God for the Muslim community (5:97; 22:36).

Sacrificial Animals

The most common sacrificial animal is a sheep or a goat. Cattle and camels also can be offered as sacrifice. Pilgrims must sacrifice a camel if they perform *tawaf* in a state of major ritual impurity (*junub*), are still menstruating or having post-childbirth bleeding, have sexual intercourse with their spouse after spending Dhu'l-Hijja 9 (eve) in 'Arafat but before shaving or clipping the hair, or if they have vowed to sacrifice a camel.

Conditions for Sacrifice

A sacrificial animal should satisfy the following conditions:

- If it is a sheep, it must be one year old, or as fat and healthy as a one-year-old sheep if it is more than six months old. A camel must be at least five years old, a cow two years old, and a goat one year old.
- The animal should be healthy and without defect (i.e., it must not be one-eyed, have a limp, be mangy, very thin, or weak).

Time and Place of Offering

The sacrifice must be made at a specific time, as follows:

- Whether one is performing *Hajj* or not, a sacrifice must be offered on any of the first three days of *'Iydu'l-Adha*. It cannot be offered before the *'Iyd Prayer* on the first day.[66] However, it is *sunna* to throw seven pebbles at *Jamratu'l-Aqaba*, then offer the sacrifice, and then shave one's head or cut one's hair on the first day of *'Iydu'l-Adha* during *Hajj*.[67]
- A sacrifice made to fulfill a vow, atone for sins, or perform a supererogatory act of worship may be offered any time during the year.
- A sacrifice that will be offered during *Hajj*, whether it is necessary (*wajib*) or voluntary or for an atonement, must be offered within Makka's Sacred Precincts. God's Messenger, upon him be peace and blessings, sacrificed his animals in Mina.[68]

Who Must Sacrifice the Animal

The one who kills the animal must be a Muslim or belong to the People of the Book (a Christian or a Jew). As decreed in the verses mentioned before (22:28, 34), he must say *Bismillah* before sacrificing, for the meat of an animal slaughtered by an atheist, an agnostic, an apostate, or one who intentionally does not say *Bismillah* cannot be eaten.

Eating the Meat of the Sacrificial Animal

God commands Muslims to eat of meat of sacrificed animals: *eat of their meat and feed the poor such as (beg not but) live in contentment and such as beg with due humility* (22:36). It is advisable to eat one-third, give one-third to the poor, and one-third to one's friends and relatives. Clearly, this command applies to both the obligatory and supererogatory sacrifice. However, one cannot eat the meat of any animal sacrificed in fulfillment of a vow, for all of the meat must be distributed among the poor and needy.

The sacrificed animal's skin can be used as a rug or in another way, after it is tanned, or given away as charity. One cannot sell it.[69]

Visiting the Prophet's Mosque and Tomb

Going to Madina and visiting the Prophet's Mosque and tomb is *sunna* and brings great reward. God's Messenger said, "The space between my room (where he died and was buried) and my pulpit is one of the gardens of Paradise (*Rawda*), and my pulpit is upon my *Hawd* in Paradise."[70] He also said that a journey can be undertaken to pray only in three mosques: his mosque in Madina—The Prophet's Mosque—the Mosque of *al-Haram* in Makka and the Mosque of Aqsa in Quds,[71] and gave the glad tidings that a Prayer performed in his mosque is a thousand times more excellent than a Prayer in any other mosque, except the *Masjid* or the Mosque of *al-Haram* in Makka.[72]

It is recommended that one calls God's blessings and peace upon the Messenger as many times as possible and approaches his mosque calmly and with composure. One should wear perfume (men only), nice clean clothes, and enter the mosque with the right foot. It is recommended that pilgrims first go to the *Rawda* and offer two *rak'a*s, with calmness and humility, to "greet" the mosque. After this one should move toward the Prophet's grave, face it, give greetings of peace to him, and call God's blessings and peace upon him. Then, moving about a yard to the right, one should offer one's greetings to Abu Bakr and, moving another yard in the same direction, offer greetings to 'Umar ibn al-Khattab. Then, facing the *qibla*, pilgrims should supplicate for themselves, their family, friends, relatives, and all Muslims, and then leave. It is highly recommended and meritorious to pray forty times in the Prophet's Mosque.

One should also visit the *Jannatu'l-Baqi* cemetery, where many Companions and members of the Prophet's Family are buried. During the visit, people should talk only loudly enough to hear themselves, and behave with the utmost humility and sincerity.

Offering Prayers in the Quba Mosque

God's Messenger, upon him be peace and blessings, used to go to Quba, riding or on foot, every Saturday and offer a two-*rak'a* supererogatory Prayer.[73] He advised others to do the same: "Whoever takes ablutions at home and then goes and prays in the Quba Mosque will have a reward like that of an *'Umra*."[74] Thus, pilgrims who visit Madina should also visit the Quba Mosque and pray there.

Worship

- Belief in God is creation's highest aim and most sublime result, and humanity's most exalted rank is knowledge of Him. The most radiant happiness and sweetest bounty for jinn and humanity is love of God contained within knowledge of God. The human spirit's purest joy and the human heart's sheerest delight is spiritual pleasure contained within love of God. All true happiness, pure joy, sweet bounties, and unclouded pleasures are contained within knowledge and love of God. Those who truly know and love God can receive endless happiness, bounties, enlightenment, and mysteries. Those who do not are afflicted with endless spiritual and material misery, pain, and fear. If any person were allowed to rule this world, despite his or her being powerless, miserable, and unprotected amid other purposeless people in this world, what would its true worth be?
  People who do not recognize their Owner and discover their Master are miserable and bewildered. But those who do, and then take refuge in His Mercy and rely on His Power, see this desolate world transformed into a place of rest and felicity, a place of exchange for the Hereafter.[75]
- Worship means one's sincere acknowledgement of himself or herself as a servant and God as the sole and true Object of Wor-

ship. It consists in a servant designing his or her life in accordance with the relations between a true servant and the True Object of Worship, in the light of the fact that one is the created and the other the Creator.

- Worship means one's thankfulness for the bounties with which one is endowed, such as life, consciousness, power of perception and faith, while neglecting the duty of worship is crude ingratitude. Worship is a road to travel, opened by the Being Who commands us to belief, and is a set of good manners that He ordered us to observe so that we could finally reach Him and obtain happiness in both this life and the next.
- Worship is the safest way to reach the most unshakable certainty in one's conscience about the greatest truth known only theoretically at the outset.
- Worship is a blessed, growing resource feeding a person's thoughts and deliberations of being good, righteous, and virtuous, and a mysterious elixir that reforms the selfhood's innate tendencies toward evil.
- Worship is developing a person's potential to be like the angels in order to be fitted for Paradise, and bringing under control the bestial inclinations and potentialities. So far in human history, by means of their worship many have surpassed angels, while many others, refusing to worship, have fallen to the lowest of the low.
- The most meritorious of the acts or services of worship is knowing and loving God Almighty and being beneficial to humanity. If there is something more meritorious and commendable than this, it is seeking God's approval and good pleasure in whatever one does and, moved by the command, "Be straightforward as you are commanded," always being in pursuit of what is the truest and highest ideal in life.[76]

CHAPTER 7

Marriage and Family Life

MARRIAGE AND FAMILY LIFE[1]

God Almighty has created humanity as vicegerent on the earth in order that human beings might populate and rule it. Obviously this purpose cannot be realized unless humanity perpetuates itself, living, thriving, cultivating, manufacturing, building, and worshipping its Creator. Accordingly, the Creator has placed certain appetites and tendencies in humanity so that its members are impelled towards activities that guarantee humanity's survival. The Qur'an declares:

> Made innately appealing to men are passionate love for women, children, (hoarded) treasures of gold and silver, branded horses, cattle, and plantations. Such are enjoyments of the present, worldly life; yet with God is the best of the goals to pursue. (3:14)

God Almighty has inculcated such desires or tendencies in human nature so that humanity can survive on the earth and develop spiritually and mentally by disciplining them to transform each one into a virtue in order to develop into being a true, perfect human from being only potentially human. Humanity is not like other species, for it has been created with a different disposition, multiple potentialities, and various mental and spiritual faculties. So, there must be a significant purpose behind its creation. Achieving this purpose and being perfected require self-discipline. Islam has the set of principles for that self-discipline.

According to Imam al-Ghazzali, Islam's legal principles seek to protect and secure five basic values in human life, namely, religion, life, intellect, personal property, and reproduction, and forbid acts that will nullify any of these rights. When we consider the Divinely established prohibitions (e.g., unbelief, hypocrisy, associating partners with God, apostasy, killing a person, taking intoxicants and drugs, usurpation, theft, adultery, fornication, sodomy, and homosexual acts, and so on), we can deduce that in one respect, these prohibitions have been given to protect and secure those values. In order to secure these values for a virtuous life based upon justice, the observation of mutual rights, mutual helping, and righteousness, we also see that Islamic jurisprudence presents us with some measures and precautions. As regards marriage and family life, we can point to the following:

Prohibition of Adultery and Fornication

Illegal sexual relationships and the relationships leading to them are prohibited, for they cause a confusion of lineage, child abuse, family break-ups, bitterness in relationships, the spread of venereal diseases, and a general laxity in morals. Moreover, they open the door to a flood of lust and self-gratification. God's command, *Do not draw near to any unlawful sexual intercourse; surely it is a shameful, indecent thing, and an evil way* (17:32), is absolutely just and true.

Prohibition of Privacy between a Man and a Woman Who Are Not Married to Each Other

Islam prohibits a man and woman who are not married to each other from being alone together in a private place where there is no fear of being interrupted by someone else. This is done to prevent such illicit sexual activities as touching, kissing, embracing, or having sexual intercourse.

Looking with Desire at the Opposite Sex

Islam prohibits people from looking lustfully at people of the opposite sex, for the eye is the key to the feelings, and the look is a messenger of desire. The Qur'an declares:

> Tell the believing men that they should restrain their gaze (from looking at the women whom it is lawful for them to marry, and

> from others' private parts), and guard their private parts and chastity. This is what is purer for them. God is fully aware of all that they do. And tell the believing women that they (also) should restrain their gaze (from looking at the men whom it is lawful for them to marry, and from others' private parts), and guard their private parts, and that they should not display their charms except that which is revealed of itself; and let them draw their headcoverings over their bosoms. (24:30–31)

Looking at the Private Parts of Others

Islam defines "the private parts" as those parts of the body that must be covered in front of others. For men, this is the area between the navel and the knees, which other men and women are not allowed to see. For a woman, this area is her whole body, except her hands, feet, and face. This prohibition applies to all men who are allowed to marry the woman in question.[2] Muslim woman must also preserve themselves against licentious women.

God's Messenger said, "A man should not look at the *'awra* (private parts) of another man, nor a woman of a woman, nor should a man go under one cloth with another man, nor a woman with another woman."[3]

The practice of Islam equips and adorns Muslim men and women with chastity, dignity, self-respect, and modesty, while most of the men and women of the "Times of Ignorance" have been vain, showy, and anxious to display their attractions.

Sexual Perversion

Islam, while regulating one's sexual drive, has prohibited illicit sexual relations and all ways that lead to them, as well as sodomy and homosexual acts. Homosexual practice is considered a reversal of the natural order, a corruption of human sexuality, and a violation of the rights of the other sex. It is a major sin. The spread of this unnatural practice disrupts a society's natural life. It also makes those who practice it slaves to their lusts, thereby depriving them of decent taste, decent morals, and a decent manner of living. The Qur'anic account of Prophet Lot's people should be sufficient for us.

No Monasticism

Although Islam is against sexual license, and thus prohibits fornication and adultery and blocks all ways leading to them, it does not seek to suppress the sexual urge. Therefore, it encourages people to get married and prohibits renunciation and castration.

Muhammad Abu Zahra, a modern scholar, defines marriage as follows: "Marriage is a contract that results in the man and woman living with each other and supporting each other within the limits of what has been laid down for them in terms of rights and obligations."

The Purpose and Goals of Marriage

Like anything a Muslim does, marriage should be undertaken only after gaining an understanding of what God has prescribed in terms of rights and obligations, as well as gaining an understanding of the wisdom behind this institution. Nearly all peoples and societies practice marriage in some form, just as they practice business. 'Umar ibn al-Khattab used to expel people from Madina's marketplace if they did not know the Islamic rules of buying and selling. Likewise, Muslims should not engage in something as important as marriage without understanding its purpose or having a comprehensive understanding of the ensuing rights and obligations.

Concerning the relationship of man and woman, the Qur'an declares:

> And among His signs is that He has created for you, from your selves, mates, that you may incline towards them and find rest in them, and He has engendered love and tenderness between you. Surely in this are signs for people who reflect. (30:21)

> They (women) are a garment for you and you are a garment for them. (2:187)

The verses state in a very captivating style that the relationship between man and woman is and should be based on mutual love and tenderness, and mutual rights and duties. Every person needs a friend, a companion. What satisfies this human need most is having an intimate life-companion with whom to share love, joys, and sorrows. Since the kindest, most compassionate and generous of hearts is the heart of a woman, what can be understood from the many relevant verses of the Qur'an is that women are a greater blessing for men than men are for women. It is because of this that the Qur'an also mentions women among the greatest blessings of Paradise for men. The pleasure coming from mutual helping, sharing joys and sorrows, companionship, love, affection, and intimacy, is much greater than the bodily pleasures with which men and women may satisfy in each other.

One important aspect of the relationship between man and woman is that the sides function as a garment for each other. In another verse, the Qur'an declares, *O children of Adam! Assuredly We have sent down on you a garment to cover your private parts, and garments for adornment. However, (remember that) the garment of piety and righteousness—it is the best of all. That is from God's signs, that they may reflect and be mindful* (7:26). That is, just as a garment saves a person from nakedness and the harmful effects of heat and cold, and beautifes him or her, so too do spouses save each other from the harmful effects of the outside world and beautify each other. Since the best of garments is piety and righteousness, spouses encourage and help each other to attain and lead a pious, righteous life, and function as a garment of piety and righteousness for each other.

One of marriage's most important purposes is to continue and increase the human population. The Qur'an mentions this as one of the blessings of God on humanity: *God has made for you, from your selves, mates (spouses), and has made for you children and grandchildren from your mates, and has provided you with good, wholesome things. Do they, then, believe in falsehood and deny the blessings of God?*(16:72). Clearly, this goal could be achieved without marriage, but when actions are undertaken in disobedience to God, they do not receive His blessing and corrupt society. The goal is not just to produce children for the next generation, but to produce righteous children who will obey God, serve the people, and be a source of reward for their parents.

Islam takes humanity's natural tendencies and needs into consideration. It is not like the human-made (or modified) religions or systems that place unnatural constraints on people or set them free without any restrictions. Men are inclined towards women, and women are inclined towards men. Marriage fulfills this desire and channels it in ways pleasing to God and befitting humanity's honor and mission in life.

The desire of men and women for each other needs to be fulfilled. If left unfulfilled, it will be a source of discord and disruption in society. For this reason, God's Messenger, upon him be peace and blessings, ordered those who can meet the responsibilities of marriage to get married: "Whichever of you is capable should marry, for it will aid him in lowering his gaze and guarding his body (from sin). As for one who is not capable, fasting is his protection."[4]

Marriage and the Home[5]

- The basic purpose of marriage is not pleasure; rather, it is to establish a family, ensure the nation's permanence and continuation, save the individual from dispersed feelings and thoughts, and to control physical pleasures. Just as with many other matters related to the basic nature that God has given to each being, the pleasure from marital relations is a payment determined by Divine Mercy to invite and encourage this duty of marriage.
- One should not marry for reasons of dress, wealth, or physical beauty; rather, marry for spiritual beauty, honor and morality, and virtue and character. Every union made in the name of marriage, but without careful thought, has left behind crying wives, orphans, and those who wound the family's heart. Some marriages based on logic and judgment and initiated by taking refuge in God are so sacred that, throughout a lifetime,

they function just like a school, and their "students" guarantee the nation's permanence and continuation.

- If a couple wishes to divorce, the most intelligent criteria are of no use to those who did not (or could not) get married for the correct reasons. The important thing is not to escape from the fire in the home with the least harm, but to prevent it from ever starting.
- The soundest foundation for a nation is a family in which material and spiritual happiness flows, for such a family serves as a sacred school that raises virtuous individuals. If a nation can make its homes as enlightened and prosperous as its schools, and its schools as warm as its homes, it has made the greatest reform and has guaranteed the contentment and happiness of future generations.
- The word *home* is used according to the people in it. They are considered happy to the degree that they share human values. We can say that people live humanly with those in their home; a home becomes a home because of its inhabitants.
- A home is a small nation, and a nation is a large home. One who successfully manages a home and who has raised its members to a level of humanity can manage a large organization with little effort.

Men and Women to be Preferred in Marriage

Making sure that Muslims are well-matched to their spouses is a most important matter. Those who want to get married must have their priorities straight and be clear on what characteristics are most important in ensuring a marriage's success. Many characteristics are important in a husband or a wife, but some are far more important than others. God's Messenger said, "A woman is married for the excellence of her religious belief and life, her wealth, or her beauty. You must prefer the one with an excellent religious belief and life."[6] Thus, the first thing to be sought for in a potential spouse is excellence of religious belief and life.

Character is of extreme importance, and goes hand in hand with belief and piety. The Messenger described it as the purpose of his mission: "I have only been sent to perfect good character,"[7] and, "That which will weigh the heaviest in the Balance in the Hereafter is good character."[8] Believers with the most perfect belief are those with the best character.

God's Messenger advised marrying child-bearing women and preferring virginity, and said that a virgin woman is more likely to be pleased by a man. Scholars stress that this applies to both the husband and the wife. If it is each person's first marriage, both the man and the woman should be virgins.[9]

Beauty has a certain undeniable role to play, since one of marriage's purposes is to keep both spouses from sin. The best way to do this is to have a strong attraction between the spouses. However, this is something that surely grows over time, some people may allow first impressions to become an obstacle to what could be a successful marriage.

Recommended Steps

The following are important steps for those who want to get married and for those seeking to facilitate a marriage.

- The entire process, in order to be successful with God's blessing, should be proper and consistent with the teachings of the Qur'an and the *Sunna*.
- Both spouses should seek to get married purely for God's good pleasure, fulfill the purposes of marriage, and put their full trust in God.
- Both the man and the woman are allowed to see their prospective spouse before taking further steps. God's Messenger strongly advised people to see their prospective spouse as this is important for mutual love and understanding.[10]
- If they do everything properly and in accordance with the rules of Islam, it is hoped God will grant them a successful marriage.

The Girl's Consent and the Permission of the Guardian

A girl has the right to decide about her marriage, and her father or guardian cannot override her objections or ignore her wishes. God's Messenger, upon him be peace and blessings, declared, "A woman without a husband (or divorced or a widow) must not be married until she is consulted, and a virgin must not be married until her permission is sought."[11] The Messenger also referred to the agreement of the girl's guardian.[12] Therefore, it is better that the guardian's agreement is also sought, although her guardian can in no wise force a girl into a marriage she does not accept.[13]

Prohibited Proposals and 'Idda for Women

A divorced or widowed woman cannot remarry during her *'idda* (the waiting period during which she is not allowed to remarry) and a man cannot propose marriage to such a woman, for this waiting period is part of the previous marriage and must not be violated.

A pregnant woman's *'idda* ends when she delivers the baby (Qur'an, 65:4). If she is widowed but not pregnant, her *'idda* is four months and ten days (2:234). If she is divorced and it is not known if she is pregnant, her *'idda* is three menstrual cycles (2:228). This *'idda* relates to women who have menstrual periods; for women who do not menstruate, the *'idda* is three months (65:4).

Women to Whom Marriage is Prohibited

Muslim men cannot marry women who belong to one of the following categories: the father's wife, whether divorced or widowed (this prevents any sexual attraction between the son and his stepmother, who should develop a relationship of respect and honor between them), the mother (including grandmothers on both sides), the daughter (including granddaughters from the son or the daughter), the sister (including half- and stepsisters), the paternal aunt (whether she is the father's real, half-, or stepsister), the maternal aunt (whether she is the father's real, half-, or stepsister), the brother's daughter (his niece), and the sister's daughter (his niece).

Marriages prohibited by reason of fosterage. These are as follows:

- THE FOSTER MOTHER: Muslim men cannot marry women who suckled them during their infancy, even if it was only once. Although some jurists opine that in order for such a woman to be forbidden she must have suckled him five or even seven times, in order to avoid committing a sin they must not be allowed to marry each other.
- FOSTER SISTERS: Just as a woman becomes a mother to a child by virtue of suckling, so do her daughters become his sisters, her sisters his aunts, and so on. God's Messenger, upon him be peace and blessings, declared, "What is forbidden by reason of genealogy is forbidden by reason of fosterage."[14] Thus, marriage to foster sisters, foster aunts, and foster nieces through a relationship of wet-nursing is forbidden.

In-law relationships. These are as follows:

- THE MOTHER-IN-LAW: Marriage to the wife's mother is prohibited from the time a man marries a woman, whether he and his wife have engaged in sexual intercourse or not (Qur'an, 4:22). The act of marriage itself gives the mother-in-law the same status as the mother, in that marriage to her is forbidden.
- THE STEPDAUGHTER: A man cannot marry his stepdaughter if he has had legal sexual intercourse with her mother (his wife). However, if a man divorces his wife before consummating the marriage, he may marry his stepdaughter. (Qur'an, 4:23)
- THE DAUGHTER-IN-LAW: This woman is the wife of the real son, not of the adopted son. In fact, Islam abolished legal, formalized adoption because it is contrary to fact and reality, and results in prohibiting what is essentially lawful and permitting what is essentially forbidden.

Sisters and aunts as co-wives. As opposed to the pre-Islamic practice, Islam forbade taking two sisters as co-wives and being married at the same time to a woman and her maternal or paternal aunt.[15]

Married women. A woman can only be married to one man at a time. She may marry another man only if her husband has died or she has been divorced, and if she has completed her *'idda* (the period of waiting before remarrying).

Female idolaters. Muslim men cannot marry women who are atheists, agnostics, or practice idolatry (associating partners with God in His Divinity or Lordship). (Qur'an, 2:221; 24:3; 60:10)

Prohibiting Muslim women from marrying non-Muslim men. Muslim women cannot marry non-Muslim men, regardless of whether they belong to the People of the Book or not. (Qur'an, 5:5; 60:10)[16] However, Islam allows Muslim men to marry chaste Jewish or Christian women, for they are considered People of the Book, or people whose tradition is based upon a Divinely revealed Scripture. (Qur'an, 5:5)

Those who engage in fornication. Islam forbids marrying those who are engaged in prostitution, adultery, and fornication (24:3). If one has engaged habitually in such activities or is a prostitute, other people are forbidden to marry them. But if one has committed it only once or twice and is not a prostitute, it still is highly advisable not to marry them. However, it is not forbidden to do so if one has sincerely repented of it and given it up without returning to it. God permits Muslims to marry chaste spouses. Similarly, He has made marriage lawful to men on the condition that they seek it in honest wedlock, not in lust (4:24; 5:5).

Temporary Marriage (*Mut'a*)

Islam considers marriage a strong bond and a binding contract based upon both partners' intention to live together permanently in order to attain, as individuals, the benefit of the repose, affection, and mercy mentioned in the Qur'an. In addition, one of its purposes is to attain the social goal of reproduction and perpetuation of the human species:

> God has made for you, from your selves, mates (spouses), and has made for you from your mates children and grandchildren, and has provided you with good, wholesome things. Do they, then, believe in falsehood and deny the blessings of God? (16:72)

Temporary marriage (*mut'a*), which is contracted by two people to marry for a specified period of time in exchange for a specified sum of money, does not realize the above-mentioned purposes of marriage. Thus, there is no room for it in Islam, and although it was practiced during the time of pre-Islamic Age of Ignorance, Islam forbade it.[17]

Children

- Adam, the first man, and Eve, the first woman, were created together at the very beginning of human existence. This indicates that marriage is natural. Reproduction is the most important purpose of this natural state. A marriage made for reasons other than bringing up new generations is no more than a temporary entertainment and adventure.
- Human generations come and go. Those who have attained high levels of spiritual and moral attainment are worthy of being considered human. Those who do not develop their spiritual faculties, due to their low level of education, scarcely merit being called human, even though they are descended from Adam.
- Those of you who bring children into this world are responsible for raising them to the realms beyond the heavens. Just as you take care of their bodily health, so take care of their spiritual, moral, and intellectual life. For God's sake, have pity and save the helpless innocents. Do not let their lives go to waste.
- If parents encourage their children to develop their abilities and be useful to themselves and the community, they have given humanity a strong new pillar. If, on the contrary, they do not

cultivate their children's human feelings, they will have released scorpions into the community.

- Parents have the right to claim their children as long as they educate and equip them with virtue. They cannot make such a claim, however, if they neglect them. But what shall we call parents who introduce their children to wickedness and indecency, and cause them to break with humanity?

The Rights of Children

- A child has the same meaning for humanity's continuation as a seed for a forest's continued growth and multiplication. People who neglect their children decay gradually.
- Children form the most active and productive part of a community after every thirty or forty years. Those who ignore their young children should consider how important an element of their own community's life they are disregarding.
- The vices observed in today's generation, the incompetence of some administrators, and other social problems are the direct result of the conditions prevailing thirty years ago, and of that time's ruling elite. Likewise, those entrusted with educating today's young people are responsible for the vices and virtues that will appear thirty years from now.
- Those who want to secure their future should apply as much energy to raising their children as they devote to other problems. While the energy devoted to many other things may go in vain, whatever is spent for raising a young generation elevates them to the rank of humanity. Such people will be like an inexhaustible source of income.
- Those people in our community who are miserable and lost, such as drug addicts, alcoholics, and other dissolute people, were once children. We failed to educate them properly. I wonder whether we are sufficiently aware of the kind of people we are preparing to walk our streets tomorrow.

- Communities that pay close attention to the family institution and their young people's education, as opposed to those who are more advanced in sciences and technology, will have the upper hand in the future.[18]

Parents must give a good name, shelter, food, and breast-feeding for two years to their children, and must provide necessary education for them; they must especially teach them the Religion. They should also provide for their marriage.

The Marriage Contract (*Nikah*)

Islam views marriage as a contract. Thus, as with any contract, several elements are considered essential to its existence. Each of these should be understood properly to ensure that the marriage is performed properly and that each spouse receives his or her full rights.

All the scholars agree that one essential act is the "offer and acceptance," for no marriage contract is valid without it. Either party can initiate this process. The presence of two witnesses and the dowry paid by the husband are necessary elements as well.

Conditions for a Sound Marriage Contract

These conditions are as follows:

- The woman cannot be one of those forbidden to the man by relation, nursing, or any of the other preventing factors mentioned above.
- The offer and acceptance is permanent and certain. If anything in the contract indicates something of a temporary and uncertain nature, the marriage is invalid. This is why the words of acceptance must be in the past tense, which expresses certainty. The Qur'an describes the marriage contract as a solemn pledge, and the marital relationship as going in to each other: "*.... when you have gone in to each other, and they (the married women) have taken from you a most solemn pledge*" (4:21).

- Two credible witnesses must be present, and the marriage should be documented, announced, and publicized.[19]
- Both parties have willingly accepted the marriage. Coercion invalidates any contract.[20]
- The bride and groom are identified and known.
- Neither of the contracting parties are in the state of *ihram*.
- The parties and witnesses are not bound to keep it quiet.
- The presence of the woman's guardian or representative (*waliy*). The *waliy* is a Muslim man charged with marrying a woman entrusted to his care to a man who will be good for her.[21]
- The man and woman must be legally competent (i.e., adult and sane). If they are not, the marriage is invalid. The woman cannot be from any category of women that her intended spouse cannot marry. For example, suppose the couple get married and he then learns that they had been breastfed by the same woman. In this case, the marriage becomes null and void, because their breastmilk relationship disqualifies them from marrying each other.
- The offer and acceptance of the contract must be done in one sitting. In general, this means that the response must be immediate. The acceptance must correspond to what is being offered, and the marriage must be effective immediately.
- The bride must receive a dowry (bridal-due *[mahr]*).

Mahr (Dowry or Bridal-Due)

The groom gives the *mahr* only to the bride to honor her, show his respect for her, his serious desire to marry her, and his sense of responsibility, obligation, or effort to her. The Qur'anic injunction, *Give to the women (whom you marry) their bridal-due all willingly and for good (i.e. without expecting a return)* (4:4), is addressed to either the husband (because it is his duty to give it) or to the guardian (because before Islam came they used to keep a woman's dowry for themselves). This verse shows that this particular pre-Islamic custom was no longer permitted. The exact amount of the dowry has not been determined, for the groom should pay it according to his capacity or wealth. The region's customs also are considered in determining its amount. If the spouses are divorced after consummation, the husband cannot take back anything of it (4:20).

Fulfilling Agreements

Generally speaking, Muslims must comply with any agreements that they make. God says about the believers: *They fulfill their covenant when they have engaged in a covenant* (2:177), and orders them, *O you who believe, fulfill the bonds (you have entered in with God and people)* (5:1). God's Messenger mentioned breaking one's promise and covenant as among the signs of hypocrisy.[22]

Wedding Ceremony and Feast

It is permissible, even advisable, to arrange a wedding ceremony within an Islamic framework. The husband is required to sponsor the wedding feast after the marriage contract. God's Messenger, upon him be peace and blessings, exhorted both giving a wedding feast and the acceptance of the invitation to it.[23]

Mutual Love, Mercy, Respect, Understanding, and Thankfulness

The Qur'an declares:

> O humanity, avoid disobedience to your Lord, Who has created you from a single, original human self, and from it created its mate, and from the pair of them scattered abroad a multitude of men and women. (4:1)

The original expression translated as "a single, original human self" is *nafs wahida* (literally, a single self or soul). *Nafs* has two cardinal meanings: a being's self, and the animating energy or faculty that is the source of each person's and jinn's worldly life. Considering both meanings together, *nafs wahida* is understood to mean a single, original human self.

This point is very important to understanding the nature of the male–female relationship. The Qur'an stresses this very point: *And of His signs is that He has created for you, from your selves, mates, that you might incline towards them and find rest in them, and He has engendered love and tenderness between you* (30:21); *God has given you, from your selves, mates, and He has made for you children and grandchildren from your mates* (16:72); *The Originator of the heavens and the earth; He has made for you, from your selves, mates, and from the cattle mates (of their own kind)* (42:11). What these refer to by *your selves* is the human kind, self, or nature. In addition, they indicate that everything in the universe was created in pairs: *And everything We have created in pairs* (51:49).

However, these verses do not mean that by being the two halves of a perfect unit, men and women are identical or the same. While a man's and a woman's rights and responsibilities are equal, they are not necessarily identical. Equality and sameness are two quite different things. This difference is understandable, because men and women are not identical but are created as equals. Bearing this in mind, there is no problem. In fact, it is almost impossible to find even two identical men or women.

This distinction between equality and sameness is vital. Equality is desirable, just, and fair; but sameness is not. People are created as equals, and not as identical to each other, and so there is no basis to consider a woman as inferior to a man. There is no reason to assume that she is less important than him just because her rights are not identical to his. Had her status been identical to his, she would have been no more than a duplicate of him, which she is not. The fact that Islam gives her equal—but not identical—rights shows that it takes her into due consideration, acknowledges her, and recognizes her independent personality.

In *And of His signs is that He has created for you, from your selves, mates, that you might incline towards them and find rest in them, and*

He has engendered love and tenderness between you (30:21), the Qur'an stresses that male–female relations are—and must be—based upon mutual love and mercy. What satisfies the needs of a human being the most is having an intimate life companion with whom one can share love, joy, and grief. However, we should acknowledge that a woman's heart is the most compassionate, loving and generous of all hearts. This is why the Qur'an stresses men's inclination towards and attachment to women, rather than the other way. In fact, it states that the most beautiful blessing in Paradise for a man will be a pure woman after God's good pleasure with him.

On the other hand, the Qur'an also says, *Men (those who are able to carry out their responsibilities) are the protectors and maintainers of women inasmuch as God has endowed some of humankind (in some respects) with greater capacity than others, and inasmuch as they (men) spend of their wealth (for the family's maintenance)* (4:34). This verse is highly significant with respect to male–female relations and family law, and draws attention to the following cardinal points:

God has not created all people exactly the same in all respects; rather, He has given each superiority in some respect to others, as required by social life, the division of labor, and the choice of occupation. Although it is not true to the same degree for all men and women, as He has created men superior to women in some respects, He also has given women superiority over men in others. For example, God has given men greater physical strength, endowed them with a greater capacity for management, and has charged them with the family's financial upkeep. This is why He has made men the head of the family. However, this does not mean that men have absolute authority over the family, for this authority must be exercised according to the Prophetic principle that "The master of a people is he who serves them." In addition, responsibility is proportionate to authority and authority is proportionate to responsibility.

In short, Islam proposes a male–female relation based upon mutual love, mercy, understanding, and respect. It also exhorts couples to be thankful to each other for their kindness and efforts to please each other. Such things should be fundamental in any marriage. Each spouse should acknowledge the other's efforts, show them gratitude, and repay them with kindness.

Islam is concerned with enabling people to attain the status of true humanity or perfection. Its legislation is, in one respect, based upon this cardinal point, and it considers legal rules or laws as a means of reinforcing it.

The Wife's Rights

These are as follows: receipt of a dowry, support or maintenance, kind and proper treatment and due respect, marital relations, privacy, justice between multiple wives, to be taught Islam, defense of her honor, and not revealing their secrets to others.[24] God's Messenger, upon him be peace and blessings, says, "The most perfect among the believers in respect of faith is the one who is the best of them in character; and the best of you are the kindest towards their wives."[25]

The Husband's Rights

These are as follows: enjoying due respect for being responsible for bringing up and maintaining the family, and marital relations. In addition, a wife must not allow in the house anyone of whom her husband disapproves, leave the house and go to places of which he disapproves without his consent, or show ingratitude to him for the favors done to her. She must be ready for him for conjugal relations, avoid actions which will stir up his jealousy, must defend his honor and not disclose their secrets to others.[26]

Housework

The above-mentioned rights are agreed upon by scholars. The wife's duties in the house (e.g., cooking, cleaning and generally serving her husband in the house), however, have been the subject of discussion. The law establishes the general rules and mutual rights and duties. Obeying them is obligatory. However, there is another set of laws which is called the Divine laws of creation and life. For example, Islamic law does not enjoin upon mothers to suckle their babies in any case; providing for the baby is among the father's duties, which he fulfills after consultation with the mother (2:233; 65:6). However, maternal compassion and the milk God stores in their breasts following birth usually lead mothers to suckle their babies willingly. So, many matters are and should be referred to the creational facts and the traditionally accepted norms that are not against Islam and the Qur'an calls *'urf* or *ma'ruf*. This is what the Qur'an actually does. So, while it has been the traditional custom that women do the housework, given that the men are obliged to look after the entire family, it is considered as *ihsan* (good treatment and excellence) for the wife to do it and meet her husband's needs (e.g., sewing, ironing, cooking, and taking care of children).

Sex

The Qur'an does not neglect humanity's sensual aspect and the married couple's sex life, for it guides humanity to the best path and enables them to fulfill their sexual urges while avoiding harmful or deviant practices.

It is reported that the Jews and Zoroastrians would go to extremes in order to avoid any physical contact with menstruating women. For example, Jewish laws and regulations are extremely restrictive in this regard. The Old Testament considers a menstruating woman unclean and impure. Moreover, her impurity "infects" other people, for whoever or whatever she touches becomes unclean (Leviticus, 15:19–24). Thus a menstruating woman was sometimes banished to the "house of impurity" so that no contact with her would be possible during this time. The Talmud considers a menstruating woman "fatal," even without any physical contact, whereas Christians generally believe that sexual intercourse is permissible during a woman's menstrual period. The pre-Islamic Arabs would not eat, drink, or sit with menstruating women and would send them to separate dwellings, just as the Jews and Zoroastrians did.

When some Muslims asked the Messenger, upon him be peace and blessings, about menstruating women, God revealed:

> They also ask you about (the injunctions concerning) menstruation. Say: "It is a state of hurt (and ritual impurity), so keep away from them during their menstruation and do not approach them until they are cleansed. When they are cleansed, then (you can) go to them inasmuch as God has commanded you (according to the urge He has placed in your nature, and within the terms He has enjoined upon you). Surely God loves those who turn to Him in sincere repentance (of past sins and errors), and He loves those who cleanse themselves. (2:222)

What is meant by *keep away from them* is sexual intercourse or benefiting from their genitals. Thus a man can caress his menstruating wife, avoiding only the place of hurt. Islam's ruling, as in all other matters, is a middle one between the two extremes of banishing a menstruating woman from the house and of having sexual intercourse with her.[27]

Islam has established no rules concerning the way or position of intercourse. However, it has forbidden anal sex.[28]

Contraception

One of the primary objectives of marriage is to preserve humanity through continued reproduction. Accordingly, Islam encourages large families and blesses both boys and girls. However, family planning is allowed for only valid reasons and recognized necessities. At the time of the Prophet, the common method of contraception was *coitus interruptus* (withdrawing the penis from the vagina just before ejaculation, thereby preventing the influx of semen).[29] The primary valid reason for contraception is that the pregnancy or delivery might endanger the mother's life or health. Past experience or a reliable physician's opinion should guide the couple in such matters.

Abortion

While Islam permits preventing pregnancy for valid reasons, Muslim jurists agree unanimously that abortion is forbidden especially after the fetus is completely formed and has been given a soul, which is, according to the *hadith*s, about six weeks after contraception.[30] This is considered a crime under Islamic law, for it is an offense against a complete, live human being. Jurists insist that blood money (*diyat*) must be paid if the baby was aborted alive and then died, and that a lesser amount must be paid if it was aborted dead.

According to the jurists, if, after the baby is completely formed, it becomes clear that continuing the pregnancy will cause the mother's death, the couple has recourse to the general Islamic legal principle that the lesser of the two evils should be chosen.

Artificial Insemination

Islam safeguards lineage by prohibiting adultery and fornication (*zina*) and legal adoption (but not fostering, which it allows), thus keeping the family line clear. Thus, artificial insemination is forbidden unless the donor is the husband.

Polygamy[31]

Islam is a way of life consonant with human nature, provides human solutions to complex situations, and avoids extremes. The Qur'an draws attention to God's creation or the universal order or the essential nature of things being identical to the Religion:

> So set your whole being upon the Religion (of Islam) as one of pure faith (free from unbelief, polytheism, and hypocrisy). This is the original pattern (*fitra*) belonging to God on which He has originated humankind. No change can there be in God's creation. This is the upright, ever-true Religion, but most of the people do not know. (30:30)

This characteristic can be observed most clearly in the issue of polygamy, which Islam allows only to resolve pressing individual and social problems. Many peoples and religions prior to Islam permitted men to marry as many women as they desired. The Qur'an, on the other hand, laid down definite restrictions and conditions.

Some people criticize Islam wrongly for allowing polygamy. However, such criticisms are not justifiable for several reasons, as follows:

- Polygamy is an ancient practice found in many societies. The Bible does not condemn it, and the Old Testament and rabbinical writings frequently attest to its legality. King Solomon and King David had many wives and concubines (2 Samuel 5:13). According to Father Eugene Hillman in his insightful book, *Polygamy Reconsidered*, "Nowhere in the New Testament is there any explicit commandment that marriage should be monogamous or any explicit commandment forbidding polygamy." Moreover, Jesus did not speak against it, even though it was practiced by the Jews of his society. Father Hillman stresses that the Church in Rome banned polygamy in order to conform to the Greco-Roman culture (which prescribed only one legal wife while tolerating concubinage and prostitution). The Qur'an, contrary to the Bible, limited the maximum number of wives to four and mandated equal and just treatment for each wife. The Qur'an does not encourage polygamy or consider it an ideal. Rather, it tolerates or allows it and no more, for the following reason: There are places and times in which there are compelling social and moral reasons for polygamy. Islam, as a universal religion suitable for all places and all times, could not ignore such compelling obligations.
- In most societies, women outnumber men. For example, America currently has around eight million more women than men. What should be done about such unbalanced sex ratios? There are various potential reactions or responses, such as lawful po-

lygamy or celibacy, female infanticide (which still happens), or sexual permissiveness (e.g., prostitution, extramarital sex, and homosexuality).

- This problem becomes truly problematic in times of war. Native American Indian tribes used to suffer highly unbalanced sex ratios after wartime losses. Their women, who enjoyed a fairly high status, accepted polygamy as the best protection against indulgence in indecent activities. After the Second World War, there were 7.3 million more women than men in Germany (3.3 million of them were widows). Many needed a man for companionship as well as to provide for the household in a time of unprecedented misery and hardship. Is not being an accepted and respected second wife more dignifying for a woman than, for instance, being in dire needs or being a virtual prostitute? In 1987, a poll conducted by the student newspaper at the University of California at Berkeley asked students whether polygamy should be permitted as a way to deal with a perceived shortage of marriageable men in California. Almost all of the students polled approved of this idea.
- Polygamy continues to be a viable solution to some of the social ills of modern societies. In his provocative *Plural Marriage for Our Time*, Philip Kilbride, an American anthropologist of Roman Catholic heritage, proposes polygamy as a solution to some of America's social ills. He argues that plural marriage may be a potential alternative for divorce, in many cases, in order to obviate divorce's damaging impact upon children.
- Polygamy is quite rare in many contemporary Muslim societies, for there is no large gender imbalance. In fact, one can say that the rate of polygamous marriages in the Muslim world is far less than the rate of extramarital affairs in the West. In other words, Muslim men are far more monogamous than their Western counterparts.

- Billy Graham, the eminent Christian evangelist, has recognized this fact:

> Christianity cannot compromise on the question of polygamy. If present-day Christianity cannot do so, it is to its own detriment. Islam has permitted polygamy as a solution to social ills and has allowed a certain degree of latitude to human nature but only within the strictly defined framework of the law. Christian countries make a great show of monogamy, but actually they practice polygamy. No one is unaware of the part mistresses play in Western society. In this respect Islam is a fundamentally honest religion, and permits a Muslim to marry a second wife if he must, but strictly forbids all clandestine amatory associations in order to safeguard the moral probity of the community.[32]

- There are even psychological factors calling for polygamy. For example, many young African brides, whether Christian, Muslim, or otherwise, prefer to marry a married man who has already proved himself to be a responsible husband. Many African wives urge their husbands to get a second wife so that they do not feel lonely. A survey of over 6,000 women, ranging in age from 15 to 59, conducted in Nigeria's second largest city showed that 60 percent of them would be pleased if their husbands took another wife. In a survey undertaken in rural Kenya, 25 out of 27 women considered polygamy better than monogamy and felt that it could be a happy and beneficial experience if the co-wives cooperated.The condition that Islam lays down for permitting polygamy is that the husband be able to treat each wife equitably as regards food, drink, housing, clothing, expenses, and spending time with them. Any man who feels that he cannot fulfill such obligations justly cannot have more than one wife: *But if you fear that you will not be able to do justice (among them), (marry) only one* (4:3). A woman can have a condition written into her marriage agreement that she can have a divorce from her husband if he takes another wife. If she does not do so, he is entitled to take another wife if he wants.

THE STATUS OF WOMEN IN ISLAM[33]

The status of women in Islam is not a problem. The relevant verses of the Qur'an and the attitude of early Muslims bear witness to the fact that women are as vital to life as men, and that they are neither inferior to men nor of a lower species. Had it not been for the impact of foreign cultures and alien influences, this question would never have arisen among Muslims. It was taken for granted that the status of women was equal to that of men. It was a matter of course and a fact, and so no one considered it a problem.

Equity, Equality, or Sameness?

In order to understand what Islam has established for woman, there is no need to deplore her plight in the pre-Islamic era or in the modern world. Islam has given woman rights and privileges that she has never enjoyed under other religious or constitutional systems. This can be understood when the matter is studied as a whole and in a comparative, rather than in a partial, manner. The rights and responsibilities of a woman are equal to those of a man, but are not necessarily identical to them, for equality and sameness are two quite different things. This difference is understandable, because man and woman are not identical, but are created as equals. With this distinction in mind, there is no problem. It is almost impossible to find even two identical men or women.

This distinction between equality and sameness is of paramount importance. Equality is desirable, just, fair, but sameness is not. People are not created identical, but they are created equal. With this distinction in mind, there is no room to imagine that woman is inferior to man. There is no ground to assume that she is less important than he just because her rights are not identical to his. Had her status been identical to his, she would have been simply a duplicate of him, which she is not. The fact that Islam gives her equal—but not identical—rights shows that it takes her into due consideration, acknowledges her, and recognizes her independent personality.

Islam's View of Woman and Original Sin

Islam does not consider a woman to be the product of the devil, the seed of evil, or man to be her dominating lord to whom she must surrender without any choice. In addition, Islam never asked whether women had souls. Never in the history of Islam has any Muslim doubted the human status of women and their possession of souls and other fine spiritual qualities.

Unlike other popular beliefs, Islam does not blame Eve alone for the first sin. The Qur'an states that both Adam and Eve were tempted, that both sinned and were pardoned by God after repenting, and that God addressed them jointly (2:35–36; 7:19, 27; 20:117–23). In fact, the Qur'an gives the impression that Adam was more to blame for the first sin, from which all prejudice against and suspicion toward women have emerged. Islam does not justify such prejudice or suspicion, because Adam and Eve were equally in error. Thus if Eve is to blame, Adam is to blame to the same degree – or even more.

The Status of Women in Islam

The Qur'an draws attention to an important point by declaring that those communities distant from Divine guidance often call upon female deities. That is, those that reject belief in the One God adopt male and female deities. While they have usually chosen their supreme deity to be male, their other deities have been female. This is because they adore their own selves and consider, first of all, the satisfaction of their interests and animal desires. Since men's primary appetite is for women, and since they tend to exploit their deities to satisfy their needs, they choose many of their deities from among women. They desire to see a physically comely woman wherever they look, and tend to eternalize them by making statues and pictures of them. This is the most abominable way of degrading women, and means viewing them as no more than physical objects to gratify men's desires and interests. They no longer receive any respect and affection during their old age, when they need them most.

People also have many fears. They feel awe before that which they fear, and so conceive of their supreme deity (of whom they are afraid) as a man. Considering him above all other deities, they fawn on him. Even if such people may be Pharaoh-like tyrants, people degrade themselves in order to kiss the feet of any power above themselves and in whose hand they see the satisfaction of their needs and desires.

Islam recognizes woman as a full and equal partner in the process of procreation. Man is the father, she is the mother, and both are essential for life. Her role is no less vital than his. This partnership gives her an equal share in every aspect. She is entitled to equal rights, undertakes equal responsibilities, and has as many qualities and as much humanity as her partner. Concerning this equal partnership in human reproduction, God says, *O humankind! Surely We have created you from a single (pair of) male and female, and made you into tribes and families so that you may know one another (and so build mutuality and co-operative relationships, not so that you may take pride in your differences of race or social rank, or breed enmities). Surely the noblest, most honorable of you in God's sight is the one best in piety, righteousness, and reverence for God. Surely God is All-Knowing, All-Aware* (49:13; see also 4:1).

She is equal to man in bearing personal and common responsibilities and in receiving rewards for her deeds. She is acknowledged as an independent personality with human qualities and spiritual aspirations. Her human nature is neither inferior to that of a man nor deviant. Both are members of one another. As we read in the Qur'an:

> And thus does their (All-Gracious and Generous) Lord answer them: "I do not leave to waste the work of any of you (engaged in doing good), whether male or female. (As males and females following the same way) you are all one from the other...." (3:195; see also 9:71–72; 33:35–36; 66:10–12).

She is equal to man in the pursuit of education and knowledge. When Islam enjoins the seeking of knowledge upon Muslims, it makes no distinction between man and woman. Almost fourteen centuries ago, Prophet Muhammad, upon him be peace and blessings, declared that pursuing knowledge is incumbent upon every Muslim. This declaration was very clear and has been implemented by Muslims throughout history.

A woman is entitled to freedom of expression as much as a man is. Her sound opinions are taken into consideration and cannot be disregarded just because of her gender. The Qur'an and history both record that women not only expressed their opinions freely but also argued and participated in serious discussions with the Prophet and other Muslim leaders (58:1–4; 60:10–12). In addition, there were occasions when Muslim women expressed their views on legislative matters of public interest and opposed the caliphs, who then accepted their sound arguments. A specific example took place during 'Umar's caliphate. When the Caliph advised the Muslim men from the pulpit not to pay more than 500 *dirhams* of bridal-due, an aged woman objected, saying, "O 'Umar! Shall we heed you or the Qur'an?" The Caliph asked, "What does the Qur'an say?" The woman replied, "The Qur'an says, 'if you still decide to dispense with a wife and marry another, and you have given the former (even so much as amounts to) a treasure, do not take back anything thereof. [4:20].' O 'Umar! Is a treasure 500 *dirhams*?" 'Umar remarked, "O 'Umar! You don't know your religion as much as this woman!"

Historical records show that women participated in the early Muslim community's public life, especially during emergencies. Women accompanied Muslim armies to nurse the wounded, prepare supplies, serve the warriors, and so on. They were not shut behind iron bars, or considered worthless and deprived of souls.

Islam grants women equal rights to contract, enterprise, earn, and possess independently. A woman's life, property, and honor are as sacred as those of a man. If she commits any offense, her penalty is no more or less than that of a man's in a similar case. If she is wronged or harmed, she receives due compensation equal to what a man in her position would receive (2:178; 4:45, 92–93).

Islam does not state these rights in a statistical form and then relax. Rather, it has taken all measures to safeguard and implement them as integral articles of faith. It does not tolerate those who are inclined to prejudice against women or gender-based discrimination. Time and again, the Qur'an reproaches those who used to believe that a woman was inferior to a man (16:57–59; 43:15–19; 53:21–23).

Apart from recognizing women as independent human beings and as equally essential for humanity's survival, Islam has given them a share of inheritance. Before Islam, a woman could inherit nothing as she was even considered property to be inherited by men. Islam made this "transferable property" an heir, thereby acknowledging woman's inherent human qualities.

Whether a wife or a mother, a sister or a daughter, a woman receives a certain share of the deceased kin's property. This share depends upon her degree of relationship to the deceased and the number of heirs. This share is hers, and no one can take it from her or disinherit her. If the deceased wishes to deprive her by willing his estate to other relatives or a cause, the law will not respect his wish. Any person can use a will to dispose of only one-third of his or her property, so that no male or female heir will be treated unjustly. This matter will be discussed below within the framework of the Islamic law of inheritance.

Bearing Witness

Women were not allowed to bear witness in early Jewish society. The rabbis counted a woman's not being allowed to bear witness among the nine curses inflicted upon all women because of the Fall.

In Israel today, women are not allowed to give evidence in rabbinical courts. The rabbis justify this prohibition by citing Genesis, 18:9–16, where it is stated that Sara, Abraham's wife, lied. The rabbis use this incident as evidence that women are unqualified to bear witness. The Qur'an also mentions this incident more than once, in 11:69–74, 51:24–30, without any hint that Sara lied. In the Christian West, both ecclesiastical and civil law debarred women from giving testimony until the late eighteenth century.

If a man accused his wife of unchastity, the Bible says that her testimony is not admissible. Furthermore, she had to undergo a trial by ordeal, a complex and humiliating ritual that supposedly proved her guilt or innocence (Numbers, 5:11–31). If she was found guilty after this ordeal, she would be sentenced to death. If she was found innocent, her husband was considered innocent of any wrongdoing.

If a man married a woman and then accused her of not being a virgin, her own testimony would not count. Her parents had to prove her virginity before the town elders. If they could not prove her innocence, she would be stoned to death on her father's doorstep. If the parents were able to prove her innocence, the husband would only be fined a hundred silver shekels and could not divorce his wife as long as he lived.

By giving women the right to testify, the Qur'an brought a revolutionary change. For example, in the case where a person accuses another of unchastity, the Qur'an's commandment is completely different from that of the Bible. It requires the accuser to produce four witnesses who will give testimony that they personally saw the act being committed. If he cannot, he is punished and no longer accepted as a witness in any case. In case a spouse accuses the other of adultery, the testimony of a woman has the same value or weight as that of a man (24:4–9).

However, in some instances of bearing witness to certain civil contracts, two men are required or one man and two women. This does not, however, indicate that a woman is inferior to a man. Rather, it is a means to secure the rights of the contracting parties, because a woman generally is not so experienced in practical life as a man. As this lack of experience may cause a loss to any of the contracting parties, the law requires that at least two women should bear witness with one man. If a woman witness forgets something, the other one would remind her; if she makes a mistake due to a lack of experience, the other would help correct her.

The reason why the Qur'an demands two women in place of one man in commercial transactions is quite clear. The Qur'an does not regard a woman as half of a man; rather, what is important here is not the status of women or men, but accuracy, justice, and equity in business.

Generally, men are supposed to be more engaged in business than women, which is actually the case, and are responsible for supporting the family. Furthermore, women are more emotional than men and more susceptible to social pressure and threats. However, there may be men who are more emotional than women. But rather than the exceptions, the law considers the majority of people in all matters relating to the community. Women also are expected to be more susceptible to mistakes and forgetfulness over a matter in which they are not so engaged as men. This precautionary measure guarantees honest transactions and proper dealings between people. In fact, it gives women a role to play in civil life and helps to establish justice. Such a lack of experience does not denote inferiority, for every person lacks one thing or another. Yet no one questions their human status.

Islam does not demand two women in place of one man in all cases. One example of this was mentioned above, which is concerned with a husband's accusing his wife of unchastity. Another example is that both men and women can scan the sky for the crescent moon to determine whether a lunar month has begun or ended. In addition, the testimony of two women can be sought in matters in which women have greater knowledge or specialty than men.

Privileges

A woman enjoys certain privileges that a man does not. For example, she is exempt from some religious duties (i.e., Prayers and fasting while menstruating or experiencing post-childbirth bleeding) and all financial liabilities. As a mother, she enjoys more recognition and higher honor in God's sight (31:14–15; 46:15). The Prophet acknowledged this honor when he declared that Paradise is under the feet of mothers.[34]

A mother is entitled to three-fourths of the son's love and kindness, with one-fourth left for the father. A man came to God's Messenger and asked him who among people was the most deserving of his kind treatment. The Messenger answered, "Your mother!" The man repeated the question three times, and the Messenger gave the same answer for the two subsequent times and said, "Your father!" only at the fourth time.[35] As a prospective wife, a woman can demand a suitable dowry, which will belong to her alone, from her husband-to-be. She is entitled to complete provision and maintenance by the husband, does not have to work or share any of the family expenses, and can retain whatever she possessed before her marriage and earns after it. Her husband has no right to any of her belongings. As a daughter or sister, she is entitled to security and provision by her father and brother(s), respectively. If she wishes to work, be self-supporting, and participate in handling the family responsibilities, she is quite free to do so, provided that her integrity and honor are safeguarded.

The fact that women stand behind men during the Prayers does not indicate inferiority. Women, as already mentioned, are exempt from attending the congregational Prayers, which are necessary for men. If they do attend, they stand in separate lines made up of women exclusively. This is a regulation of discipline in Prayers, not a classification of importance. In men's rows, the head of state stands shoulder to shoulder with the pauper. Men of the highest social ranks stand in Prayer side by side with men of the lowest ranks.

The order of the Prayer lines is intended to help every person concentrate while praying. Such discipline is very important, because the Prayers are not simply chanting or singsong, but involve specific actions and motions (e.g., standing, bowing, prostrating). If men and women prayed in the same line, they might be distracted by something and lose their concentration. Thus the Prayer's purpose would not be fulfilled.

Moreover, a man cannot touch a woman's body while praying, and vice versa. If they stand side by side while praying, they cannot avoid touching each other. Furthermore, if a woman prays in front of a man or beside him, he will most likely be distracted and exposed to evil thoughts. In order to concentrate on praying, prevent any unforeseen accidents, maintain harmony and order among worshippers, to fulfill the Prayer's true purposes, Islam ordains praying in rows: the men in the front, then the male children, and then the women and girls. Anyone who understands what praying means to a Muslim can easily understand the wisdom of organizing the lines of worshippers in this manner.

The Veil

The Muslim woman is always associated with an old tradition known as "*hijab*," (literally the veil), referring to the adherence to certain standards of modest dress that cover the body, which is nontransparent and loose-fitting that do not delineate the parts of body. She is to beautify herself with the veil of honor, dignity, chastity, purity, and integrity; and refrain from all deeds and gestures that might stir the passions of people other than her husband or cause people to suspect her morality. She is warned not to display her charms or expose her physical attractions before strangers. The *hijab,* in addition to being one way to save women's soul from weakness, and preserve her dignity, is also a *form of courtesy* to men (in that it is less provoking and helps them to avoid sin and Hellfire). Men are also ordered by Islam to dress modestly (and not provoke women's desire). Thus modesty supports a kind of solidarity among Muslims seeking God's good pleasure and Paradise and respect for chastity as an ideal. Islam is most concerned with its followers' integrity, safeguarding of their morals and morale, and protecting their character and personality (cf. Qur'an, 24:30–31).

Inheritance and Women

Among the pre-Islamic Arabs, inheritance rights were confined exclusively to the male relatives. Since Biblical days, Judaism has given no female members of the household, including the wife and daughters, the right to inherit any part of the family estate. Christianity followed suit for long time. Both the ecclesiastical and civil laws of Christendom barred daughters from sharing with their brothers in their father's patrimony. Wives also had no inheritance rights. These laws survived until late in the twentieth century. Islam also made a great revolution in this respect, for the Qur'an declared:

> For the male heirs is a share of what parents and near kindred (who die) leave behind, and for the female heirs is a share of what parents and near kindred (who die) leave behind, whether it (the heritage) be little or much— a share ordained by God. (4:7)

This short verse contains the basic principles of the Islamic law of inheritance and a significant warning:

- Both women and men have a share in the inheritance.
- A deceased person's property is inherited, whether it be little or much.
- It makes no difference whether the inherited property is movable or immovable.
- The survivors (e.g., parents, grandparents, and nearest relatives) can inherit. If there are any "nearest kindred," "distant relations" cannot inherit.
- Heirs cannot be deprived of their share of the inheritance.

The significant warning is: Women in pre-Islamic, idolatrous, Christian, and Jewish societies could not inherit. By mentioning female heirs separately, but in the same words as it mentions male heirs, at the risk of repetition and emphasizing that the estate's size does not matter, the verse warns that women cannot be deprived of their share of the inheritance on such pretexts as "the estate is too small."

Then, the Qur'an details the laws for inheritance (4:11–12). Its basic principles and standards were laid down, and its precise details were established on these standards and the Prophet's practice.

With the exception of the parents, and the siblings in some cases, a son receives twice as much as a daughter, a brother twice as much as a sister, and a husband twice as much as a wife. This has been the target of unjust objections. However:

- First, it should be noted that Islam is not a religion that has to have answers to objections, for whatever it decrees is right and just. So, while explaining Islam's position in matters to which objections have been raised, we intend to illuminate sincere minds.
- Second, the verses present Islam's law of inheritance as God's absolute command, and in their conclusive pronouncements declare that they are based on God's Knowledge and Wisdom. So, we should try to find the instances of Divine wisdom in them. Breaching them means disobeying God and His Messenger, while rejecting them knowingly that they are God's commands amounts to unbelief.
- Third, Islam is universal and thus considers and addresses the conditions of all ages and communities. Its worldview is holistic and does not ignore the universal frame while dealing with particular matters. Therefore, in viewing its law of inheritance, we should consider such psychological and sociological factors as the psychology of women and men; their positions and financial, familial, and social responsibilities; and their contributions to the economy. As the matter is never a matter of equality between men and women, we should evaluate every matter with respect to its own nature and context.
- Fourth, the distribution of inheritance is a highly complicated matter; it does not consist in only the rule that a son receives twice as much as a daughter, a brother twice as much as a sister, and a husband twice as much as a wife. There are many cas-

es where men and women have equal shares or even women are preferred.

In order to understand the rationale behind Islam's giving a woman half of a man's share in some cases only, one must remember that a man's financial obligations far exceed those of a woman. A groom must provide his bride with a marriage gift (bridal-due), which then becomes her exclusive property and remains so even if she is divorced. The bride is under no obligation to present any gifts to the groom.

Moreover, the husband must maintain his wife and children. The wife, on the other hand, is not obliged to help him do so. Her property and earnings are for her use alone, except for what she may offer to her family members or others voluntarily. Besides, one has to realize that Islam strongly advocates family life, encourages young people to get married, and discourages divorce. Therefore, in a truly Islamic society, family life is the norm and single life is the rare exception, for almost all women and men get married. In light of these facts, men generally have greater financial burdens than women, and the inheritance rules are meant to offset this imbalance.

When a woman receives less than a man, she is not deprived of anything for which she has worked. The property she inherits is not the result of her earning or endeavor, but something coming from a neutral source, something additional or extra. Thus it is a type of aid, and any aid has to be distributed according to needs and responsibilities.

The Qur'anic injunction of inheritance is a perfect mercy for women, in addition to its being perfectly just, for a girl is delicate, vulnerable, and thus held in great affection by her father. Her father, in turn and thanks to the Qur'an, does not see her as a child who will cause him any loss by carrying away some of his wealth to others. In addition, her brothers feel compassion for her and protect her without feeling envious, as they do not consider her as a rival in the division of the family's possessions. Thus, the affection and compassion which the girl enjoys through her family compensate her for the apparent loss in the inheritance.

Some still object on the grounds that a woman's share of the inheritance should be equal to that of a man so that there would be no need to compensate her through a bridal-due and maintenance by her husband.

Those who make this objection think that the bridal-due and maintenance are the effects of women's peculiar position with regard to inheritance, whereas the real position is just the reverse. Further, they seem to be under the impression that the financial aspect is the only consideration. If this were so, there would have been no need for bridal-due and maintenance or for any disparity between the shares of men and women. As in every other case, however, Islamic jurisprudence considers all aspects connected to the individual's nature and psychology. It has considered women's unique needs arising out of their procreative function. Moreover, a woman's earning capacity is less than a man's, and her consumption of wealth is usually more. In most cases, in her parents' house her contribution to the family income is far less than her brother(s). In addition, there are several other finer aspects of their respective mental make-up. For example, a man always wants to spend on the woman of his choice. Other psychological and social aspects that help consolidate domestic relations also have been considered. Taking all of these points into consideration, Islam has made bridal-due and maintenance obligatory.

Thus it is a severe injustice, not a kindness, to give a girl or woman more than her due out of unrealistic feelings of compassion—unrealistic because no one can be more compassionate than God, the Creator, the Upbringer, and the Provider. Rather, if the Qur'anic bounds are exceeded, women may become vulnerable to exploitation and tyranny in the family. As for the Qur'anic injunctions, all of them, like those pertaining to inheritance, prove the truth expressed in *We have not sent you (O Muhammad), save as an unequalled mercy for all the worlds* (21:107).

Islam does not approve of wealth circulating only among a few people; rather, it wants wealth to be distributed among as many people as possible. In inheritance, considering that God's grace and bountifulness have a share in it, it strongly advises and even orders that distant relatives, orphans, and the poor should also benefit from it.

Conclusion

By now it is clear that the status of women in Islam is unprecedentedly high and realistically suitable to their nature. A woman's rights and duties are equal to those of a man, but not necessarily or absolutely identical to them. If she is "deprived" of one thing in some aspect, she is fully compensated for it with more things in many other aspects. The fact that she is a woman has no bearing on her human status or independent personality, and is no basis for justifying any prejudice or injustice towards her. Islam gives her as much as is required of her. Her rights match beautifully with her duties. This balance between rights and duties is maintained, and no side outweighs the other. As we read in the Qur'an:

> In a fair manner women have the same rights against men as men have against them, but men (due to the heaviness of their duty and responsibility) have a degree above them (which they should not misuse). (2:228)

This degree is not a title of supremacy or an authorization to dominate women, but rather corresponds with a man's extra responsibilities and compensates him for his unlimited liabilities. The above-mentioned verse is always interpreted in the light of:

> Men (those who are able to carry out their responsibilites) are the protectors and maintainers of women inasmuch as God has endowed some of humankind (in some respects) with greater capacity than others, and inasmuch as they (the men) spend of their wealth (for the family's maintenance). (4:34)

These extra responsibilities give men a degree over women in some economic aspects, not in humanity or character. Nor is it a dominance of one over the other, or a suppression of one by the other. Rather, it is a distribution of God's abundance according to the needs of each gender's nature, of which God is the Maker. As He alone knows what is best for men and women, the following words are absolutely true:

> O humankind! In due reverence for your Lord, keep from disobedience to Him Who created you from a single human self, and from it created its mate, and from the pair of them scattered abroad a multitude of men and women. In due reverence for God, keep from disobedience to Him in Whose name you make demands of one another, and (observe) the rights of the wombs (i.e. of kinship, thus observing piety in your relations with God and with human beings). God is ever watchful over you. (4:1)

Women

- Women train and educate children, and establish order, peace, and harmony at home. They are the first teachers in the school of humanity. A house that contains an honorable, well-mannered woman loyal to her home is a corner from Heaven. The sounds and breaths heard there are no different from the musical voices of the young people of Paradise and the burbling of the Kawthar stream in Heaven.
- A woman's inner depth, chastity, and dignity elevate her higher than angels and cause her to resemble an unmatched diamond. A woman awake to virtue in her inner world resembles a crystal chandelier that, with every movement, sends light throughout the house.
- Women often have been used as objects of pleasure, means of entertainment, and material for advertising. Most champions of woman's rights and freedom only excite women with physical pleasures and then stab her spirit.

- In the past, a son was called *makhdum* and a daughter *karima*. Meaning "pupil (of the eye)," this word expresses a member that is very valuable, as necessary as it is valuable, and as delicate as it is necessary.
- A good woman speaks wisdom and has a delicate, refined spirit. Her behavior inspires admiration and respect. Familiar looks sense this sacred side of her, and turn instinctive feelings to contemplation.
- Like a flower worn on the breast, a physically beautiful woman may receive admiration and respect for some short period. But, if she has not been able to get the seeds of her heart and spirit to blossom, she will eventually fade and, like falling leaves, be trampled underfoot. What a sad ending for those who have not found the road of immortality!
- Thanks to the good successors she raised and left behind, the home of a spiritually mature woman constantly exudes a scent of joy like an incense burner. The "heavenly" home where this aroma "blows" is a garden of Paradise beyond description.
- A woman whose heart is illuminated with the light of faith and whose mind is enlightened with knowledge and social breeding builds her home anew each day by adding new dimensions of beauty to it.[36]

Divorce

Christianity abhors divorce, and in the Gospels Jesus, upon him be peace, spoke against divorce except in the case of adultery, and the Catholic Church forbids divorce completely. Judaism, on the other hand, allows divorce without cause. The Old Testament gives the husband the right to divorce his wife if he just dislikes her (Deuteronomy, 24:1–4).

Islam, which rejects and is free from all extremities, occupies the middle ground between Christianity and Judaism with respect to divorce. It considers marriage a bond that should not be broken except for compelling reasons. Couples are instructed to pursue all possible remedies whenever their marriages are in danger. Divorce is not to be resorted to except when there is no other solution. In a nutshell, Islam recognizes divorce and yet it discourages it by all means. For example, the Qur'an warns: *Consort with them (your spouses) in a good manner, for if you are not pleased with them, it may well be that you dislike something but God has set in it much good* (4:19).

God's Messenger emphasizes, "Among all of the permitted acts, divorce is the most hateful to God"[37]; and: "The most perfect among the believers in respect of faith is the one who is the best of them in character; and the best of you are the kindest towards their wives."[38]

However, Islam recognizes that there can be circumstances in which a marriage will be on the verge of collapse. In such cases, mere advice to be kind or show self-restraint may not be a viable solution. So, what should be done to save the marriage in such cases? The Qur'an offers some practical advice for the spouses, suggests some measures, and gives the spouses the possibility to reconsider their decision.

No Divorce during Menstruation

A man cannot divorce his wife at any time; rather, he must wait for a suitable time. According to the law, the suitable time is when the wife has cleansed herself after her menstrual or post-childbirth bleeding period and before they resume sexual relations, or when she is not pregnant.[39]

The reason for prohibiting divorce during menstruation or post-childbirth bleeding is that since sexual intercourse is forbidden during such periods, a husband is given the time and opportunity to withdraw his decision by waiting until his wife is clean and there can be a new atmosphere of love, understanding, and reconciliation between them. Divorce is also forbidden between menstrual periods (i.e., "the period of purity") if the husband has had sexual intercourse with his wife since the end of her previous period.[40]

Repeated Divorce

A man is given three chances on three different occasions to divorce his wife,[41] provided that each divorce is pronounced during the time when his wife is in "the period of purity" and he has not had intercourse with her.

He may divorce her once and let the *'idda* pass. The *'idda* is three monthly courses. During that time, the divorced wife must stay in her home (i.e., her husband's house). She cannot move somewhere else (Qur'an, 65:1), except that she can go out for a need,[42] and her husband cannot evict her without a just cause, such as indecency on the part of the woman (65:1). During *'idda*, he must provide for her (65:3). This requirement leaves the way open for reconciliation. They have the option of reconciliation without having to remarry. If, however, this waiting period expires without reconciliation, they are considered divorced and therefore each former spouse can marry someone else or remarry each other . The former husband cannot debar her if she would like to marry another man, nor can he force her to remarry him (2:232). If they decide to remarry, a new marriage contract is required.

If they remarry, the husband has one more chance to divorce his wife, as in the first instance. But if he divorces his wife for a third time, they can no longer return to each other unless the woman marries another man and divorces or is divorced by him in normal conditions (2:230). However, this second marriage to another man must be genuine; it must have been consummated before the divorce in order that the woman can return to her former husband after her divorce from the second man.[43] All these rules show what great importance Islam attaches to the preservation of marriage and how it calls the spouses to think over and over before dissolving it.

Appointing Arbitrators and Witnesses

The Qur'an advises that two arbitrators be appointed if discord occurs between the two spouses, and calls on the spouses to settle the problem between them peacefully. One arbitrator should be from the husband's family and the other from the wife's family (4:35,128). If that is not possible, other people may be appointed, depending on what is in the best interest of those concerned. They also agree that when a possible resolution has been devised to reconcile the spouses, it should be implemented. However, if they disagree, their opinions are not to be implemented (4:130).

The Qur'an also advises that there are to be two witnesses in case of either divorce or a new marriage contract when women divorced for the first or second time reach the end of their waiting-term (*'idda*). These witnesses should be two Muslim men of probity and establish the testimony for God with due consciousness of their responsibility to Him (65:2).

Imam as-Shafi'i records in his book *al-Umm* from Ubayda al-Salmani, who said:

> A man and a woman came to 'Ali ibn Abi Talib, each of them accompanied by a group of people. 'Ali told them to appoint a male arbitrator from his family and one from her family. Then he said to the arbitrators, "Do you know what your responsibilities are? If you find that you can bring them back together, do so. If you find that they should be separated, do so."

Reconciling Honorably or Separating with Kindness

If a reconciliation does not occur and the period of *'idda* ends, they have two alternatives if only one or two instances of divorce have occurred: either to reconcile honorably (i.e., to remarry with the intention of living in peace and harmony), or for the husband to let his wife go and part with her in kindness, without argument and harsh words, and without taking back anything of what he has given her as bridal-due or other gifts, and without setting aside any of their mutual rights (2:229, 231; 65:2).

The Divorced Woman's Freedom to Remarry

After a divorced woman's *'idda* ends, her ex-husband, guardian, or anyone else cannot prevent her from marrying anyone she chooses. As long as she and the man who proposes to her follow the procedure required by the law, no one has the right to interfere (2:232).

The Woman's Right to Demand Divorce

If the wife chooses to end the marriage, she resorts to the court and may return the marriage gifts to her husband. Habiba daughter of Sahl saw her husband as so ugly that it was impossible for her to continue to live with him, or her husband beat her. She came to the Prophet, upon him be peace and blessings, and complained to him of her husband. The Prophet asked her, "Would you give him his garden (his marriage gift to her) back?" "Yes," she replied. The Prophet then instructed the man to take back his garden and accept the dissolution of the marriage.[44] This is a fair compensation for a husband who is keen to keep his wife, while she chooses to leave him. The Qur'an instructs the man not to take back any of the gifts he has given to his wife, unless she chooses to end the marriage (2:229).

In some cases, a wife might want to keep her marriage but find herself forced to seek divorce for a compelling reason (e.g., cruelty, desertion without a reason, non-fulfillment of his conjugal responsibilities). In such cases, the Islamic court dissolves the marriage.

As another case, a husband can confer the power of divorce on the wife. This delegation of power can be general or limited to certain specified circumstances. To make it irrevocable, it is included in the marriage contract as a binding clause that empowers the wife to dissolve the marriage based upon the agreed-upon specified circumstances. The husband can also give his wife the option to continue the marriage or be divorced (33:28–29).[45]

Adoption

Islam has abolished the type of adoption that makes an adopted child a member of the family, which would give him or her full rights of inheritance and to mix freely with other members of the household, and prohibit him or her to marry certain women or men, and so on (Qur'an, 33:4–5).

But the word *adoption* is also used in another sense, one that is not prohibited by Islam. In this context, adoption means bringing home an orphan or an abandoned child to rear, educate, and treat as one's own child as regards protection, feeding, clothing, teaching, and loving. However, one does not consider the child to be one's own and does not give the child any of the rights that Islamic law reserves for natural children.

One of the wisdoms in the jurisprudence on adoption is that the orphaned or abandoned child is cared for in a family but does not lose knowledge of his or her family, parents and forebears (thus "observing the rights of the wombs" which bore them), a loss which can cause great distress, as well as potential problems of unintended incest between brothers and sisters later. So, adopted children do not change their names in Muslim societies and intra-family adoption is preferred. This is another example of the wisdom of Islamic jurisprudence and an impressive example of guarding children's rights – as well as, for example, the rights of grandparents who wish to continue contact with their grandchildren who have been adopted out of their family, often against their will and without their consent.

The Prophet, His Wives, and Children[46]

Prophet Muhammad personifies the perfect father and husband. He was so kind and tolerant to his wives that they could not envisage their lives without him, nor did they want to live away from him.

He married Sawda, his second wife, while in Makka. After a while, he considered divorcing her for certain reasons. She was extremely upset at this news, and implored him, "O Messenger of

God, I wish no worldly thing of you. Please don't deprive me of being your wife. I want to go to the Hereafter as your wife. I care for nothing else."[47] The Messenger did not divorce her.

Once he noticed that Hafsa was uncomfortable over their financial situation. "If she wishes, I may set her free," he said, or something to that effect. This suggestion so alarmed her that she requested mediators to persuade him not to do so. He kept his faithful friend's daughter as his trusted wife.[48]

His wives viewed separation from the Messenger of God as a calamity, so firmly had he established himself in their hearts. They were completely at one with him. They shared in his blessed, mild, and natural life. If he had left them, they would have died of despair. If he had divorced one of them, she would have waited at his doorstep until the Last Day.

After his death, there was much yearning and a great deal of grief. Abu Bakr and 'Umar found the Messenger's wives weeping whenever they visited them. Their weeping seemed to continue for the rest of their lives. Prophet Muhammad, upon him be peace and blessings, left a lasting impression on everyone. He dealt equally with his wives and without any serious problems. He was a kind and gentle husband, and never behaved harshly or rudely. In short, he was the perfect husband.

Each wife, because of his generosity and kindness, thought she was his most beloved. The idea that any man could show complete equality and fairness in his relationships with more than one woman seems impossible. For this reason, the Messenger of God asked God's pardon for any unintentional leanings. He would pray, "I may have unintentionally shown more love to one of them than the others, and this would be injustice. So, O Lord, I take refuge in Your grace for those things beyond my power."[49]

His gentleness affected his wives' souls so deeply that his departure led to what they must have felt to be an unbridgeable separation. They did not commit suicide, as Islam forbids it, but their lives now became full of endless sorrow and ceaseless tears.

The Messenger was kind and gentle to all women, and advised all other men to follow him in this regard. Sa'd ibn Abi Waqqas described his kindness as follows:

> 'Umar said, "One day I went to the Prophet and saw him smiling. 'May God make you smile forever, O Messenger of God,' I said, and asked why he was smiling. 'I smile at those women. They were chatting in front of me before you came. When they heard your voice, they all vanished,' he answered still smiling. On hearing this answer, I raised my voice and told them, 'O enemies of your own selves, you are scared of me, but you are not scared of the Messenger of God, and you don't show respect to him.' 'You are harsh and strict,' they replied.[50]

'Umar was manly, strong, generous, courageous, forthright, and honest. He was also gentle to women. However, the most handsome man looks ugly when compared to Prophet Joseph's beauty. Likewise, 'Umar's gentleness and sensitivity seem like violence and severity when compared to those of the Prophet, upon him be peace and blessings.

The Prophet's Consultation with His Wives

The Messenger discussed matters with his wives as friends. Certainly he did not need their advice, since he was directed by Revelation. However, he wanted to teach his nation that Muslim men were to give women every consideration. This was quite a radical idea in his time, as it is today in many parts of the world. He began teaching his people through his own relationship with his wives.

For example, the conditions laid down in the Treaty of Hudaybiya[51] disappointed and enraged many Muslims, for, in addition to some others which annoyed them, one condition stipulated that they could not make the pilgrimage that year. They wanted to reject the treaty, continue on to Makka, and face the possible consequences. But the Messenger ordered them to kill their sacrificial animals and take off their pilgrim attire. Some Companions hesitated, hoping that he would change his mind. He repeated his order, but they continued to hesitate. They did not oppose him; rather, they still hoped he might change his mind, for they had set out with the intention of pilgrimage and did not want to stop halfway.

Noticing this reluctance, the Prophet, upon him be peace and blessings, returned to his tent and asked Umm Salama, his wife accompanying him at that time, what she thought of the situation. He did so for he would teach Muslim men an important social lesson: there is nothing wrong with exchanging ideas with women on important matters or on any matters at all.

She said, "O Messenger of God, don't repeat your order. They may resist and thereby perish. Offer your sacrificial animal and change out of your pilgrim attire. They will obey, willingly or not, when they see that your order is final."[52] He did what his wife suggested, and the Companions began to do the same, for now it was clear that his order would not be changed.

Women are secondary beings in the minds of many, including those self-appointed defenders of women's rights as well as many self-proclaimed Muslim men. Whereas a woman is part of a whole, a part that renders the other half useful. We believe that when the two halves come together, the true unity of a human being appears. When this unity does not exist, humanity does not exist—nor can Prophethood, sainthood, or even Islam.

Our master, upon him be peace and blessings, encouraged us through his enlightening words to behave in a kindly way to women. He declared, "The most perfect among the believers in respect of faith is the one who is the best of them in character; and the best of you are the kindest towards their wives."[53] It is clear that women have received the true honor and respect they deserve, not just in theory but in actual practice, only once in history—during the period of Prophet Muhammad.

A Perfect Head of Family

Some of his wives had enjoyed an extravagant lifestyle before their marriage to him. One of these was Safiya, who had lost her father and husband and had been taken prisoner during the Battle of Khaybar. She must have been very angry with the Messenger, but when she saw him, her feelings changed completely. She undertook the same destiny as the other wives. They undertook it because love of the Messenger had entered their hearts.

Safiya was a Jewess. Once, she was dismayed when this fact was mentioned to her sarcastically. She informed the Messenger, expressing her sadness. He comforted her saying, "If they repeat it, tell them, 'My father is Prophet Aaron, my uncle is Prophet Moses, and my husband is, as you see, Prophet Muhammad, the Chosen One. What do you have more than me to be proud of?'"[54]

The Qur'an declares that his wives are the mothers of the believers (33:6). Although fourteen centuries have passed, we still feel delight in saying "my mother" when referring to Khadija, 'A'isha, Umm Salama, Hafsa, and his other wives, may God be pleased with them. We feel this because of him. Some feel more love for these women than they do for their real mothers. Certainly, this feeling must have been deeper, warmer, and stronger in the Prophet's own time.

The Messenger was the perfect head of a family. Managing many wives with ease, being a lover of their hearts, an instructor of their minds, an educator of their souls, he never neglected the affairs of the community or compromised his duties.

The Messenger excelled in every area of life. People should not compare him to themselves or to the so-called great personalities of their age. Researchers should look at him, the one to whom angels are grateful, always remembering that he excelled in every way. If they want to look for Prophet Muhammad, the pride of existence, they must search for him in his own dimensions. Our imaginations cannot reach him, for we do not even know how to imagine properly. God bestowed upon him, as His special favor, superiority in every field.

God's Messenger and Children

The Messenger, upon him be peace and blessings, was an extraordinary husband, a perfect father, and a unique grandfather. He was unique in every way. He treated his children and grandchildren with great compassion, and never neglected to direct them to the Hereafter and good deeds. He smiled at them, caressed and loved them, but did not allow them to neglect matters related to the afterlife.

In worldly matters he was extremely open. But when it came to maintaining their relationship with God Almighty, he was very serious and dignified. He showed them how to lead a humane life, and never allowed them to neglect their religious duties and become spoiled. His ultimate goal was to prepare them for the Hereafter. His perfect balance in such matters is another dimension of his Divinely inspired intellect.

In a *hadith*, Anas ibn Malik, honored by being the Messenger's servant for ten unbroken years, said, "I've never seen a man who was more compassionate to his family members than God's Messenger, upon him be peace and blessings."[55] If this admission were made just by us, it could be dismissed as unimportant. However, millions of people, so benign and compassionate that they would not even offend an ant, declare that he embraced everything with compassion. He was a human like us, but God inspired in him such an intimate affection for every living thing that he was able to establish a connection with all of them. As a result, he was full of extraordinary affection toward his family members and others.

All of the Prophet's sons died. Ibrahim, his last son born to his Coptic wife Mary, also died in infancy. The Messenger often visited his son before the latter's death, although he was very busy. Ibrahim was looked after by a nurse. The Prophet would embrace, kiss, and caress him before returning home.[56] When Ibrahim died, the Prophet took him on his lap again, embraced him, and described his sorrow while on the brink of tears. Some were surprised. He gave them this answer, "Eyes may water and hearts may be broken, but we do not say anything except what God will be pleased with." He pointed to his tongue and said, "God will ask us about this."[57]

He carried his grandsons Hasan and Husayn on his back. Despite his unique status, he did this without hesitation to herald the honor that they would attain later. One time when they were on his back, 'Umar came into the Prophet's house and, seeing them, exclaimed, "What a beautiful mount you have!" The Messenger added immediately, "What beautiful riders they are!"[58]

The Messenger was completely balanced in the way he brought up his children. He loved his children and grandchildren very much, and instilled love in them. However, he never let his love for them be abused. None of them deliberately dared to do anything wrong. If they made an unintentional mistake, the Messenger's protection prevented them from going even slightly astray. He did this by wrapping them in love and an aura of dignity. For example, once Hasan or Husayn wanted to eat a date that had been given to distribute among the poor as alms. The Messenger immediately took it from his hand and said, "Anything given as alms is forbidden to us."[59] In teaching them while they were young to be sensitive to forbidden acts, he established an important principle of education.

Whenever he returned to Madina, he would carry children on his mount. On such occasions, the Messenger embraced not only his grandchildren but also those in his house and those nearby. He conquered their hearts through his compassion. He loved all children.

He loved his granddaughter Umama as much as he loved Hasan and Husayn. He often went out with her on his shoulders, and even placed her on his back while praying. When he prostrated, he put her down; when he had finished, he placed her on his back again.[60] He showed this degree of love to Umama to teach his male followers how to treat daughters. This was a necessity, for only a decade earlier it had been the social norm to bury infant or young girls alive. Such public paternal affection for a granddaughter had never been seen before in Arabia.

The Messenger proclaimed that Islam allows no discrimination between son and daughter. How could there be? One is Muhammad, the other is Khadija; one is Adam, the other is Eve; one is 'Ali, the other is Fatima.

He loved them and directed them toward the Hereafter, to the otherworldly and eternal beauty, and to God. For example, he once saw Fatima, his beloved daughter, wearing a necklace (a bracelet, according to another version), and asked her, "Do you want the inhabitants of the earth and the Heavens to say that my daughter is holding (or wearing) a chain from Hell?" These few words, coming from a man whose throne was established in her heart and who had conquered all her faculties, caused her to report, in her own words, "I immediately sold the necklace, bought and freed a slave, and then went to God's Messenger. When I told him what I had done, he rejoiced. He opened his hands and thanked God, 'All thanks be to God, Who protected Fatima from Hell.'"[61]

Fatima did not commit any sin by wearing this necklace. However, the Messenger wanted to keep her in the circle of the *muqarrabin* (those made near to God). His warning to her was based on *taqwa* (righteousness and devotion to God) and *qurb* (nearness to God). This was, in a sense, a neglect of worldly things. It is also an example of the sensitivity befitting the mother of the Prophet's household, which represents the Muslim community and the source of its spiritual leaders until the Last Day. To be mother to such godly men like Hasan, Husayn, and Zayn al-'Abidin was certainly no ordinary task. The Messenger was preparing her to be the mother first of his own household (*Ahl al-Bayt*), and then of those who would descend from them.

Bukhari and Muslim gave another example of how he educated them. 'Ali narrates:

> We had no servant in our house, and so Fatima did all the housework by herself. We lived in a house with just a small room. There, she would light a fire and try to cook. She often singed her clothes while trying to increase the fire by blowing.

She also baked our bread and carried water. Her hands became covered with calluses from turning the millstone, as did her back from carrying water.

Meanwhile some prisoners of war were brought to Madina. The Messenger gave them to those who applied. I suggested to Fatima that she ask for a servant from her father. And she did.

Fatima continues:

I went to my father, but he was not at home. 'A'isha said she would tell him when he came, so I returned home. As soon as we went to bed, the Messenger came in. We wanted to get up, but he did not let us and instead sat between us. I could feel the coolness of his foot on my body. He asked what we wanted, and I explained the situation. The Messenger, in an awesome manner, replied: "Fatima, fear God and be faultless in all your duties to Him. I will tell you something. When you want to go to bed, say *subhana'llah* (All-Glorified is God), *al-hamdu li'llah* (All praise is for God), and *Allahu akbar* (God is the All-Great) thirty-three times each. This is better for you than having a maid."[62]

Affection toward and Respect for Parents[63]

Your Lord has decreed that you worship none but Him alone, and treat parents with the best of kindness. Should one of them, or both, attain old age in your lifetime, do not say, "Ugh!" to them (as an indication of complaint or impatience), nor push them away; and always address them in gracious words. Lower to them the wing of humility out of mercy, and say, "My Lord, have mercy on them even as they cared for me in childhood." Your Lord best knows what is in your souls (in respect of all matters, including what you think of your parents). If you are righteous (in your thoughts and deeds), then surely He is All-Forgiving to those who turn to Him in humble contrition. And give his due to the relative, as well as the destitute and the wayfarer; and do not squander (your wealth) senselessly. Surely squanderers are ever brothers of satans; and Satan is ever ungrateful to his Lord. (17:23–27)

O you who are unaware of filial responsibility toward parents, whose house contains an elderly parent, a helpless and invalid relative, or a brother or sister in faith unable to earn a living. Heed these verses and see how they insist in five ways that you show filial affection.

As paternal affection for children is a sublime reality of worldly life, filial gratitude is a most urgent and heavy duty. Parents lovingly sacrifice their lives for their children. Given this, children who preserve their humanity and have not become monsters of ingratitude should try to please them and gain their approval by showing them sincere respect and serving them willingly. Islam assigns uncles and aunts the same honorable value as parents.

Know, you who neglect such duties, how terribly disgraceful and unscrupulous it is to be bored with their continued existence and so hope for their deaths. Know this and come to your senses! Understand what an injustice it is to desire the deaths of those who sacrificed their lives for you.

O you immersed in earning your livelihood! Know that your disabled relative, whom you consider a burden, is a means of blessing and abundance. Never complain about the difficulty of making a living, for were it not for the blessing and abundance bestowed upon you, you would face even more hardship. If I did not want to keep this letter brief, I would prove this to you.

I swear by God that this is a reality that even my devil and evil-commanding self accept. All existence can see that the infinitely Merciful and Compassionate Creator of Majesty and Munificence sends children here along with their sustenance: their mothers' breast milk. He sends sustenance for the elderly, who are like children and even more worthy and needy of compassion, in the form of blessing and unseen, immaterial abundance. He does not load their sustenance onto mean, greedy people.

The truth expressed in *God is the All-Providing, the Possessor of Strength and the Steadfast* (51:58) and in *How many an animate creature bears not its own provision, but God provides for it and you* (29:60) is proclaimed by all living creatures through the tongue of their disposition. So not only is the sustenance of elderly relatives sent in the form of blessings, but also that of pets, created as friends to people who feed and take care of them. I have personally observed this: Years ago, my daily ration was half a loaf of bread. I barely managed with this until four cats became my daily guests. As soon as they began sharing my bread, the same ration was always enough for all of us. I saw this so often that I became convinced that I benefited from the blessing coming through the cats. I declare that they were not a burden upon me; rather, I was indebted to them.

O people, you are the most esteemed, noble, and worthy-of-respect of all creatures. Among people, believers are the most perfect. Among believers, the helpless and elderly are the most worthy and needy of respect and compassion. Among the helpless and elderly, relatives deserve more affection, love, and service than others. Among relatives, parents are the most truthful confidants and most intimate companions. If an animal is a means of blessing and abundance when it stays as a guest in your house, consider how invaluable a means of blessing and mercy your elderly parents are if they stay with you. The following *hadith* shows what an important means for removing calamities they are: "But for the old bent double, calamities would pour down upon you."[64]

So come to your senses. If you have been assigned a long life, you also will grow old. If you do not respect parents, then, according to the rule that one is rewarded or punished in accordance with one's action, your children will not respect you. Further, serious reflection on your afterlife shows that gaining your parents' approval and pleasing them through service is a precious provision for your afterlife. If you love this worldly life, please them so that you may lead a pleasant life. If you consider them a burden, break their easily offended hearts, and desire their deaths, you will be the object of the Qur'anic threat, *He [She] loses both the world and the world to come* (22:11). So, those who wish for the All-Merciful's mercy must show mercy to those entrusted to them by God.

I noticed that Mustafa Cavus, my brother in religion, usually succeeded in both his worldly and otherworldly affairs. I did not understand why until I learned that he strictly observed his parents' rights. Whoever desires prosperity in both worlds should follow his example.

> O God, bestow blessings and peace on him who declared, "Paradise is beneath the feet of mothers," and on his Family and Companions. We have no knowledge save what You have taught us. You are the All-Knowing, the All-Wise.

Chapter 8

Halal (Lawful) and *Haram* (Forbidden)

HALAL (LAWFUL) AND *HARAM* (FORBIDDEN)[1]

Halal is a Qur'anic term that means permitted, allowed, (religiously) lawful, or legal. Its opposite is *haram* (forbidden, unlawful or illegal). Determining what is *halal* and *haram* is one matter over which, prior to the advent of Islam, the peoples of the world were very far astray and utterly confused. Thus, they permitted many impure and harmful things and forbade many things that were good and pure.

They erred grievously, either going far to the right or the left. At one extreme was India's ascetic Brahmanism and Christianity's self-denying monasticism. In addition, other religions were based on mortifying the flesh, abstaining from good food, and avoiding other enjoyments of life that God has provided for humanity. At the other extreme was Persia's Mazdak philosophy, which advocated absolute freedom and allowed people to take whatever they wanted and to do whatever they pleased. It even exhorted them to violate what is naturally held inviolable.

When Islam came, errors, confusion, and deviations with respect to *halal* and *haram* were widespread. One of Islam's initial accomplishments was, therefore, to establish certain legal principles and measures for rectifying this situation. These principles were made the determining criteria on which defining *halal* and *haram* were based. Thus this vital aspect was determined according to the correct perspective, and the related rules were established on the basis of such principles as justice, morality, righteousness, and perfect goodness. As a result, the Muslim community occupied a position between the extreme deviations mentioned above and was described by God as a *middle community, the best community that has been brought forth for humanity* (2:143; 3:110).

Basic Principles

- The first principle is that all that God has created and the benefits derived from them are for humanity's use and permissible. Nothing is haram except what is forbidden by a sound and explicit *nass*, that is, either a Qur'anic verse or a clear, authentic, and explicit *Sunna* [practice or saying] of the Prophet, upon him be peace and blessings. (These are the two main sources of Islamic law.) Juridical principles such as the consensus of scholars (*ijma*) and analogy (*qiyas*) are operative in judging about novel things as based on the Qur'an and the *Sunna*.
- In Islam, the sphere of forbidden things is small, while that of permissible things is vast. In relation to acts of worship, the principle is limitation: nothing can be legislated in this regard except what God Himself or the Messenger have legislated. But as far as habits of life are concerned, the principle is freedom, because nothing can be restricted in this regard except what God Himself and the Messenger, as based upon His Revelation, have forbidden. No rabbi, priest, king, or sultan has the right to forbid something permanently to God's servants. The Qur'an took to task the People of the Book (the Christians and Jews) for giving their priests and rabbis the power to make things and actions religiously lawful or forbidden without considering the Divine ordinances.

'Adiy ibn Hatim, who was a Christian before accepting Islam, once came to God's Messenger, upon him be peace and blessings. When he heard him reciting:

> The Jews take their rabbis (teachers of law), and the Christians take their monks, as well as the Messiah, son of Mary, for Lords besides God, whereas they were commanded to worship none but the One God. There is no deity but He. All-Glorified He is in that He is absolutely above their association of partners with Him (9:31),

he said, "O Messenger of God, but they do not worship them." The Messenger replied, "Yes, but they forbid to the people what is *halal* and permit them what is *haram*, and the people obey them. This is indeed their worship of them."[2]

- One of Islam's beauties is that it forbids only that which is unnecessary, harmful, and discardable (useless and unwanted), while providing alternatives that are better and give greater ease and comfort. For example: God forbids seeking omens by drawing lots, but provides the alternative of *istishara* (consultation) and *istikhara*. Islam teaches that Muslims facing a problem should consult those of expert knowledge and seek God's guidance. *Istikhara* means to ask for God's guidance in choosing between two conflicting decisions. For this there is a *salat* and a *du'a* (a supplication for guidance). God forbids usury, but encourages profitable trade; forbids (to men) the wearing of silk, but gives them the choice of wool, linen, cotton, and so on; forbids adultery, fornication, and homosexual acts, but encourages lawful marriage; forbids intoxicating drinks, but provides other delicious drinks that are wholesome for the body and mind; and forbids unclean food, but provides alternative, wholesome food.

Thus, when we survey all of Islam's injunctions, we find that if God limits His servants' choice in some matters, He provides them with a still wider range of more wholesome alternatives. Assuredly, God has no will to make peoples' lives difficult, narrow, and circumscribed; on the contrary, He wills ease, goodness, guidance, and mercy for them.

- Another Islamic principle is that whatever leads to something that is forbidden is also forbidden. In this way, Islam intends to block all avenues leading to what is *haram*. For example, it forbids extramarital sex, as well as anything that leads to it or makes it attractive (e.g., seductive clothing, private meetings and casual mixing between men and women, depicting nudity, pornography, obscene songs, and so on).

- Just as whatever leads toward the *haram* is forbidden, so is resorting to technical legalities in order to do what is *haram* by devious means and excuses. For example, God forbade the Jews to hunt on the Sabbath (Saturday). To get around this, they would dig traps on Friday so that the fish would fall into them on Saturday and be caught on Sunday. Those who resort to rationalizations and excuses to justify their actions consider such practices permissible. However, Muslim jurists consider them *haram*, since God's purpose was to prevent them from hunting on the Sabbath, whether by direct or indirect means.
- Renaming a *haram* thing or changing its form while retaining its essence is a devious tactic, since both actions are of no consequence as long as the thing and its essence remain unchanged. Thus, when some people invent new terms in order to deal in usury or to consume alcohol, the sin of dealing in usury and drinking remains. As we read in the *hadith,* "A time will come when people will devour usury, calling it 'trade,'" and, "A group of people will make peoples' intoxication *halal* by giving it other names."[3]
- In all of its legislation and moral injunctions, Islam emphasizes nobility of feelings, loftiness of aims, and purity of intentions. Indeed, in Islam, having a good intention transforms life's routine matters and mundane affairs into acts of worship and devotion to God. Accordingly, if a person eats food with the intention of sustaining life and strengthening his or her body so that he or she can fulfill his or her obligations to the Creator and other people, eating and drinking are considered worship and devotion to the Almighty. If one enjoys sexual intimacy with one's spouse, desiring a child and seeking to keep both spouses chaste, it is considered an act of worship that deserves a reward in the Hereafter.

When Muslims perform a permissible action along with a good intention, the action becomes an act of worship. But the case of the *haram* is entirely different: it remains *haram* no matter how good the intention, how honorable the purpose, or how lofty the aim may be. Islam can never consent to employing a *haram* means to achieve a praiseworthy or lawful end. Indeed, it insists that both the aim and the means chosen to attain it must be honorable and pure. "The end justifies the means," has no place in Islam.

- It is God's mercy to people that He did not leave them in ignorance concerning what is lawful and forbidden. Indeed, He has made these matters very clear. Accordingly, one may do what is lawful and must avoid what is forbidden insofar as one has the choice to do so. However, there is a gray area of doubt between the clearly *halal* and the clearly *haram*. Some people may not be able to decide whether a particular matter is permissible or forbidden, either because of doubtful evidence or of doubt concerning the text's applicability to the circumstance or matter in question. In such cases, Islam considers it an act of piety to avoid doing what is doubtful in order to stay clear of doing something *haram*.[4]
- In Islam, the *haram* has universal applicability, for that which is forbidden to a non-Arab cannot be permitted to an Arab, or that is restricted for a black person cannot be allowed to a white person. Islam contains no privileged classes or individuals who, in the name of religion, can do whatever they please according to their whims. No Muslim can forbid something to others but allow it for himself or herself, for God is the Lord of all and Islam is the guide for all. Whatever God has legislated through the Religion that He has sent for humanity is lawful for all people, and whatever He has forbidden is forbidden to all people until the Day of Resurrection.

Eating and Drinking

The following products are definitely lawful: milk (from cows, camels, sheep, and goats), honey, fish, plants that do not intoxicate, fresh or naturally frozen vegetables, fresh or dried fruits; legumes and nuts (e.g., peanuts, cashew nuts, hazel nuts, walnuts), and grains (e.g., wheat, rice, rye, barley, oats). Such animals as cows, sheep, goats, deer, geese, chickens, ducks, and birds such as partridges are lawful, but they must be slaughtered or killed according to Islamic rites before being eaten.

Slaughtering animals in the Islamic manner (*zabiha*) and following Islam's dietary rules are excellent ways to avoid certain diseases. Slaughter is performed to ensure the meat's quality and to avoid any microbial contamination. Lawful animals must be killed in such a way that all of the blood is drained from the animal's body.

The Islamic method of slaughtering an animal is to cut its throat, so that the blood runs out and does not congeal in the veins. Thus, animals that have been strangled, beaten to death, or died in a fight or accident cannot be eaten. The one who slaughters the animal must be a mature sane Muslim, who slaughters it while reciting *Bismillah* (In God's Name) with a sharp device and without severing its head. The animal must be completely dead before it is skinned.

A product is considered *haram* if it has any contact with, or contains anything from:

- Pigs, dogs, donkeys, and carnivorous animals (e.g., bears and lions).
- Animals that are ugly or filthy in nature or live on filthy things, and those that are detestable by human nature (e.g., reptiles, insects, worms, lice, flies, rats, scorpions, centipedes, frogs, turtles, hedgehogs, moles, and cockroaches) (Qur'an, 7:157).
- Animals killed by strangulation, a blow to the head (clubbing), a headlong fall, natural causes (carrion), or being gored or attacked by another animal (5:3–4). Fish are exempted from this class. When the Messenger was asked about the sea, he replied, "Its water is pure and its dead are *halal*."[5]
- All animals, except fish, that are not sacrificed according to Islamic rules, or those that are slaughtered without God's Name being pronounced over them (Qur'an, 6:121).

- Alcohol, harmful substances, and poisonous and intoxicating plants or drinks (e.g., opium, and all contemporary intoxicating hard and soft drugs, whether natural or chemical) (5:90–91).
- Animals with protruding canine or molar teeth (e.g., monkeys, cats, lions);[6] birds and other animals with talons or those which hunt and tear up their prey with their paws or claws (e.g., owls and eagles).[7]
- Animals slaughtered for worship of, or in the name of, that which is not God (2:173; 5:3; 6:145).
- Any meat that has been cut off a live animal.[8]
- Carrion, blood outpoured (not that which is left in the veins of such organs as the liver and spleen when an edible animal is slaughtered), and animals won in a bet or a game of chance (5:3; 7:157).
- Food additives whose raw materials are forbidden and produced through a process incompatible with Islam.
- Human and animal urine and waste matter, parts obtained from still-living animals (except for wool, hair, horns, and so on), and the milk of animals that cannot be eaten (e.g., donkeys, cats, and pigs).

Medical Necessity

Jurists differ over whether some of the forbidden food substances can be used as medicine. Some do not classify medicine as a "compelling necessity" like food based upon the following *hadith*: "Assuredly, God did not provide a cure for you in what He has forbidden to you."[9] Others consider the need for medicine equal to that of food, for both are necessary for preserving life. However, they maintain that any medicine containing a *haram* substance is permissible only under the following conditions: if the patient's life is endangered when the medicine is not taken; if there is no entirely *halal* alternative or substitute medication available; and if the medication is prescribed by a Muslim physician who is both knowledgeable and God-conscious.

Hunting and Game Animals

- For game animals to be lawful, the hunter must be a Muslim or one of the People of the Book. A Muslim cannot hunt while in the state of *ihram* (Qur'an, 5:1, 5).
- The hunter should not hunt merely for sport, meaning that he or she kills animals but has no intention of eating them or otherwise benefiting from them.
- The weapon should pierce the animal's body, making a wound, for death by impact (e.g., hitting a deer with a car) does not make it *halal* (5:3–4).
- The hunter must say *Bismillah* when hurling or striking with the weapon, or dispatching the hunting animal (5:4).
- If a dog, a falcon, or a similar animal is used, it should be a trained animal and catch the game animal only for its owner (5:4).

Intoxicants

Khamr, translated as intoxicants, signifies any alcoholic drink that causes intoxication. Humanity has been afflicted with no greater calamity than alcohol. If statistics were collected worldwide of all the patients in hospitals who, due to alcohol, suffer from mental disorders, delirium tremens, nervous breakdowns, and digestive ailments and added to those collected worldwide regarding the suicides, homicides, bankruptcies, sales of properties, and broken homes related to alcohol consumption, the number of such cases would be so staggering that, in comparison, all exhortation and preaching against it would seem too little.

Whatever intoxicates is haram. The first declaration made by the noble Messenger of God, upon him be peace and blessings, concerning this matter was that in whatever form or under whatever name it may appear, whatever intoxicates is *khamr* and therefore forbidden. Thus, beer and similar drinks are *haram*. When the Messenger was asked about certain drinks made from honey, corn, or barley by the process of fermentation until they became alcoholic, he replied succinctly, "Every intoxicant is *khamr*, and every *khamr* is *haram*."[10]

Whatever Intoxicates in Large Amounts Is Haram in Any Amount. Islam takes an uncompromising stand on prohibiting intoxicants, regardless of whether the amount is little or much. If an individual is permitted to take just one step down this road, other steps follow. The person starts walking and then running, and does not stop at any stage. This is why the Messenger said, "Of that which intoxicates in a large amount, a small amount is *haram*."[11]

Drugs or "Khamr Is What Befogs the Mind." 'Umar ibn al-Khattab declared from the Messenger's pulpit, that "*Khamr* is what befogs the mind," thus providing us with a decisive criterion for classifying items as *khamr*.[12] There is no room for any uncertainty, for any substance that befogs or clouds the mind, as well as impairs its faculties of thought, perception, and discernment, is forbidden by God and His Messenger until the Day of Resurrection. This definitely includes such drugs as marijuana, cocaine, and opium.

Trading in Alcohol. The Messenger forbade any trading in alcohol, even with non-Muslims.[13]

The Consumption of Tobacco and Other Harmful Things. A general Islamic rule is that it is *haram* to eat or drink anything that may cause death, either quickly or gradually, such as poison, or substances that injure one's health or harm one's body. Thus, if tobacco or another substance is proven to harm one's health, it is *haram*, especially if a physician has told the patient to quit smoking. Even if it were not injurious to one's health, it is still a waste of money and brings no religious or secular benefit, and the Qur'an forbids wasting one's property (7:31; 17:26–27). This becomes more serious when the money spent on such items is needed to support oneself and one's family.

Clothing and Adornment

From the Islamic point of view, clothing has two purposes: to cover the body and to beautify the appearance. God Almighty counts

His bestowal of clothing and adornment upon human beings as one of His favors to humanity: *O children of Adam! Assuredly, We have sent down on you clothing to cover your private parts, and garments for adornment* (7:26).

Before dealing with questions of adornment and good appearance, Islam addressed itself in considerable depth to the question of cleanliness, for cleanliness is the essence of good appearance and the beauty of every adornment.

Gold Ornaments and Pure Silk Clothing. Islam forbids gold ornaments and clothing of pure silk to men, but permits them to women.[14]

Women's Clothing. Islam makes it *haram* for women to wear clothes that do not cover the body, that are transparent, and that are tight fitting enough to delineate the parts of the body, and that display their charms. (Qur'an, 24:31).[15]

Dressing for Ostentation and Pride. The general rule for enjoying life's good things (e.g., food, drink, and clothing) is that they should be enjoyed without extravagance or pride. Extravagance consists of exceeding the limits of what is beneficial in the use of the *halal*, while pride is something related to the intention and the heart rather than to what is apparent. Pride is defined as the intention to look superior and above others, and God does not love any proud boaster (57:23). In order to avoid even the suspicion of pride, the Messenger forbade garments of "fame" (i.e., clothes worn to impress others and that generate competition in vain and idle pursuits).[16]

Going to Extremes in Beautification. Islam denounces such excesses in beautifying oneself that require altering one's physical features as God has created them. The Qur'an considers such alterations as inspired by Satan, who will command them (his devotees) to change what God Almighty has created (4:119).

Items Related to Luxurious Living and Paganism. Muslims may adorn their houses with flowers, decorated fabrics, and other permitted ornamental objects. They are free to desire beauty in their homes and elegance in clothing. However, Islam disapproves of excess, and the Messenger did not like Muslims to fill their houses with luxurious and extravagant items or items related to paganism, for Islam has condemned luxury, extravagance, and paganism.[17]

Useful Information

Gold and Silver Utensils. In accordance with what has been stated above, Islam has forbidden the use of gold and silver utensils and pure silk spreads.[18]

Commemorating Great People. Islam abhors any excessive glorification of people, no matter how "great" they may be or whether they are living or dead. The Messenger, upon him be peace and blessings, also gave similar warnings. For example, he said, "Do not glorify me in the same manner as the Christians glorify Jesus, son of Mary, but say, 'He is a servant of God and His Messenger.'"[19] A religion that views even the Messenger of God in such a light is one of such moderation that it cannot tolerate the erecting of idol-like statues for some individuals, so that people may point to them with admiration and esteem. Many pretenders to greatness and self-proclaimed makers of history have slipped into the hall of fame through this open door, since those who are able to do so erect statues or monuments to themselves, or let their admirers do so, so that people do not appreciate those who are truly great.

It should, however, be noted here that some people talk about God's Messenger in a way that is not respectful. The Qur'an warns us against any word or action which may suggest disrespect for him (49:1–5). The Prophet's warning above is in order to prevent Muslims from going to extremes concerning him as Christians did in respect of Prophet Jesus, and therefore preserve *tawhid*. He also warned against having any unbecoming opinion about any Prophet, saying, "It is not right for a person that he should say, 'I am better than Yunus (Jonah) ibn Matta.'"[20] The Bible contains many calumnies against some Prophets, and just as the Qur'an restores the Prophets to their genuine rank, our noble Prophet, upon him be peace and blessings, also warned his Community against any wrong opinion about them. However, he also declared:

> I am Muhammad and I am Ahmad, and I am *al-Mahi* (the obliterator) by whom unbelief will be obliterated, and I am *al-Hashir* (the gatherer) at whose feet humankind will be gathered, and I am *al-'Aqib* (the last to come) after whom there will be no Prophet.[21]
>
> I am the most lovable to God, but I am not boastful of this. I will be the first to be resurrected when humans are raised from the dead on the Resurrection Day, but I am not boastful of this. When they come up to God's Presence, I will be their spokesman. When they despair of mercy and forgiveness, I will give them the glad tidings of God's mercy and forgiveness, and I will be the first who will intercede (on people's behalf) and whose intercession will be accepted, but I am not boastful of this. I hold the flag of praise on that day, and Adam and everyone else will stand under it, but I am not boastful of this. I am the most valuable of Adam's children in my Lord's sight, but I am not boastful of this.[22]

Therefore, while avoiding going into extremes concerning our Prophet and other great persons, we should also avoid not paying the necessary respect to them, particularly to the noble Prophet, whom God Almighty sent as a mercy for all worlds (Qur'an, 21:107). We must love him as much as possible and try to follow him or his *Sunna* in every dimension of our life. The Qur'an declares, *The Prophet has a higher claim on the believers than they have on their own selves* (33:6). The noble Prophet himself, upon him be peace and blessings, said, "No one can be a believer unless I am dearer to him than the members of his household, his wealth and the whole of humankind."[23]

Children's Toys. Children's toys in the form of human beings, animals, and the like are allowed in Islam.[24]

Keeping Dogs without Necessity. Keeping dogs inside the house as pets was forbidden by the Messenger. Dogs kept for a purpose (e.g., hunting or guarding cattle or crops) are allowed.

Condemned Industries and Professions. Islam has forbidden certain professions and industries because they are harmful to society's beliefs, morals, honor, or good manners. Among these are prostitution, erotic arts, and manufacturing intoxicants and drugs.

TRADE

The Qur'an and the *hadith* urge Muslims to engage in trade and commerce, and to travel in order to "seek God's bounty."

Forbidden Trades. Islam forbids all trade that involves injustice, cheating, making exorbitant profits, or promoting that which is *haram*. Examples of such trades are doing business in alcoholic beverages, intoxicants, drugs, pigs, idols, or anything whose consumption and use has been forbidden. Any related earnings are considered sinful.

Even if the trading is in entirely *halal* things, merchants must still adhere to many moral considerations, such as not lying and cheating, for those who cheat are considered to be outside the Islamic community; not tampering with the scales when weighing; not hoarding, lest they forfeit the protection of God and His Messenger; and not dealing in usury or interest (*riba*), for God has forbidden it. The Qur'an repeatedly warns against dealing in fraud, saying for example: *Woe to those who deal in fraud—those who, when they are to receive their due from others, demand that it be in full; but when they measure or weigh out for others, they make it less than the due* (83:1–3). God's Messenger declared, "He who deceives us (who acts dishonestly towards us) is not of us."[25]

Sales Involving Uncertainty. The Messenger forbade any kind of transaction that could lead to a quarrel or litigation due to some uncertainty.[26]

Price Manipulation. In Islam, the market is to be free and allowed to respond to the natural laws of supply and demand. Unnecessary interference in the freedom of individuals is unjust.[27] However, if any forbidden artificial forces (e.g., hoarding and price manipulation) interfere in the free market, public interest takes precedence over the individual's freedom. In such a situation, price control becomes permissible in order to meet society's needs and to protect it from greedy opportunists by thwarting their schemes. Scholars have concluded that, depending upon the nature of the circumstances, price controls may be either unjust and forbidden or just and permissible, depending upon the relevant circumstances.

Hoarding. Freedom for the individual and natural competition in the marketplace are guaranteed by Islamic jurisprudence. Nevertheless, it severely condemns those who, driven by ambition and greed, accumulate wealth at the expense of others and become rich by manipulating the price of food and other necessities.[28]

Interfering in the Free Market. The noble Messenger of God, upon him be peace and blessings, forbade another practice related to hoarding: allowing a person in the town to sell on behalf of a person from the desert. Scholars have explained this as follows: A stranger would bring some goods to be sold in town at the current market price, or that stranger is unaware of the market prices. A townsman would approach him, saying, "Leave them with me and I will sell them for you." If this resulted in the deception of the stranger, it was also possible that if the stranger had sold his own goods, the price would have been lower, the people would have benefited, and he would have made a reasonable profit.[29]

Brokerage. With the exception of such unlawful cases as mentioned above, brokerage is permissible, since it is a kind of mediation and connection between the buyer and the seller, which in many cases facilitates a profitable transaction for at least one of them or for both.[30] In modern times, brokers have become far more necessary than before due to the complexities of trade and commerce, which involve all types of exports and imports, and wholesale and retail sales and purchases. Brokers play an important role in keeping things moving. There is nothing wrong, therefore, if they charge a commission for their services. The commission may be a fixed amount, proportional to the volume of sales, or whatever is agreed upon among the parties involved.

Exploitation and Fraud. In order to prevent the market's manipulation, the Messenger forbade *najash*. This is when someone bids for an item in excess of its price without having any intention of actually buying it, but merely in order to induce others to bid still higher. Many times this is prearranged for the purpose of deceiving others.[31]

Frequent Swearing. The sin of deceiving becomes greater when a seller supports it by swearing in God's name that something is true. God's Messenger told merchants to avoid swearing in general, saying, "Swearing produces a ready sale but blots out the blessing."[32] Swearing in support of a lie, in particular, is a grave sin.[33]

He disapproved of frequent swearing in business transactions because it is probably done to deceive people, and because it reduces respect for God's Name.

Withholding Full Measure. One way of defrauding customers is to measure or weigh inaccurately. The Qur'an orders full measure and full weight (6:152; 17:35) and severely warns against any fraud in this aspect of business transactions (83:1–6):

Buying Stolen Property. In order to combat crime and to confine criminals within a very narrow sphere of activity, Islam has forbidden Muslims to buy any article that they know to be usurped, stolen, or taken unjustly from its owner. Anyone who does so abets the usurper, the thief, or the one committing injustice.

Interest. Islam permits an increase in capital through trade. At the same time, it blocks the way for anyone who tries to increase his or her capital through lending on usury or interest (*riba*), whether at a low or a high rate. The Qur'an contains severe threats concerning interest. For example:

> O you who believe! Keep from disobedience to God and try to attain piety in due reverence for Him, and give up what remains (due to you) from interest, if you are (in truth) believers. If you do not (and you persist in taking interest, whether regarding it

> as lawful or not) be warned of war from God and His Messenger. If you sincerely repent (and give up all interest transactions completely), you will have your principal. Then you will neither be doing wrong nor being wronged. If the debtor is in straitened circumstances, let him have respite until the time of ease; if you make any remission (of his debt) by way of charity, this is better for you, if only you knew. And guard yourselves against a Day in which you will be brought back to God (with all your deeds referred to His judgment). Then every soul will be repaid in full what it has earned (while in the world), and they will not be wronged. (2:278–281)

Sale for Deferred Payment (Credit). While it is best to buy an article with cash, it is also permissible to buy on credit by mutual consent. Some jurists opine that if the seller increases his or her price and if the buyer asks for deferred payments, as is common in installment buying, the price differential due to the time delay resembles interest, which is likewise a price for time. Accordingly, they declare such sales to be *haram*. However, most scholars permit it because there is, on the whole, no resemblance to interest in such a transaction, since the seller is free to increase the price as he or she considers proper, as long as it does not cause blatant exploitation or clear injustice. If it does, it becomes *haram*. In order for such trade to be lawful, there should be mutual consent and the amount and the duration should be fixed and known to both sides.[34]

Granting Time to the Debtor in Difficulty and Showing Him or Her Tolerance. Both the Qur'an and the Messenger, upon him be peace and blessings, encourage creditors to give a debtor in strained circumstances respite until the time of ease, and even make any remission by way of charity (Qur'an, 2:280).[35]

A Debtor Must Try to Pay His or Her Debt in Time. Even though it is a meritorious act that a creditor shows tolerance in collecting his credit, a debtor must try to pay his or her debt in time. The Messenger declared, "Good amongst God's servants is he who is best in paying off debt."[36]

Auction. Selling something at a reasonable auction is permissible.[37]

Untrue Advertising Is Forbidden. Trying to sell something or raise its price through untrue advertising is forbidden.[38]

Everything Must Be Clear in Transactions. There must not be any unclear point in transactions. The buyer and seller must know the price, the goods in all their aspects—including the exact amount or size according to their kind, and their defects if there are any—and the time and amount of the payment.[39] A person cannot sell any goods which are not in his or her possession and disposal.[40] If the seller does not disclose any defect in his or her goods, which is a sin, the buyer can return them when he or she comes to know it.[41]

The Option to Cancel the Transaction. Both the buyer and seller have the option to cancel or confirm the transaction before leaving the meeting where the bargain is struck.[42]

Trading in Forbidden Things. Trading in forbidden things is also forbidden (*haram*). For example, God's Messenger forbade the sale of intoxicants, idols, and carcasses.[43]

Paying in Advance. There is a kind of transaction called *salam*, in which payment is made in advance. It is permissible on condition that the exact amount of the goods and the time of payment are specified.[44]

Bribery. Giving or taking a bribe is one way of consuming someone else's wealth wrongfully. A bribe refers to any kind of property offered to a judge or public servant in order to obtain a favorable decision for oneself or against a rival, to expedite one's own affair, or to delay any competition, and so on. Islam strictly forbids bribery. The Qur'an declares:

> Do not consume your wealth among yourselves in false ways; nor proffer it to those in authority so that you may sinfully consume a portion of other people's goods, and that knowingly. (2:188)

God's Messenger cursed both the one who gives a bribe and the one who takes it.[45] He also forbade public officials to receive gifts from people.[46]

Wasteful Spending. Just as the wealth of others is sacred and any violation of it, whether secret or open, is forbidden, a person's wealth is sacred with respect to oneself. Thus, one should not waste it by extravagant or other wasteful spending. The Qur'an repeatedly bans wasteful spending (6:141; 7:31; 17:26), asserting that squanderers are the brothers and sisters of Satan (17:27)

Salaried Employment. Muslims are free to seek employment with a government, an organization, or an individual, as long as they can do their job satisfactorily and carry out their duties. However, they cannot seek a job for which they are unfit, especially if the job carries judicial or executive authority.[47]

Forbidden Types of Employment. Muslims cannot take jobs that are injurious to the cause of Islam or harm Muslims. Accordingly, they cannot work for companies that manufacture *haram* items. Similarly, any service rendered in support of injustice or in promoting what is *haram* is itself *haram*. For example, Muslims cannot work in organizations that deal with interest, in bars or liquor shops, nightclubs, and the like.

Pre-emption in Every Joint Ownership. There is a pre-emption in every joint undivided property. It is not lawful for one who has a partner in a dwelling or a garden to sell it until he or she is permitted by his or her partner. However, when the boundaries are well marked or the ways and streets are fixed, there is no pre-emption.[48]

Intervention in a Bargain Already Concluded. God's Messenger, upon him be peace and blessings, declared, "No town-dweller should sell for a desert-dweller. Do not offer a high price for a thing which you do not want to buy, in order to deceive the people. No Muslim should offer more for a thing already bought by his Muslim brother, nor should he demand the hand of a girl already engaged to another Muslim. A Muslim woman shall not try to bring about the divorce of her sister (i.e. another Muslim woman) in order to take her place herself."[49]

A General Rule in Earning a Living. A Muslim must be careful that whatever he or she does or says is lawful. God's Messenger warns, saying, "A time will come when one will not care how one gains one's money, legally or illegally."[50] Another important thing to note is that every man must try to earn his living by working and avoid asking others to provide for him. The Messenger declares, "Nobody has ever eaten a better meal than that which one has earned by working with one's own hands. The Prophet of God, David used to eat from the earnings of his manual labor."[51] As is known, Prophet David, upon him be peace, was a caliph or the ruler of a very powerful state. The Messenger also says, "It is better to take a rope and cut wood and carry it than ask from others."[52]

One of the other important rules is that any transaction in which one person's gain results in another's loss is unlawful, while any transaction that is fair and beneficial to all the parties concerned and that is transacted by mutual consent is lawful.

The verses:

> O you who believe! Do not consume one another's wealth in wrongful ways, except it be dealing by mutual agreement; and do not destroy yourselves (individually or collectively by following wrongful ways. Be ever mindful that) God has surely been All-Compassionate toward you (particularly as believers). Whoever acts wrongfully through enmity (toward others) and by way of deliberate transgression and wronging (both himself and others), We will surely land him in a Fire to roast therein; that indeed is easy for God. (4:29–30)

Other Activities

Illicit Sexual Intercourse. All revealed religions have forbidden fornication and adultery (*zina*). Islam, the last of the Divinely revealed religions, is very strict in prohibiting *zina* (4:3, 15–16, 25; 17: 24:2–9; 17:32; 60:12), for it leads to confusion of lineage, child abuse, family break-ups, bitterness in relationships, the spread of venereal diseases, and a general laxity in morals. Moreover, it opens the door to a flood of lust and self-gratification.

When Islam prohibits something, it closes all the avenues of approach to it. This is achieved by prohibiting every step and every means leading to what is *haram*. Accordingly, whatever excites passions, opens ways for illicit sexual relations outside marriage, and promotes indecency and obscenity is *haram*.

Superstitions, Divination, and Myths. Soothsayers or diviners existed in Arab society during the Messenger's time. They deceived people by pretending to reveal information about past and future events through their contact with jinn or other secret sources. The Messenger struggled against this deception, which had no basis in knowledge, Divine guidance, or revealed Scripture. For the same reason, divination with arrows and making decisions based upon what is observed in sand, seashells, tea leaves, cards, and palms, as well as fortune-telling by cards and similar methods, are all forbidden.[53] The Qur'an describes them as among loathsome evils of Satan's doing (5:90).

Magic. Although Islam admits the effect of magic and the evil eye, it absolutely condemns magic and those who practice it. God's Messenger, upon him be peace and blessings, counted the practice of magic among those major deadly sins that destroy nations before destroying individuals, and that degrade those who practice them.[54] Some jurists consider magic as unbelief (*kufr*) or as leading toward unbelief.

Omens. Drawing evil omens from certain articles, places, times, individuals, and the like was, and still is, a current superstition.[55]

Relaxing the Mind. Following the Messenger's example, his noble and pure Companions relaxed their bodies and minds. 'Ali ibn Abi Talib said, "Minds get tired, as do bodies, so treat them with humor," and, "Refresh your minds from time to time, for a tired mind becomes blind." Abu al-Darda said, "I entertain my heart with something trivial in order to make it stronger in the service of the truth."

Thus, there is no harm if Muslims entertain themselves to relax their mind or refresh themselves with some permissible sport or activity. However, the pursuit of pleasure should not become the goal of their life so that they devote themselves to it, forgetting their religious obligations. Nor should one joke about serious matters. It has been aptly said, "Season your conversation with humor in the same proportion as you season your food with salt."

Muslims are forbidden to joke and laugh about other people's values and honor. Such sports and games as racing on foot, archery, spear play, and swimming are permissible.

Singing and Music. Among the entertainments that may comfort the soul, please the heart, and refresh the ear is singing. Islam permits music under certain conditions. In order to bring about an atmosphere of happiness and refreshment, it is recommended on such festive occasions as the *'Iyd* days, weddings and wedding feasts, births, and *'aqiqat* (thanksgiving to God for the birth of a baby by sacrificing a sheep). However, there are some limitations placed upon music:

- The song's subject matter should not be against Islam's teachings. For example, if the song praises wine and invites people to drink, singing or listening to it is *haram*. It also must not stir up pessimism and despair.
- Although the subject matter may not be against Islamic teachings, the way of singing (e.g., bodily movements that stir up lust or impulses to commit *haram* acts) may render it *haram*.
- Islam opposes excess and extravagance in anything, so it cannot tolerate excessive involvement with entertainment. Too much time should not be wasted in such activities.
- Each individual is the best judge of himself or herself. If a certain type of singing arouses one's passions, leads one toward sin, excites the animal instincts, and dulls spirituality, one must avoid it so that one will not cave into temptation.

- There is unanimous agreement that if singing is done in conjunction with *haram* activities like attending a drinking party, or if it is mixed with obscenity and sin, it is *haram*.
- Music like religious hymns or tunes which arouse feelings of love of God, consideration of the afterlife, serving the Religion, and heroism and the like is regarded as advisable.[56]

Gambling, the Companion of Drinking. While permitting a variety of games and sports, Islam prohibits any game that involves betting (e.g., has an element of gambling). Muslims cannot seek relaxation and recreation in, or acquire money by, gambling.

The Qur'an mentions drinking and gambling together (5:90–91), since their harmful effects on the individual, family, and society are very similar. What is more like alcoholism than an addiction to gambling? This is why one is rarely found without the other. The Qur'an is absolutely right when it teaches us that both drinking and gambling are inspired by Satan, that they are akin to idolatry and divining by arrows, and that they are abominable habits that must be shunned.

The Lottery. Lotteries and raffles are also forms of gambling. There should be no laxity or permissiveness toward them in the name of "charitable institutions" or "humanitarian causes."

Movies. Movies may be regarded as permissible if the following conditions are met:

- The content must be free of sin and immorality—indeed, of anything that is against Islamic beliefs, morals, and manners. Portrayals that excite sexual desire or greed, glorify crime, or propagate deviant ideas, false beliefs, and the like are not permissible, and Muslims cannot watch or encourage them.
- Watching movies should not result in the neglect of religious obligations or worldly responsibilities.
- Physical intermingling and free mixing among men and women in movie theaters must be avoided in order to prevent sexual undertones and temptation.

Some other matters included in *Halal* and *Haram*, such as settling disputes, the sanctity of life, backbiting, suspicion, and so on, will be mentioned in the third volume of this series concerning Islamic morality.

Sin

What Is Sin?

Sin is committing something that God and His Messenger have forbidden and not doing what they ordered to do. Since a believer's heart and conscience are sensitive to sin and obedience to God, God's Messenger said, "Righteousness is good morality, and sin is that which causes discomfort (or pinches) within your soul and which you dislike people to become informed of."[57] In other words, sin is what Muslims try to refrain from at all costs.

The Major Sins (al-Kaba'ir)

The major sins are those acts that God Has forbidden and threatened to punish severely if they are committed. God instructs us to avoid them:

> If you avoid the major sins which you have been forbidden, We will blot out from you your minor evil deeds and make you enter by a noble entrance to an abode of glory. (4:31)

Scholars differ in this regard. There are Prophetic Traditions (*hadith*) that mention the major sins, which are as follows: Associating anything with God as a partner, disrespecting one's parents and violating their rights, despairing of God's mercy or regarding oneself as secure from His punishment, unjust killing, fornication and adultery, devouring usury, consuming an orphan's property, magic, drinking alcohol, gambling, turning back when the army advances, and slandering chaste women who are believers but indiscreet.[58]

However, the Traditions do not limit the major sins only to those mentioned. Rather, they point to the types of sin that fall into the category of "major" without excluding others, such as betraying public trusts, breaking one's word, giving false evidence in a court, not carrying out any of the obligatory religious duties, all of which are also included in this category.

What follows is a list of major sins:

- Unbelief in any of the essentials requiring belief (*kufr*)
- Hypocrisy (*nifaq*)
- Associating partners with God (*shirk*)
- Neglecting any of the pillars of Islam (i.e., the prescribed Prayers, paying *Zakah*, fasting Ramadan, and *Hajj*)
- Violating one's parents' rights
- Murder
- Practicing magic
- Adultery, fornication, and homosexual acts
- Dealing with usury and interest
- Theft and usurpation
- Consuming alcohol
- Gambling
- Slandering innocent people, especially chaste women
- Fleeing the battlefield
- Wrongfully consuming an orphan's property
- Lying
- Backbiting
- Gossiping
- Mocking others
- Spying and suspicion
- Abandoning relatives
- Wrongdoing and injustice
- Fraud and cheating
- Violating other people's rights
- Pride and arrogance
- Bearing false witness and taking a false oath

- Oppression
- Consuming wealth acquired unlawfully
- Giving short weight or measure
- Committing suicide
- Giving and accepting bribes
- Showing-off
- Using the Religion or "God's signs" for worldly benefits
- Betraying a trust, especially public trusts
- Despairing of God's mercy or regarding oneself as secure from His punishment
- Listening to private conversations
- Breaking one's promise
- Fortune-telling and believing in fortune-tellers
- Making idols and engaging in idolatrous practices
- Trading in unlawful things
- Displaying overbearing conduct toward one's spouse, servant, children, weak people, and animals
- Offending neighbors
- Offending and abusing Muslims
- Wearing silk and gold (men only)
- Sacrificing an animal in the name of that which is not God
- Knowingly ascribing one's paternity to one who is not one's real father.

Muslims must try not to commit any sins. When they fall or sin, they must repent immediately and seek God's forgiveness. Scholars say that any sin, no matter how small, is great so long as it is committed with ease and indifference, without repentance, and without seeking God's forgiveness, while any major sin, no matter how great, is not great so long as it is avoided as much as possible and the one who commits it repents and seeks God's forgiveness.

Chapter 9

Prayers, Supplications, and Remembrance of God

PRAYERS, SUPPLICATIONS, AND REMEMBRANCE OF GOD

PRAYER

Belief requires prayer as a means of attainment and perfection, and our essence desperately needs it. God Almighty decrees, *Say (O Muhammad): "My Lord would not concern Himself with you but for your prayer"* (25:77), and, *Pray to Me and I will answer your (prayer)* (40:60).

If people say that they pray so many times but that their prayers are unanswered, despite the assurance given in the above verse, we should point out that an answered prayer does not necessarily mean its acceptance. There is an answer for every prayer. However, accepting the prayer and giving what is requested depends upon the All-Mighty's Wisdom. Suppose a sick child asks a doctor for a certain medicine. The doctor will give what is asked for, something better, or nothing. It all depends upon how the medicine will affect the child. Similarly, the All-Mighty, Who is the All-Hearing and the All-Seeing, answers His servant's prayer and changes his or her loneliness into the pleasure of His company. But His answer does not depend on the individual's fancies; rather, according to His Wisdom, He gives what is requested, what is better, or nothing at all for the supplicator's good.

Moreover, prayer is a form of worship and worship is rewarded mainly in the Hereafter. In essence, prayer is not done for worldly purposes, but worldly purposes are causes for the prayer. For example, praying for rain is a kind of worship occasioned by the lack of rain. If rain is the prayer's only aim, the prayer is unacceptable, for it is not sincere or intended to please God and obtain His approval.

Sunset determines the time for the evening Prayer, while solar and lunar eclipses occasion two particular kinds of worship. Since such eclipses are two means of manifesting Divine Majesty, the All-Mighty calls His servants to perform a form of worship particular to these occasions. The Prayer offered has nothing to do with causing the eclipse to end, for this is known already through astronomical calculations. The same argument applies to drought and other calamities, for all such events occasion certain kinds of prayer. At such times, we best realize our impotence and so feel the need to take refuge in the high Presence of the Absolutely Powerful One through prayer and supplication. If a calamity is not lifted despite many prayers, we should not say that our prayer has not been accepted. Rather, we should say that the time of prayer has not yet ended. God removes the calamity because of His endless Grace and Munificence. The end of that event marks the end of that special occasion for prayer.

We must pursue God's good pleasure through worship, affirm our poverty and weakness in our prayer, and seek refuge in Him through prayer. We must keep in mind that whatever God wills, happens, and thus never attempt to interfere in His Lordship, but rather pray to God and leave the result to Him with absolute confidence and reliance on His Wisdom. In addition, we should not accuse His Mercy.

Every creature offers its own kind of praise and worship to God. What reaches the Court of God from the universe is a kind of prayer. Some creatures, like plants and animals, pray through the tongue of their potential to achieve a full form and then display and show certain Divine Names (e.g., a plant's seeds grow into plants, and the joined semen and eggs of animals grow into animals. Since they have this potential, their natural disposition to mature is, in essence, a prayer. By doing so they affirm the manifestation of such Divine Names as the All-Sustaining and All-Forming).

Another kind of prayer is done in the tongue of natural needs. All living beings ask the Absolutely Generous One to meet their vital needs, as they cannot do so. Yet another kind of prayer is done in the tongue of complete helplessness. A living creature in straitened circumstances takes refuge in its Unseen Protector with a genuine supplication and turns to its All-Compassionate Lord. These three kinds of prayer are always acceptable, unless somehow impeded.

The fourth type of prayer is the one engaged in by humanity. This type falls into two categories: active and by disposition, and verbal and with the heart. For example, acting in accordance with causes is an active prayer. We try to gain God's approval by complying with causes, for causes cannot produce the result—only God can do that. Another type of active prayer is plowing the soil, for this is nothing other than knocking at the door of the treasury of God's Mercy. Such a prayer is usually acceptable, for it is an application to the Divine Name the All-Generous.

The second type of prayer, done with the tongue and the heart, is the ordinary one. This means that we ask God from the heart for something we cannot reach. Its most important aspect and finest and sweetest fruit is that we know that God hears us, is aware of our heart's contents, that His power extends everywhere, that He can satisfy every desire, and that He comes to our aid out of mercy for our weakness and inadequacy.

We should never abandon prayer, for it is the key to the Treasury of Mercy and the means of obtaining access to the Infinite Power. We should hold on to it and ascend to the highest rank of humanity and, as creation's most favored and superior member, include the whole universe's prayer in our prayer. We should say, on behalf of all beings, *From You alone do we seek help* (1:5), and become a beautiful pattern for all of creation.[1]

Supplications and Remembrance of God

All words of praise and glorification of God, extolling His Perfect Attributes of Power and Majesty, Beauty and Sublimity, whether one utters them with the tongue or says them silently in one's heart, are known as *dhikr* (remembrance of God). He has commanded us to remember Him always and forever: *O you who believe, celebrate the praises of God, and do so often; and glorify Him morning and evening* (33:41).

In a *hadith qudsi* (a Tradition whose meaning God inspired in the heart of the Messenger together with its wording) the Messenger narrated:

> God says, "I am to My servant as he expects of Me, I am with him when he remembers Me. If he remembers Me in his heart, I remember him to Myself; if he remembers Me in an assembly, I mention him in an assembly better than his; if he draws nearer to Me a hand's span, I draw nearer to him an arm's length; if he draws nearer to Me an arm's length, I draw nearer to him a fathom length; and if he comes to me walking, I rush to him with [great] speed."[2]

God has bestowed a special distinction upon those who remember Him. The Messenger, upon him be peace and blessings, said, "The example of him who remembers and mentions God in comparison to him who does not do so is that of a living one compared to a dead one."[3]

How Much Dhikr Is Required?

God, the Exalted, ordered that He should be remembered a great deal. Describing the wise men and women who ponder His signs, the Qur'an mentions: *those who remember God standing, sitting, and on their sides* (3:191), and, *those men and women who engage much in God's praise. For them has God prepared forgiveness and a great reward* (33:35). Mujahid, one of the earliest interpreters of the Qur'an, explained, "A person cannot be one of 'those men and women who remember God much' as mentioned in the above verse of the Qur'an, unless he or she remembers God at all times, standing, sitting, or lying in bed."[4]

The Excellence of Dhikr Assemblies

Joining assemblies or circles of *dhikr* is commendable, as shown by the following *hadith*: Ibn 'Umar reported, "The Prophet, peace be upon him, said, 'When you pass by a garden of Paradise, avail yourselves of it.' The Companions asked, 'What are the gardens of Paradise, O Messenger of God?' The Prophet, upon him be peace and blessings, replied, 'The assemblies or circles of *dhikr*. There are some angels of God who go about looking for such assemblies of *dhikr*, and when they find them they surround them.'"[5]

The Excellence of Istighfar

Asking God's forgiveness for one's sins is also of great importance. Said Nursi says that we should take prayer in one of our hands and seeking God's forgiveness in the other. Prayer urges and reinforces one's intention to do good deeds, while seeking His forgiveness discourages one from committing sins. God's Messenger is reported to have said, "God says, 'O Adam's child! So long as you pray to me in expectation from Me I overlook your sins and forgive you. O Adam's child! Even if your sins fill the space as far as the clouds, I overlook them and forgive you so long as you continue to ask Me to forgive you. O Adam's child! Even if you have sins to the fullness of the world, I overlook them and forgive you so long as you turn to Me without associating any partners with Me.'"[6] The Messenger also said, "God Almighty sent down to me two securities for my Community: *God is not to punish them so long as you are among them, and God is not to punish them while they implore Him for forgiveness for their sins* (8:33). When I depart from among them, I will leave asking Him for forgiveness as a means of security among them."[7]

Supplicating at the Most Opportune Times and Locations

These are, for instance, the day of 'Arafat, Ramadan, Friday, the last part of the night, dawn, after the prescribed Prayers, while in prostration, while it is raining, between the *adhan* and the *iqama*, when armies meet each other, times of strain and great need, and when one's heart is soft and tender.[8]

Praying for a Fellow Muslim in His or Her Absence

Safwan ibn 'Abdullah reported, "I visited Abu Darda's house in Syria. I did not find him there, but Umm Darda (his wife) was home.

She asked, 'Do you intend to perform *Hajj* this year?' I replied, 'Yes.' She said, 'Please supplicate to God for us, for God's Messenger, upon him be peace and blessings, used to say, "A Muslim's supplication for his or her fellow Muslim in his (her) absence is accepted. When he (she) asks for blessings for his (her) brother (sister), the commissioned angel says, 'Amen, may it be for you too!'"'"[9]

Beginning a Supplication

It is highly recommended that one should begin the prayer and supplication with praises of God, seeking His forgiveness for sins, calling God's blessings and peace upon His Messenger, as well as on his Family and Companions, and reciting some of His Names.[10]

Examples of God's Messenger's Prayers and Supplications

God's Messenger, upon him be peace and blessings, always prayed to God before any action. The books of Tradition (*hadith*) record no case in which he did not pray. As mentioned earlier, prayer is a mystery of servanthood to God, and the Messenger is the foremost in servanthood. This is made clear with every repetition of the declaration of faith: "I bear witness that there is no deity but God; I also bear witness that Muhammad is His servant and Messenger." Note that he is called servant before Messenger. Whatever he intended to do, he referred it to God through prayer.

God created us and our actions. Although we should take the necessary precautions and follow precedents to accomplish things in this world, where cause and effect have a special place, we should never forget that everything ultimately depends upon God for its existence. Therefore, we must combine action and prayer. This is also required by our belief in God's absolute Oneness.

The Messenger's knowledge of God can never be equaled. As a result, he was the foremost in love of, and paradoxically, in fear of Him. He was perfectly conscious that everything depends upon God for its existence and subsistence. Whatever God wills, happens: *When He wills a thing to be, He but says to it "Be!" and it is* (36:82). Fully aware of this, the Messenger did what he had to do and then, combining action with prayer, left the result to God with absolute confidence.

His supplications have been transmitted to us. When we read them, we see that they have deep meaning and accord exactly with the surrounding circumstances. They reflect profound belief, deep sincerity, absolute submission, and complete confidence. Some examples are given below:

In the Morning and Evening

- He used to recite *Surat al-Ikhlas*, *Surat al-Falaq*, and *Surat an-Nas* three times every morning and at night before going to bed.[11]
- We have reached evening and the whole creation, which is God's property, also has reached evening. All praise is due to God. There is no deity but God, the One Who has no partner with Him. His is the sovereignty, and all praise is due to Him. He has power over all things. O God, I ask You for the good of this night, and seek refuge in You from the evil of this night and the evil that follows it. O God, I seek refuge in You from sloth and from the evil of vanity. O God, I seek refuge in You from the torment of Hellfire and from the torment of the grave.[12]
- God, with Your help we have reached evening, and with Your help we will reach morning. With Your help we live and by Your command we die. To You is our return.[13]
- God, You are my Lord. There is no deity but You. You have created me, and I am Your servant. I try my best to keep my covenant with You and to live in the hope of Your promise. I seek refuge in You from the evil I have done. I acknowledge Your favors upon me and acknowledge my sins. So forgive me, for none forgives sins but You.[14]
- God, Creator of the heavens and the earth, Who knows the unseen and the seen, Lord and Possessor of everything. I testify that there is no deity but You. I seek refuge in You from the evil

within myself, from the evil of Satan, and from his inciting one to attribute partners to God.[15]

- In the Name of God, by Whose Name nothing in the earth or in the heaven can do any harm, and He is the All-Hearing, the All-Knowing.[16]
- I am pleased with God as Lord, with Islam as religion, and with Muhammad as Prophet.[17]
- God, I have reached morning and call You to bear witness, and the bearers of Your Throne, Your angels, and all Your creatures to bear witness, that You are God, other than Whom there is no deity, and that Muhammad is Your servant and Messenger.[18]
- God, I ask You for security in this world and in the Hereafter. O God, I ask You for forgiveness and security in my religion and my worldly affairs, in my family and my property. O God, cover my faults and keep me safe from the things I fear. O God, guard me from the front and the behind, from the right and the left, and from above. I seek in Your greatness the protection from unexpected harm from beneath.[19]
- God, grant me sound health. O God, grant me sound hearing. O God, grant me sound eyesight. There is no deity but You.[20]
- God, I have risen with Your help, blessings, security, and protection, so complete Your blessings upon me, Your security for me, and your protection in this world and in the Hereafter.[21]
- God suffices me. There is no deity but He. In Him is my trust, and He is the Lord of the Mighty Throne. (To be said seven times.)[22]
- God, You are my Lord. There is no deity but You. I put my trust in You. You are the Lord of the Mighty Throne. Whatever God wills happens, and whatever He does not will does not happen. There is neither power nor strength save with You, the Exalted, the Mighty. I know that God has power over all things, and God comprehends all things in knowledge. O God, I seek refuge with You from the evil of myself and from the evil of all creatures under Your control. Surely the straight way is my Sustainer's way.[23]

At Bed Time

- God, I have submitted my soul to You, turned my face towards You, entrusted my affair to You, and retreated unto You, in fear of You and with hope in You. There is no resort and no deliverer (from hardship) but You only. O God, I have believed in Your Book which You revealed and in Your Prophet whom You sent. O God, save me from Your punishment on the day when You will raise Your creatures. By Your Name I live and die.[24]
- God, Lord of the heavens, the earth, and the Mighty Throne, our Lord and the Lord of everything, Who causes the seed to grow and the date-stone to split and sprout, Who sent down the Torah and the Gospel and the Qur'an. I seek refuge in You from the evil of all evildoers under Your Control. You are the First and there is nothing before You, and You are the Last and there is nothing after You. You are the Outward and there is nothing beyond You, and You are the Inward and there is nothing more inward than You. Relieve us of our debt and poverty.[25]
- Every night when he went to bed, the Messenger would hold out his hands together imploringly and blow over them after reciting *Surat al-Ikhlas*, *Surat al-Falaq*, and *Surat an-Nas*. Then he would rub his hands three times over whichever parts of his body he was able to rub, starting with his head, face, and front of his body.[26]
- In Your name, O Lord, I lay myself down to sleep, and by Your permission I raise myself up. So if You take away my soul during sleep, forgive it. If You keep it alive after sleep, protect it just as You protect Your pious servants.[27]
- (*In bed*:) *Allahu akbar* (God is the Greatest) thirty-four times, *subhana'llah* (Glory be to God) thirty-three times, *al-hamdu li'llah* (All praise be to God) thirty-three times.[28]

Upon Waking Up

- Thanks be to God, Who returned my soul, made my body sound, and permitted me to remember Him.[29]

- There is no deity but You. Glory be to You. O God, I seek Your forgiveness for my sins and ask for Your mercy. O God, increase me in knowledge and let not my heart swerve after You have guided me on the right path. Grant me mercy from You, for You are the Grantor of bounties without measure.[30]
- There is no deity but God. He is One and has no partner. To Him belongs all praise and all authority, and He has power over all things. Praise be to God, glory be to God, there is no deity but God. God is the Greatest. There is neither power nor strength save with God.[31]

Upon Getting Dressed

- All thanks and praise be to God, Who has clothed me and given me sustenance, whereas I have no power, nor strength.[32]
- All praise and thanks be to God, Who has clothed me to cover my nakedness and made it a means of adornment for me.[33]

Upon Seeing Another Muslim Wearing Some New Clothes

- May you wear out this in health, may you wear out this in health![34]

Upon Leaving One's House

- There is no deity but God alone. He has no partners. His is the sovereignty, and His is all praise. He gives life, and causes to die, while He is ever-living, without dying. All good is in His hand, and He is powerful over everything.[35]
- In the Name of God. In God do I trust, and on God do I rely. O God, I seek Your refuge against going astray or leading others astray, slipping or causing others to slip, doing wrong or being wronged by others, and behaving arrogantly or being treated arrogantly by others.[36]

- In the name of God; I put my trust in God; there is no might and strength but with God.[37]

Upon Entering One's House

- One enters one's house saying, "In the Name of God, the All-Merciful, the All-Compassionate," "Peace be upon you," and then, "O God! I seek of You the best of entrances and the best of departures. In the Name of God we enter and in the Name of God we go out, and we put our trust in God, our Lord."[38]

When the Wind Blows

- God, I ask You for its good, and the good that is in it, and the good with which it is sent. I seek Your refuge against its evil, and the evil with which it is sent.[39]

Upon Hearing Thunder

- God, do not destroy us with Your wrath or let us perish with Your punishment. Give us good health before it comes to pass.[40]

During Sorrow, Grief, and Difficulties

- There is no deity but God, the Mighty, the Forbearing. There is no deity but God, the Lord of the Mighty Throne. There is no deity but God, the Lord of the heavens and the earth, and the Lord of the Throne of Honor.[41]
- The Ever-Living, O the Self-Subsisting by Whom all else subsist, I seek Your help by Your Grace.[42]
- God, I hope for Your Mercy, so do not entrust me to myself even for a twinkle of the eye. Set right all my affairs. There is no deity but You.[43]
- There is no deity but You. All glory be to You. I have indeed been one of the wrongdoers.[44]

- God, I am Your servant, son of Your servant, son of your maidservant. My rein is in Your hand. Your command concerning me prevails, and Your decision concerning me is just. I call upon You by every one of the All-Beautiful Names by which You have described Yourself, or which You have revealed in Your Book, or have taught any one of Your creatures, or which You have chosen to keep in the knowledge of the unseen with You, to make the Qur'an the delight of my heart, the light of my breast, and the remover of my griefs, sorrows, and afflictions.[45]

Upon Encountering the Enemy, and When One is Afraid of the Ruler

- O God, we make You our shield against them, and take refuge in You from their evils.[46]
- God is the All-Great, God is the All-Great; God is mightier than all His creation. God is mightier than whatever I fear and avoid. I seek refuge in God, Who is the only Deity besides whom there is no deity, and Who keeps the heaven against falling onto the earth without His leave, from the evil of Your servant "so and so" and his followers, and from the jinn and human beings. O God, be my protector against their evil. Exalted is Your glory, and the one who seeks refuge in You is honored, and there is no deity but You. (To be said three times).[47]
- God suffices us for everything, and an excellent Guardian is He.[48]

When in Debt

- God, make Your lawful bounties sufficient for me so as to save me from what is unlawful. From Your grace, grant me sufficient abundance to free me from the need of all except You.[49]
- God, I seek refuge in You from all worry and grief. I seek refuge in You from incapacity and slackness. I seek refuge in You from cowardice and miserliness. I seek refuge in You from being overcome by debt and being subjected to people.[50]

Comprehensive Prayers That Can Be Said at Any Time

- God, put between me and errors a distance as great as that which you have put between East and West. O God, cleanse me of my errors, just as a white garment is cleansed of dirt.[51]
- God, I ask You for all good, including what is at hand and what is deferred, what I already know and what I do not know. I take refuge in You from every evil, including what is at hand and what is deferred, what I already know and what I do not know.[52]
- God, nothing hinders what You grant, nor is anything granted that You hinder. A wealthy person cannot do us good, as wealth belongs to You.[53]
- God, I have not told anything, taken an oath, made a vow, or done anything that You did not previously will. Whatever You willed is, and whatever You did not will is not. There is neither power nor strength save with You. You are indeed All-Powerful over everything.[54]
- God, I ask You for contentment after misfortune, a peaceful life after death, the pleasure of observing Your Face, and a desire to meet You. I take refuge in You from wronging others and from being wronged, from showing animosity and being subject to animosity, and from erring or committing unforgivable sins. If You leave me to myself, you leave me in weakness, need, sinfulness, and error. I depend only upon Your Mercy, so forgive all my sins, for only You can do so. Accept my repentance, for You are the One Who accepts repentance, the All-Compassionate.[55]
- God, You deserve most to be mentioned, and none but You deserves to be worshipped. You are more helpful than anyone whose help may be sought, more affectionate than any ruler, more generous than anyone who may be asked for something, and more generous than anyone who gives. You are the Sovereign without partners, the Unique One without like. Everything is perishable except You. You are obeyed only by Your permis-

sion, and disobeyed only within Your knowledge. When somebody obeys You, You reward them; when someone disobeys You, You forgive them. You witness everything, being nearer to it than any other witness; and protect everything, being nearer to it than any other protector. You ordained the acts of all people and determined their time of death. You know what is in every mind, and all secrets are manifest to You. The lawful is what You have made lawful; the forbidden is what You have forbidden. Religion is what You have laid down; the command is what You have decreed. The creation is Your creation; the servants are Your servants. You are God, the All-Pitying, All-Compassionate. I ask You, for the sake of the light of Your Face, by which the heavens and the earth were illuminated, for the sake of every right belonging to You and for the sake of those who ask of You, to forgive me just in this morning and just in this evening, and to protect me, by Your Power, from Hellfire.[56]

- God, I seek refuge in You from all knowledge that gives no benefit, from a heart that does not feel awe of You, from an unsatisfied soul, and from a prayer that will not be answered.[57]
- God, I ask You for steadfastness in my affairs, resolution in guidance, gratitude for Your bounties and acceptable service to You, and a truthful tongue and a sound heart. I seek refuge in You from the evil of what You know. I ask You for the good of what You know, and Your forgiveness for what You already know. Surely You are the Knower of the Unseen.[58]
- God, I ask You to enable me to do good, refrain from vice, and love the poor. Forgive me and have mercy upon me. When You will people's deviation, dissension, and disorder in public life, make me die before taking part in that disorder. I ask You for Your love and for the love of those whom You love, and for the love of the acts that will bring me closer to Your love.[59]
- God, I ask You for the good in the beginning and in the end, in its most comprehensive form with its beginning and result, its manifest and secret kinds, and for the highest rank in Paradise.[60]

- God, help me remember and mention You, thank You, and worship You most properly.[61]
- God, I ask You for guidance, piety and reverence for You, chastity, and independence of others.[62]
- God, bring all of our affairs to a good conclusion. Protect us from disgrace and ignominy in the world, and from being tormented in the Hereafter.[63]
- God, we ask You for all of the good for which Your Prophet Muhammad asked You, and seek refuge in You from every evil from which Your Prophet Muhammad sought refuge in You.[64]

Invoking God's Blessings and Peace upon God's Messenger, His Family, and Companions

God Almighty says, *God and His angels send blessings to the Prophet. O you who believe, invoke the blessings of God on him, and pray to God to bestow His peace on him, greeting him with the best greeting* (33:56). God's sending blessings on the Prophet, upon him be peace and blessings, means that He praises him in front of the angels and has mercy upon him, and the blessings of angels mean their supplications invoking blessings upon the Prophet.

The Messenger himself said, "If anyone invokes blessings upon me once, God will bestow blessings upon him ten times over,"[65] and, "Whoever desires to be given (his or her reward) in full measure, should send salutations to us—the members of my family—and should say, 'O God, shower blessings upon Muhammad the Prophet, his wives, the mothers of the believers, his descendants, and the members of his family, as you showered blessings upon the family of Abraham. You are All-Praiseworthy, All-Sublime.'"[66]

Invoking God's Blessings and Peace upon the Messenger Whenever His Name Is Mentioned

Some Muslim scholars hold that it is obligatory to invoke God's blessings and peace upon the Messenger whenever his name is mentioned. They base their argument upon the *hadith*, "May the nose of the person in whose presence I am mentioned be covered with dirt if he (she) does not invoke blessings upon me. Let the nose of that person be smeared with dust who finds Ramadan but lets it come to an end without securing pardon for himself (or herself). May the nose of the person be smeared with dust whose aged parents, either one or both of them are still living, and who fails (i.e., by serving them) to enter Paradise."[67]

Other scholars opine that this *hadith* means urging and therefore invoking God's blessings and peace upon the Messenger only once during a gathering is obligatory. After that it is no longer necessary, although it is preferred and better to do so. In addition, it is preferred to invoke God's peace upon other Prophets and angels separately.

How Do I Become a Muslim?

Becoming a Muslim requires no special ceremony because it is a personal commitment. It is enough for one to believe and declare, "I bear witness that there is no deity but God, and I bear witness that Muhammad is His servant and Messenger" (*Ashhadu an la ilaha illa'llah wa ashhadu anna Muhammadan 'abduhu wa Rasuluh*). This declaration of faith should be made before two or more Muslim witnesses in order that one who makes it may be known as a Muslim, but the absence of such witnesses must not cause one to delay becoming a Muslim.

After becoming a Muslim, one should perform the major ablution (*ghusl*), begin to acquire more knowledge about Islam's principles and beliefs, as well as how to conduct one's life, and how to perform the lesser ablution (*wudu'*) and pray. After this, the new Muslim must do his or her best to learn other individual responsibilities. One of the best ways to do this is to seek out the company of Muslims who actively practice their faith and can explain its underlying principles and ultimate goals.

Notes

Introduction

1 Ahmad Ibn Hanbal, *al-Musnad*, 5:411.

2 Said Nursi, *Khutba-i Shamiya* ("The Sermon of Damascus"), included in *Risale-i Nur Külliyati* ("The Collection of the Risale-i Nur"), *Nesil Yayinlari*, Istanbul 1996, p. 1980.

Chapter 1: Cardinal articles of Islamic faith and virtues of belief

1 *Muslim*, "Iman" 1; *at-Tirmidhi*, "Iman" 4; *Abu Dawud*, "Sunna" 17.

2 Summarized from *al-Fiqhu'l-Akbar* by Imam Abu Hanifa, *Kitabu't-Tawhid* by Imam al-Maturidi, and *Sharhu Aqaid an-Nasafi* by Imam at-Taftazani.

3 Said Nursi, *The Words* (trans.), The Light, New Jersey 2005, pp. 327–332.

Chapter 2: *at-Tahara* (Cleanliness or Purification)

1 *Abu Dawud*, "Libas" 25.

2 *al-Bukhari*, "Iman" 26.

3 *Muslim*, "Tahara" 1; *at-Tirmidhi*, HN: 3517.

4 Imam al-Ghazali, *Ihya'u Ulumi'd-Din*, "Asraru't-Tahara."

5 Ibn Hanbal, *al-Musnad*, 1:34; 6:155.

6 ad-Daraqutni, *al-Mu'jam al-Kabir*, HN:7503; *Ibn Maja*, HN: 521.

7 *Abu Dawud*, "Tahara" 40; *an-Nasai*, "Tahara" 147.

8 *Muslim*, "Tahara" 97.

9 *al-Muwatta'*, "Tahara" 13; *at-Tirmidhi*, "Tahara" 69; *an-Nasa'i*, "Tahara" 54.

10 *Abu Dawud*, "Tahara" 38.

11 *al-Bukhari*, "Wudu" 33; *Muslim*, "Tahara" 97.

12 *Abu Dawud*, "Tahara" 34; *at-Tirmidhi*, "Tahara" 49.

13 *Abu Dawud*, "Tahara" 33: *at-Tirmidhi*, "Tahara" 509; *an-Nasa'i*, "Miyah" 3.

14 *al-Bukhari*, "Wudu" 68; *Muslim*, "Tahara" 95; *Abu Dawud*, "Tahara" 36.

15 *Abu Dawud*, "Sayd" 23; *at-Tirmidhi*, "At'ima" 4.

16 *al-Muwatta'*, "Tahara" 12; *at-Tirmidhi*, "Tahara"52; *an-Nasa'i*, "Miyah" 5.

17 *Muslim*, "Hayd" 105; *Abu Dawud*, "Libas" HN: 4114; *al-Bukhari*, vol. 3, HN: 424.

18 *Ibn Maja*, "At'ima" 29: Ibn Hanbal, 2:97.

19 *Muslim*, "Tahara" 105, 109; *an-Nasa'i*, "Tahara" 188/1, 5–6.

20 *Abu Dawud*, "At'ima" 25; *at-Tirmidhi*, "At'ima" 24; *an-Nasa'i*, "Dahaya" 44.

21 *al-Bukhari*, "Wudu" 33; *Muslim*, "Tahara" 27; *at-Tirmidhi*, "Tahara" 68; *an-Nasa'i*, "Tahara" 27.

22 Related by at-Tabarani in his *Mu'jam al-Awsat*; at-Haythami, *Majma' az-Zawaid*, 1:286.

23 *Muslim*, "Tahara" 22; *al-Bukhari*, "Wudu" 57.

24 *Abu Dawud*, "Tahara," HN: 382.

25 *Abu Dawud*, "Tahara," HN: 385.

26 *al-Bukhari*, "Wudu" 67; at-Tirmidhi, "At'ima" 8; *Abu Dawud*, "At'ima" 48.

27 Abu Dawud, "At'ima" 48.

28 *Muslim*, "Hayd" 105; *al-Muwatta'*, "Sayd" 17; *Abu Dawud*, "Libas" 4113, 4114.

29 *Fatawa-yi Hindiya*, 1:44.

30 *at-Tirmidhi*, "Tahara" 67; *an-Nasa'i*, "Tahara 33; *Ibn Maja*, "Tahara" 27.

31 *Muslim*, "Tahara" 105; *al-Bukhari*, "Wudu" 11; *at-Tirmidhi*, "Tahara" 8.

32 *Abu Dawud*, "Tahara" 1, 2; *at-Tirmidhi*, "Tahara" 16; *an-Nasa'i*, "Tahara 16.

33 *Muslim*, "Tahara" 68; *Abu Dawud*, "Tahara," 14; *at-Tirmidhi*, "Tahara" 17.

34 *at-Tirmidhi*, "Tahara" 8 (12); *an-Nasa'i*, "Tahara" 25; *al-Bukhari*, "Wudu" 62; *Muslim*, "Tahara" 73.

35 *al-Bukhari*, "Wudu" 15, 60; *Muslim*, "Tahara" 69, 73, 74.

36 *Muslim*, "Tahara" 57; *at-Tirmidhi*, "Tahara" 12; *Abu Dawud*, "Tahara" 4.

37 *al-Bukhari*, "Wudu" 9; *Muslim*, "Hayd" 32; *Abu Dawud*, "Tahara" 17; *at-Tirmidhi*, "Tahara" 5.

38 Related by Abu Dawud and an-Nasa'i; Ibn Qudama, *al-Mughni*, 1:202.

39 *al-Bukhari*, "Wudu" 58; *at-Tirmidhi*, "Tahara" 53; *an-Nasa'i*, "Jana'iz" 116.

40 *Abu Dawud*, "Tahara" 1, 2; *at-Tirmidhi*, "Tahara" 16; *an-Nasa'i*, "Tahara 16.

41 *Muslim*, "Tahara" 11; *al-Bukhari*, "Libas" 63; *at-Tirmidhi*, "Adab" 14.

42 *al-Bukhari*, "Anbiya" 30.

43 *Abu Dawud*, "Tarajjul" 4:4163.

44 *at-Tirmidhi* "Adab" 56; Ibn Hanbal, 2:179.

45 *al-Bukhari*, "Jumu'a" 8: *Muslim*, "Tahara" 42; *al-Muwatta'*, "Tahara" 15.

46 *al-Bukhari*, "Anbiya" 52; *Muslim*, "Fada'il" 27.

47 *Abu Dawud*, "Libas" 22: *an-Nasa'i*, "Ishrat at-Nisa' " 1 (7, 61).

48 *al-Bukhari*, "Hayd" 7; *al-Muwatta'*, "Tahara" 100.

49 *Muslim*, "Hayd" 14; *Abu Dawud*, "Tahara" 104: *at-Tirmidhi*, "Sawm" 67.

50 *al-Bukhari*, "Hayd" 7; *Abu Dawud*, "Manasik" 23.

51 *Abu Dawud*, "Manasik" 10; *at-Tirmidhi*, "Hajj" 100.

52 *at-Tirmidhi*, "Tahara" 98; *Ibn Maja*, "Tahara" 105.

53 *al-Bukhari*, "Hayd" 24; "Hajj" 81.

54 *Muslim*, "Hayd" 16; *Abu Dawud*, "Nikah" 47; *an-Nasa'i*, "Tahara" 181.

55 *al-Bukhari*, "Hayd" 5; *Muslim*, "Hayd" 1, 4; *Abu Dawud*, "Tahara" 107.

56 Qur'an, 2:222; *al-Bukhari*, "Hayd" 19; *Muslim*, "Hayd" 62.

57 *al-Bukhari*, "Wudu" 63; *Muslim*, "Hayd" 62, 63; *Abu Dawud*, "Tahara" 109.

58 *ash-Shawkani*, *Nayl al-Awtar*, 1:274; Fakhruddin az-Zaylai, *Tabyinu'l-Haqa'iq ala Kanzi'd-Daqa'iq*, 1:202.

59 *al-Bukhari*, "Ghusl" 4; *at-Tirmidhi*, "Tahara" 80; *Ibn Maja*, "Tahara" 80.

60 *al-Bukhari*, "Wudu" 34; *Muslim*, "Hayd" 81–83; *Abu Dawud*, "Tahara" 84.

61 *al-Bukhari*, "Ghusl" 22.

62 *Abu Dawud*, "Tahara" 95; at-Tirmidhi, "Tahara" 82.

63 *al-Bukhari*, "Wudu" 46; *Muslim*, "Tahara" 8, 12; *an-Nasa'i*, "Jumu'a" 9.

64 Qur'an, 4:43; *al-Bukhari*, "Hayd" 19; *at-Tirmidhi*, "Tahara" 93.

65 *al-Bukhari*, "Hayd" 20; *Muslim*, "Hayd" 15; *at-Tirmidhi*, "Sawm" 67.

66 *al-Bukhari*, "Hayd" 7, 8; *Ibn Maja*, "Manasik" 36; *Abu Dawud*, "Manasik" 23.

67 Ibn Jarir at-Tabari and Ibn Kathir, while commenting on the verse 4:43 in their *tafsirs*, based on Ibn 'Abbas. Also, *al-Bukhari*, "Hayd" 24.

68 *at-Tirmidhi*, "Tahara" 98; *Ibn Maja*, "Tahara" 105; ad-Darimi, *Sunan*, "Talaq" 3.

69 *Muslim*, "Hayd" 58; *Abu Dawud*, "Tahara" 120; *at-Tirmidhi*, "Tahara" 77.

70 al-Mawsili, *al-Ikhtiyar*, vol. 1, "Ghusl."

71 *al-Bukhari*, "Ghusl" 1, 5, 7; *Muslim*, "Hayd" 4; *Abu Dawud*, "Tahara" 98.

72 *al-Bukhari*, "Tayammum" 1; *an-Nasa'i*, "Tahara" 196; *Abu Dawud*, "Tahara" 123.

73 *Abu Dawud*, "Tahara" 128; *an-Nasa'i*, "Ghusl" 27.

74 *al-Bukhari*, "Wudu" 3.

75 *Muslim*, "Tahara" 41; *an-Nasa'i*, "Tahara" 107; *at-Tirmidhi*, "Tahara" 51.

76 *Muslim*, "Musafirun" 294; *an-Nasa'i*, "Tahare" 108.

77 *al-Bukhari*, "Wudu" 24; *Muslim*, "Tahara" 3–4; *Abu Dawud*, "Tahara" 50; *at-Tirmidhi*, "Tahara" 37; *an-Nasa'i*, "Tahara" 105.

78 Qur'an, 5:6; *al-Bukhari*, "Wudu" 4, 34; "Ghusl" 13; *Muslim*, "Hayd" 17, 99; *Abu Dawud*, "Tahara" 68, 93; *at-Tirmidhi*, "Tahara" 56, 83.

79 *Abu Dawud*, "Tahara" 109; az-Zaylai, *Nasbu'r-Ra'ya*, 1:37.

80 *Abu Dawud*, "Sawm" 32; *at-Tirmidhi*, "Tahara" 33.

81 *at-Tirmidhi*, "Tahara" 63; Ibn Hanbal, 6:210..

82 *Abu Dawud*, "Tahara" 79; ad-Darimi, *Sunan*, "Wudu"' 48; Ibn Hanbal, 1:111.

83 *Muslim*, "Hayd" 125; *Abu Davud*, "Tahara" 80; *at-Tirmidhi*, "Tahara" 58; *al-Bukhari*, "Adhan" 39:51.

84 *Nasbur-Raya*, Vol. I, p. 47; also reported by al-Bayhaqi and ad-Daraqutni.

85 *al-Bukhari*, "Wudu" 49; *Muslim*, "Tahara" 72, 79; *Abu Dawud*, "Tahara" 60, 63; Ibn Hanbal, 4:247; *at-Tirmidhi*, "Da'awat" 98.

86 *al-Bukhari*, "Wudu" 49; *at-Tirmidhi*, "Da'awat" 98; *Abu Dawud*, "Tahara" 60, 63; Kamaladdin ibnu'l-Humam, *Fathu'l-Qadir*, 1:102–107.

Chapter 3: *As-Salah* (The Prayer)

1 Ibn Hanbal, 5:231, 237; *at-Tirmidhi*, "Iman" 8.

2 *al-Bukhari*, "Mawaqit" 6; *Muslim*, "Masajid", 283; *an-Nasa'i*, "Salah" 7.

3 *Abu Dawud*, "Witr" 2; *an-Nasa'i*, "Salah" 6.

4 *at-Tirmidhi*, "Salah" 188; *Abu Dawud* "Salah" 145; *an-Nasa'i*, "Salah" 9.

5 Said Nursi, *The Words* (trans.), "The Fourth Word," The Light, 25–26.

6 *Muslim*, "Tahara" 7, 11; *an-Nasa'i*, "Tahara" 108.

7 *Abu Dawud*, "Salah" 26; *at-Tirmidhi*, "Salah" 299.

8 *al-Bukhari*, "Bad'u'l-khalq" 6, "Anbiya" 22; *Muslim*, "Iman" 259.

9 *Abu Dawud*, "Salah" 2; *at-Tirmidhi*, "Salah" HN: 149; Ibn Hanbal, 1:382.

10 *Muslim*, "Masajid" 178; *an-Nasa'i*, "Mawaqit" 15.

11 *al-Bukhari*, "Mawaqit" 35; *Muslim*, "Masajid" 309; *Abu Dawud*, "Salah" 11.

12 *Muslim*, "Musafirun" 293; *Abu Dawud*, "Janaiz" 51; *at-Tirmidhi*, "Mawaqit" 31.

13 *Muslim*, "Fitan" 110; *at-Tirmidhi*, "Fitan" 59, 109.

14 *al-Bukhari*, "Hajj" 93, 96; *Muslim*, "Hajj" 45; *al-Muwatta'*, "Hajj" 196; *Abu Dawud*, "Manasik" 65; *at-Tirmidhi*, "Hajj" 56; *an-Nasa'i*, "Mawaqit" 49.

15 *al-Bukhari*, "Mawaqit" 12; *Muslim*, "Musafirin" 45, 49, 52.

16 *al-Bukhari*, "Hajj" 99; *Muslim*, "Hajj" 292; *Abu Dawud*, "Manasik" 65.

17 Said Nursi, *The Words* (trans.), "The Ninth Word", 57–63.

18 *al-Bukhari*, "Adhan" 9.

19 *al-Bukhari*, "Adhan" 5; *an-Nasa'i*, "Adhan" 14.

20 *Abu Dawud*, "Salah" 28; *at-Tirmidhi*, "Salah" 139.

21 Muslim, "Salah" 6; *Abu Dawud*, "Salah" 28; *at-Tirmidhi*, "Salah" 140.

22 *al-Bukhari*, "Adhan" 7; *Muslim*, "Salah" 10; *Abu Dawud*, "Salah" 36.

23 *Muslim*, "Salah" 11; *Abu Dawud*, "Salah" 36; *at-Tirmidhi*, "Salah" 154.

24 *Muslim*, "Salah" 13; *Abu Dawud*, "Salah" 36; *at-Tirmidhi*, "Salah" 156.

25 *al-Bukhari*, "Adhan" 8; *Abu Dawud*, "Salah" 28; *at-Tirmidhi*, "Salah" 157.

26 *al-Bukhari*, "Adhan" 8; *Muslim*, "Salah" 11; *Abu Dawud*, "Salah" 28.

27 *al-Bukhari*, "Jumu'a" 8: *Muslim*, "Tahara" 42; *al-Muwatta'*, "Tahara" 15.

28 *Ibn Maja*, "Tahara" 132; *Abu Dawud*, "Salah" 84; *at-Tirmidhi*, "Salah" 277.

29 *al-Bukhari*, "Salah" 12; *Abu Dawud*, "Salah" 26; *at-Tirmidhi*, "Adab" 40.

30 *Abu Dawud*, "Jana'iz" 32.

31 *al-Bukhari*, "Bad'u'l-Wahy" 1; *Muslim*, "Iman" 155.

32 *Abu Dawud*, "Salah" 73; *at-Tirmidhi*, "Mawaqit" 62; *Ibn Maja* "Tahara" 3.

33 *al-Bukhari*, "Taqsir" 19; *Abu Dawud*, "Salah" 175; *at-Tirmidhi*, "Salah" 157.

34 *Muslim*, "Salah" 38; *al-Muwatta'*, "Salah" 38, 39; *Abu Dawud*, "Salah" 136; *at-Tirmidhi*, "Salah" 283.

35 *Abu Dawud*, "Salah" 68, 175; *Ibn Maja*, "Iqama" 13, 18; *Muslim*, "Salah" 11.

36 *al-Bukhari*, "Salah" 14; *Abu Dawud*, "Salah" 148; Ibn Hanbal, 1:123.

37 *al-Bukhari*, "Salah" 14; *Abu Dawud*, "Salah" 164; *at-Tirmidhi*, "Salah" 226.

38 *al-Bukhari*, "Salah" 53; *Muslim*, "Salah" 44; *at-Tirmidhi*, "Salah" 203.

39 *Abu Dawud*, "Salah" 178; *at-Tirmidhi*, "Salah" 215–222; *an-Nasa'i*, "Tatbiq" 15.

40 *al-Bukhari*, "Adhan" 92, "'Amal fi's-Salah" 2, 8, 11; *Muslim*, "Masajid" 46, 47, 49; *Abu Dawud*, "Salah" 165, 167, 175; *at-Tirmidhi*, "Salah" 279, 413.

41 *al-Bukhari*, "Salah" 87; *Muslim*, "Salah" 272; *Abu Dawud*, "Salah" 49; *at-Tirmidhi*, "Salah" 245; *Ibn Maja*, "Masajid" 16.

42 *Muslim*, "Salah" 24; *Abu Dawud*, "Salah" 122; Ibn Hanbal, 4:381.

43 *Muslim*, "Iqama" 27, *Abu Dawud*, "Salah" 41; *at-Tirmidhi*, "Mawaqit" 105.

44 *al-Bukhari*, "Mawaqit" 24, *Muslim*, "Salah" 27–32, 54, "Masajid" 225; *Abu Dawud*, "Salah" 118–120; *Ibn Maja*, "Iqama" 15; *an-Nasa'i*, "Iftitah" 107.

45 *Muslim*, "Salah" 54; *Abu Dawud*, "Salah" 117; *an-Nasa'i*, "Sahw" 29.

46 *Abu Dawud*, "Salah" 120; *at-Tirmidhi*, "Salah" 179.

47 *at-Tirmidhi*, "Salah" 180, 181; *an-Nasa'i*, "Iftitah" 22.

48 *al-Bukhari*, "Adhan" 112, *Muslim*, "Salah" 72; *al-Muwatta'*, "Salah" 44.

49 *al-Bukhari*, "Adhan" 106, "Mawaqit" 11, 13; *Muslim*, "Salah" 163, "Masajid" 2; *Abu Dawud*, "Salah" 89, 218; *at-Tirmidhi*, "Salah" 375; *an-Nasa'i*, "Iftitah" 76.

50 *al-Bukhari*, "Adhan" 107–110; *Muslim*, "Salah" 154; *Abu Dawud*, "Salah" 131.

51 *al-Bukhari*, "Adhan" 98, 99; *Muslim*, "Salah" 173, *Abu Dawud*, "Salah" 133.

52 *al-Bukhari*, "Adhan" 100, 102; *Muslim*, "Salah" 175; *at-Tirmidhi*, "Salah" 231; *an-Nasa'i*, "Iftitah" 71, 72.

53 *al-Bukhari*, "Adhan" 115; *Muslim*, "Salah" 27–32; *at-Tirmidhi*, "Salah" 177, 191; Abu Dawud, "Salah" 119; *an-Nasa'i*, "Iftitah" 110.

54 *al-Bukhari*, "Sıfatu's-Salah" 42; *at-Tirmidhi*, "Salah" 194; *an-Nasa'i*, "Iftitah" 102.

55 *al-Bukhari*, "Sıfatu's-Salah" 44, 45; *Muslim*, "Salah" 42; *at-Tirmidhi*, "Salah" 198.

56 *al-Bukhari*, "Sıfatu's-Salah" 37–50, 60; *Abu Dawud*, "Salah" 141; *at-Tirmidhi*, "Salah" 199, 201; *an-Nasa'i*, "Iftitah" 128.

57 *al-Bukhari*, "Anbiya" 10; *Muslim*, "Salah" 65; *Abu Dawud*, "Salah" 179; *at-Tirmidhi*, "Tafsir" 33; *an-Nasa'i*, "Sahw" 49.

58 *al-Bukhari*, "Adhan" 148, 150; *Muslim*, "Salah" 55–61; *Abu Dawud*, "Salah" 182.

59 *Muslim*, "Masajid" 135; *at-Tirmidhi*, "Salah" 224; *Abu Dawud*, "Salah" 360.

60 *Muslim*, "Masajid" 135; *at-Tirmidhi*, "Salah" 224, "Da'awat" 25; *an-Nasai*, "Sahw" 95.

61 *al-Bukhari*, "Adhan" 119, 132, "Taqsir as-Salah" *Muslim*, "Salah" 227–233; *at-Tirmidhi*, "Salah" 200, 203, 205; *Abu Dawud*, "Salah" 187; *an-Nasai*, "Iftitah" 13, 140.

62 *al-Bukhari*, " 'Amal fi's-Salah" 2, 15; *Muslim*, "Masajid" 34, 35, 37; *at-Tirmidhi*, "Mawaqit" 180; *Abu Dawud*, "Salah" 166; Ibn Hanbal, 1:435, 4:368.

63 *Muslim*, "Masajid" 160, 176–177; *at-Tirmidhi*, "Salah" 115, 148, *Abu Dawud*, "Salah" 28, 44; *an-Nasai*, "Mawaqit" 12.

64 *al-Bukhari*, "Isti'dhan" 28; *Muslim*, "Masajid" 59; *at-Tirmidhi*, "Salah" 215; *an-Nasai*, "Iftitah" 189; *Abu Dawud*, "Salah" 182.

65 *al-Bukhari*, "Anbiya" 10; *Muslim*, "Salah" 65; *Abu Dawud*, "Salah" 179; *at-Tirmidhi*, "Tafsir" 33; *an-Nasa'i*, "Sahw" 49.

66 *Muslim*, "Salah" 119; *Abu Dawud*, "Salah" 189; *an-Nasa'i*, "Sahw" 5.

67 *al-Bukhari*, "Adhan" 97, 109; *Muslim*, "Salah" 154; *Abu Dawud*, "Salah" 129; *an-Nasa'i*, "Iftitah" 56–60.

68 *al-Bukhari*, "Salah" 31; *Muslim*, "Salah" 63; *Abu Dawud*, "Salah" 198.

69 *Muslim*, "Salah" 63; *Abu Dawud*, "Salah" 197; *an-Nasa'i*, "Sahw" 24; *at-Tirmidhi*, "Salah" 291.

70 az-Zaylai, *Nasbu'r-Raya*, 2:174.

71 *al-Bukhari*, "Sujudu'l-Qur'an" 8–9; *Muslim*, "Masajid" 103–104; *an-Nasa'i*, "Iftitah" 491.

72 *al-Bukhari*, "Taqsir" 19; *Abu Dawud*, "Salah" 175; *at-Tirmidhi*, "Salah" 157.

73 *Muslim*, "Tahara" 85; *Abu Dawud*, "Tahara" 61; *an-Nasa'i*, "Tahara" 98.

74 *al-Bukhari*, "Taqsir" 4; *Muslim*, "Hajj" 413; *Abu Dawud*, "Manasik" 2.

75 *Muslim*, "Salah" 108; *an-Nasa'i*, "Qiyamu'l-Layl" 66; *at-Tirmidhi*, "Salah" 306; *Ibn Maja*, "Iqama" 100.

76 *an-Nasa'i*, "Qiyamu'l-Layl" 66; *at-Tirmidhi*, "Salah" 306; *Ibn Maja*, "Iqama" 100.

77 *al-Bukhari*, "Tahajjud" 27; *Muslim*, "Salatu'l-Musafirin" 96; *an-Nasa'i*, "Qiyamu'l-Layl" 56; *at-Tirmidhi*, "Salah" 307.

78 *at-Tirmidhi*, "Salah" 315, 317; *Abu Dawud*, "Tatawwu'" 7; *Ibn Maja*, "Iqama" 105, 108.

79 *at-Tirmidhi*, "Salah" 318; *Ibn Maja*, "Iqama" 109; *an-Nasa'i*, "Imama" 65.

80 *at-Tirmidhi*, "Salah" 324.

81 *Abu Dawud*, "Salah'" 307.

82 *al-Bukhari*, "Tahajjud" 16; *Muslim*, "Sifatu'l-Munafiqin" 79.

83 *al-Bukhari*, "Tahajjud" 14; *Muslim*, "Salah" 15; *at-Tirmidhi*, "Salah" 329.

84 *al-Bukhari*, "Tahajjud" 10; *Muslim*, "Salah" 112; *at-Tirmidhi*, "Salah" 323.

85 *Muslim*, "Salah" 113; *Abu Dawud*, "Tatawwu'" 26; *at-Tirmidhi*, "Salah" 325.

86 *Abu Dawud*, "Salah" 340.

87 *al-Bukhari*, "Salatu't-Tarawih" 1; *Muslim*, "Musafirun" 177.

88 *Abu Dawud*, "Salah" 340.

89 *al-Bukhari*, "Tahajjud" 25; *at-Tirmidhi*, "Witr" 18 (349); Abu Dawud, "Salah" 366.

90 *Abu Dawud*, "Salah" 303; *at-Tirmidhi*, "Witr" 19; *Ibn Maja*, "Iqama" 190.

91 *at-Tirmidhi*, "Witr" 19 (350).

92 *at-Tirmidhi*, "Witr" 17 (348); *Ibn Maja*, "Iqama" 189.

93 *al-Bukhari*, "Wudu" 24; *Abu Dawud*, "Salah" 162; *an-Nasa'i*, "Tahara" 27.

94 *al-Bukhari*, "Kusuf" 1; *Abu Dawud*, "Istisqa" 4; *an-Nasa'i*, "Kusuf" 5.

95 *al-Bukhari*, "Istisqa" 6; *Muslim*, "Istisqa" 2, 8.

96 *Abu Dawud*, "Istisqa" 2; *Ibn Maja*, "Iqama" 154; Ibn Hanbal, 4:395.

97 *al-Bukhari*, "Riqaq" 38.

98 *Muslim*, "Musafirun" 84; *Abu Dawud*, "Salah" 301.

99 *al-Bukhari*, "Salah" 60; *Muslim*, "Musafirun" 69; *at-Tirmidhi*, "Salah" 235.

100 *Muslim*, "Musafirun" 210.

101 *al-Bukhari*, "Tahajjud" 16; *Muslim*, "Sifatu'l-Munafiqin" 79.

102 *Abu Dawud*, "Salah" 210; *at-Tirmidhi*, "Jumu'a" 7; *an-Nasa'i*, "Jumu'a" 2.

103 *al-Bukhari*, "Jumu'a" 4; *Muslim*, "Jumu'a" 17; *at-Tirmidhi*, "Jumu'a" 1.

104 *al-Bukhari*, "Jumu'a" 14, 16, 17; *Abu Dawud*, "Salah" 215.

105 *al-Bukhari*, "Jumu'a" 4, 19; *Muslim*, "Jumu'a" 10, 12, 24; *Abu Dawud*, "Tahara" 129.

106 Abdu'r-Razzaq, *Musannaf*, 3:167; as-Sarakhsi, *al-Mabsut*, 2:24; *Abu Dawud*, "Salah" 205, 206.

107 *Ibn Maja*, "Iqama" 78; Ahmet Naim, *Tecrid-i Sarih Tercümesi ve Şerhi* ("Annonated Translation of *Tajrid as-Sarih*"), 3:48; *al-Fatawa al-Hindiya*, 1:145.

108 *al-Bukhari*, "Jumu'a" 38; *Muslim*, "Jumu'a" 36.

109 *Muslim*, "Jumu'a" 39; *an-Nasa'i*, "Jumu'a" 18.

110 *al-Bukhari*, "Jumu'a" 30; *Muslim*, "Jumu'a" 33, 47; *Abu Dawud*, "Salah" 229.

111 *al-Bukhari*, "Jumu'a" 36; *Muslim*, "Jumu'a" 8, 11; *Abu Dawud*, "Salah" 235.

112 *Muslim*, "Jumu'a" 67–69; *Abu Dawud*, "Salah" 237; *Ibn Maja*, "Iqama" 94.

113 Ibn 'Abidin, Raddu'l-Mukhtar (Rejection of the Book al-Mukhtar"), 1:595; Yusuf an-Nabhani, *Husnu'sh-Shir'a fi Mashru'iyyeti Salati'z-Zuhr* ("The Better Opinion in the Lawfulness of *Salatu'z-Zuhr*"), 6.

114 *Muslim*, "Salatu'l-'Iydayn" 13; *Abu Dawud*, "Salah" 238–241.

115 *al-Bukhari*, "Salatu'l-'Iydayn" 4; *Muslim*, "Salatu'l-'Iydayn" 4.

116 M. Fethullah Gülen, *Towards the Lost Paradise*, Kaynak Yayınları, İzmir, Turkey, 1995, pp.

117 *Muslim*, "Salatu'l-'Iydayn" 13; *Abu Dawud*, "Salah" 238–241.

118 *al-Bukhari*, "Salatu'l-'Iydayn" 4; *Muslim*, "Salatu'l-'Iydayn" 4.

119 See, Said Nursi, *The Letters* (trans.), "The First Letter," 5–6.

120 *al-Bukhari*, "Libas" 36, "Janaiz" 2.

121 *al-Bukhari*, "Marda wa Tib" 2.

122 *al-Bukhari*, "Marda wa Tib" 4; *Abu Dawud*, "Janaiz" 8, *at-Tirmidhi*, "Tib" 35.

123 *Muslim*, "Janaiz" 1.

124 *al-Bukhari*, "Marda wa Tib" 19; *Muslim*, "Dhikr" 10; *at-Tirmidhi*, "Janaiz" 3.

125 *al-Bukhari*, "Janaiz" 86; *Muslim*, "Janaiz" 59, 60; *Abu Dawud*, "Janaiz" 45, 80.

126 *Muslim*, "Janaiz" 72; *Abu Dawud*, "Janaiz" 57, 58, *at-Tirmidhi*, "Tib" 37, 45.

127 *Muslim*, "Janaiz" 73–81; *an-Nasa'i*, "Janaiz" 45.

128 *al-Bukhari*, "Adhan" 30; *Muslim*, "Masajid" 249; *at-Tirmidhi*, "Salah" 161.

129 *al-Bukhari*, "Salah" 87; *Muslim*, "Masajid" 246; *Abu Dawud*, "Salah" 423.

130 *al-Bukhari*, "Adhan" 9; *Muslim*, "Masajid" 129; *at-Tirmidhi*, "Salah" 166.

131 *Muslim*, "Salah" 134–137.

132 *Muslim*, "Salah" 141–142; *Abu Dawud*, "Salah" 52; Ibn Humam, "*ibid*," 1:529.

133 *al-Bukhari*, "Adhan" 5; *Abu Dawud*, "Salah" 31; *at-Nasa'i*, "Adhan"14.

134 *al-Bukhari*, "Adhan" 11, 13; *Abu Dawud*, "Salah" 41; *at-Tirmidhi*, "Salah" 149.

135 *Abu Dawud*, "Salah" 39; *at-Tirmidhi*, "Salah" 155; *Abu Dawud*, "Salah" 39.

136 *at-Tirmidhi*, "Salah" 147.

137 *al-Bukhari*, "Adhan" 18–19; *Muslim*, "Salah" 249; *Abu Dawud*, "Salah" 34; *at-Tirmidhi*, "Salah" 144.

138 *al-Bukhari*, "Adhan" 5; ad-Darimi, *Sunan* "Salah" 7; *al-Muwatta'*, "Nida" 5.

139 *al-Bukhari*, "Adhan" 30; *Muslim*, "Masajid" 249; *at-Tirmidhi*, "Salah" 161.

140 *al-Bukhari*, "Adhan" 7; *Muslim*, "Salah" 40; *an-Nasa'i*, "Adhan" 33.

141 *at-Tirmidhi*, "Salah" 146; *Abu Dawud*, "Salah" 30.

142 Zayd ibn 'Ali, *Musnad*, Beirut, 111–112.

143 *at-Tirmidhi*, "Salah" 174; *Ibn Maja*, "Iqama" 46; *an-Nasa'i*, "Imama" 3.

144 *an-Nasa'i*, "Mawaqit" 176; Ibn Hanbal, 5:174.

145 *al-Bukhari*, "Adhan" 17; *Muslim*, "Masajid" 292; *Ibn Maja*, "Iqama" 46.

146 *at-Tirmidhi*, "Salah" 170–173; *Abu Dawud*, "Salah" 97; *an-Nasa'i*, "Imama"19–20.

147 *at-Tirmidhi*, "Salah" 167; *Ibn Maja*, "Iqama" 50; *an-Nasa'i*, "Imama" 25.

148 *Muslim* "Salah" 28; *at-Tirmidhi*, "Salah" 168; *an-Nasa'i*, "Imama" 23.

149 *al-Bukhari*, "Salah" 100; *Muslim*, "Salah" 50; 259; *Abu Dawud*, "Salah" 108, 112; *at-Tirmidhi*, "Salah" 50–52..

150 *at-Tirmidhi*, "Salah" 236; *Abu Dawud*, "Salah" 24; *ad-Darimi*, "Salah" 111.

151 *Muslim*, "Hajj" 95; *at-Tirmidhi*, "Salah" 243; *Ibn Maja*, "Iqama" 195.

152 *Abu Dawud*, "Salah" 11; *an-Nasa'i*, "Mawaqit" 54; 259; Ibn Hanbal, 4:444.

153 *at-Tirmidhi*, "Mawaqit" 18; Ibn Hanbal, 1:375.

Chapter 4: *Sawm ar-Ramadan* (Fasting the Month of Ramadan)

1 *at-Tirmidhi*, "Iman" 7.

2 *al-Bukhari*, "Sawm" 2, 9; *Muslim*, "Siyam" 164; *Abu Dawud*, "Sawm" 25.

3 Bediüzzaman Said Nursi, *The Letters* (trans.), 390–396.

4 The Verse of the Throne is as follows:

God, there is no deity but He; the All-Living, the Self-Subsisting (by Whom all subsist). Slumber does not seize Him, nor sleep. His is all that is in the heavens and all that is on the earth. Who is there that will intercede with Him save by His leave? He knows what lies before them and what lies after them (what lies in their future and in their past, what is known to them and what is hidden from them); and they do not comprehend anything of His Knowledge save what He wills. His Seat (of dominion) embraces the heavens and the earth, and the preserving of them does not weary Him; He is the All-Exalted, the Supreme. (2:255)

5 *al-Bukhari*, "Sawm" 11, 13; *Muslim*, "Siyam" 9; *al-Muwatta'*, "Siyam" 1; *Abu Dawud*, "Sawm" 4, 6.

6 *at-Tirmidhi*, "Sawm" 20; *Muslim*, "Siyam" 15.

7 *at-Tirmidhi*, "Sawm" 2; *an-Nasa'i*, "Siyam" 62; *Abu Dawud*, "Sawm" 43.

8 *al-Bukhari*, "Tafsir" 21: *Abu Dawud*, "Sawm" 2; Ibn Hanbal, 2:183.

9 *al-Bukhari*, "Sawm" 33, 36; *Muslim*, "Siyam" 92, 103; *Abu Dawud*, "Sawm" 42, 43.

10 *at-Tirmidhi*, "Sawm" 23; *Ibn Maja*, "Siyam" 50.

11 *al-Bukhari*, "Sawm" 67: *Muslim*, "Siyam" 22 (182); *Abu Dawud*, "Sawm" 48.

12 *al-Bukhari*, "Sawm" 63: *Muslim*, "Siyam" 23 (195); *Abu Dawud*, "Sawm" 50.

13 *Abu Dawud*, "Sawm" 51; *at-Tirmidhi*, "Sawm" 43; *Ibn Maja*, "Siyam" 38.

14 *at-Tirmidhi*, "Sawm" 3; *Abu Dawud*, "Sawm" 10; *an-Nasa'i*, "Sawm" 37.

15 *an-Nasa'i*, "Sawm" 37.

16 *al-Bukhari*, "Sawm" 14: *Muslim*, "Siyam" 21; *Abu Dawud*, "Sawm" 11.

17 *Abu Dawud*, "Sawm" 63.

18 *Muslim*, "Siyam" 204; *Abu Dawud*, "Sawm" 58; *at-Tirmidhi*, "Sawm" 53.

19 *al-Bukhari*, "Sawm" 69; *at-Tirmidhi*, "Sawm" 48, 49; *Abu Dawud*, "Sawm" 64.

20 *Muslim*, "Siyam" 204; *Abu Dawud*, "Sawm" 61; *an-Nasa'i*, "Sawm" 83.

21 *al-Bukhari*, "Sawm" 52: *Muslim*, "Siyam" 175; *Abu Dawud*, "Sawm" 56.

22 *at-Tirmidhi*, "Sawm" 44; *an-Nasa'i*, "Sawm" 70; *Ibn Maja* "Siyam" 42.

23 *at-Tirmidhi*, "Sawm" 54; *an-Nasa'i*, "Sawm" 82, 83; *Abu Dawud* "Sawm" 68.

24 *Muslim*, "Siyam" 192; *an-Nasa'i*, "Sawm" 76, 77; *Ibn Maja* "Siyam" 43.

25 *al-Bukhari*, "Sawm" 19, 20: *Muslim*, "Siyam" 46, 47; *Abu Dawud*, "Sawm" 17.

26 *al-Bukhari*, "Sawm" 44: *Muslim*, "Siyam" 48, 51; *Abu Dawud*, "Sawm" 22.

27 *al-Bukhari*, "Sawm" 21: *Muslim*, "Siyam" 29 (212); *at-Tirmidhi*, "Sawm" 35.

28 *al-Bukhari*, "Sawm" 8; *Abu Dawud*, "Sawm" 25; *at-Tirmidhi*, "Sawm" 16.

29 *al-Bukhari*, "Sawm" 2, 9: *Muslim*, "Siyam" 164; *Abu Dawud*, "Sawm" 25.

30 *al-Bukhari*, "Tarawih" 6: *Muslim*, "I'tikaf" 8; *at-Tirmidhi*, "Sawm" 73.

31 *Abu Dawud*, "Sawm" 31.

32 *al-Bukhari*, "Sawm" 24: *Muslim*, "Siyam" 62–65; *Abu Dawud*, "Sawm" 35.

33 *Abu Dawud*, "Sawm" 32; *at-Tirmidhi*, "Sawm" 25; *Ibn Maja*, "Sawm" 16.

34 *Abu Dawud*, "Sawm" 32; *at-Tirmidhi*, "Sawm" 25; *Ibn Maja*, "Sawm" 16.

35 *al-Bukhari*, "Sawm" 26: *Muslim*, "Siyam" 171; *at-Tirmidhi*, "Sawm" 26.

36 *Abu Dawud*, "Sawm" 32; *at-Tirmidhi*, "Sawm" 24, 25; *Ibn Maja*, "Sawm" 16.

37 *Ibn Maja*, "Siyam" 14: *Darimi*, "Sawm" 18; Ibn Hanbal 1:92.

38 *al-Bukhari*, "Sawm" 29: *Muslim*, "Siyam" 81; *at-Tirmidhi*, "Sawm" 28.

39 *al-Bukhari*, "Tarawih" 3, 4; *Muslim*, "I'tikaf" 5, 9; *at-Tirmidhi*, "Sawm" 71.

40 *al-Bukhari*, "Tarawih" 6; *Muslim*, "Musafirun" 174; *at-Tirmidhi*, "Sawm" 83.

41 *al-Bukhari*, "Tarawih" 2; *Muslim*, "I'tikaf" 8; *Abu Dawud*, "Salah" 318.

42 *al-Bukhari*, "I'tikaf" 17; *Abu Dawud*, "Sawm" 78; *Ibn Maja*, "Siyam" 58.

43 *al-Bukhari*, "Ayman" 1; *Muslim*, "Ayman" 15, 16.

44 *al-Bukhari*, "Ayman" 28; *Abu Dawud*, "Ayman" 19; *an-Nasa'i*, "Ayman" 27.

Chapter 5: *Az-Zakah* (The Prescribed Purifying Alms)

1 *al-Bukhari*, "Zakah" 1; *Muslim*, "Iman" 31; *at-Tirmidhi*, "Zakah" 6.

2 Bediüzzaman Said Nursi refers to WWI.

3 Said Nursi, *The Letters* (trans.), 450.

4 *al-Bukhari*, "Zakah" 19.

5 *Ibn Maja*, "Zakah" 5; *al-Muwatta'*, "Zakah" 4.

6 *Muwatta'*, 18.

7 *al-Bukhari*, "Bad'u'l-Wahy" 1; *Muslim*, "Imara" 155.

8 *al-Bukhari*, "Zakah" 52; *Muslim*, "Zakah" 103; *an-Nasa'i*, "Zakah" 83.

9 *al-Bukhari*, "Zakah" 50.

10 Said Nursi, *"Lema'at* (Flashes)", *Sözler* ("The Words"), Define Yayınları, Istanbul, 789–790.

11 Shah Waliyyullah Dahlawi, *Hujjatullahi'l-Baligha* ("God's Conclusive Argument"), Beirut, 1990, 2:110–114.

12 *Abu Dawud*, "Zakah" 5; Ibn Hanbal, 1:148.

13 *at-Tirmidhi*, "Zakah" 3; *Abu Dawud*, "Zakah" 4; *an-Nasa'i*, "Zakah" 18.

14 *al-Bukhari*, "Zakah 33; *at-Tirmidhi*, "Zakah" 12; *an-Nasa'i*, "Zakah" 18.

15 *Abu Dawud*, "Zakah" 3; *at-Tirmidhi*, "Zakah" 12; *an-Nasa'i*, "Zakah" 19.

16 *Abu Dawud*, "Zakah" 4; *at-Tirmidhi*, "Zakah" 4; *Ibn Maja*, "Zakah" 4.

17 *at-Tirmidhi*, "Zakah" 5; *Abu Dawud*, "Zakah" 4; *an-Nasa'i*, "Zakah" 8.

18 *al-Bukhari*, "Zakah" 56; *Muslim*, "Zakah" 7; *at-Tirmidhi*, "Zakah" 14.

19 *al-Bukhari*, "Zakah" 66; *Abu Dawud*, "Luqata" 1; *Muslimi*, "Hudud" 11.

20 *al-Bukhari*, "Zakah" 71–76; *Muslim*, "Zakah" 13; *at-Tirmidhi*, "Zakah" 35.

21 *Abu Dawud*, "Zakah" 17, 20; *Ibn Maja*, "Zakah" 21.

22 This section is taken (edited and summarized) from Muhammad Hamidullah, *Introduction to Islam*, and from Ahmad Shafa'at and Asgar Qureshi, *Hamdard Islamicus* 20, no. 3 (Jul–Sept 1997).

23 *Abu Dawud*, "Zakah" 27; *at-Tirmidhi*, "Manaqib" 16.

24 *al-Bukhari*, "Janaiz" 37; *Muslim*, "Wasiya" 5; *Abu Dawud*, "Wasaya" 2.

25 *at-Tirmidhi*, "Birr" 63.

26 *at-Tirmidhi*, "Wasaya" 5; *an-Nasa'i*, "Wasaya" 5.

27 *al-Bukhari*, Wasaya" 1; *Muslim*, "Wasiya" 16.

28 *al-Bukhari*, "Sulh" 10, "Buyu'" 18; *Muslim*, "Musaqat" 19, 31.

29 *al-Bukhari*, "Jihad wa Siyar" 180.

30 *al-Bukhari*, "Iman" 24; *Muslim*, "Iman" 106; *at-Tirmidhi*, "Iman" 14.

31 Muhammad Y. al-Kandahlawi, *Hayatu's-Sahaba* ("The Life of the Companions"), Beirut, 1999, 2:338 (quoting from *Muntahab Kanzi'l-'Ummal*).

32 ad-Daylami, *al-Firdaws bi-Ma'thuri'l-Khitab*, Beirut, 4:300.

33 Abu'l-Fazl Ezzati, *An Introduction to the History of the Spread of Islam*, London, 1978, 199–200.

Chapter 6: *al-Hajj* (Pilgrimage to Makka)

1 *al-Bukhari*, "Hajj" 37; *Muslim*, "Hajj" 79; *at-Tirmidhi*, "Hajj" 2.

2 *Ibn Maja*, "Manasik" 5.

3 *al-Bukhari*, "I'tis am" 4; *Muslim*, "Hajj" 412; *an-Nasa'i*, "Hajj" 1.

4 *Abu Dawud*, "Manasik" 5; Ibn Hanbal, 1:214; *Ibn Maja*, "Manasik" 1.

5 *Abu Dawud*, "Manasik" 26; *Ibn Maja*, "Manasik" 9.

6 *al-Bukhari*, "Ayman" 30; *Muslim*, "Nadhr" 1; *an-Nasa'i*, "Hajj" 7, 8.

7 *Abu Dawud*, "Hudud" 17; *Ibn Maja*, "Talaq" 15.

8 *al-Bukhari*, "Hajj" 1; *at-Tirmidhi*, "Hajj" 4; *Ibn Maja*, "Manasik" 6.

9 *al-Bukhari*, "Hajj" 33.

10 *Muslim*, "Hajj" 310; *an-Nasa'i*, "Manasik" 220.

11 See *Salatu'l-Musafir* (The Prayer of a traveler) in the section 3.

12 *al-Bukhari*, "Taqsir" 4; *Muslim*, "Hajj" 413; *Abu Dawud*, "Manasik" 2.

13 *al-Bukhari*, "Hajj" 7, 9, 11, 12, 13; *Muslim*, "Hajj" 11, 18.

14 *al-Bukhari*, "Hajj" 13.

15 *al-Bukhari*, "Hajj" 18; *Muslim*, "Hajj" 37; az-Zaylai, *Nasbu'r-Raya*, 3:17, 30.

16 *al-Bukhari*, "Hajj" 28; *al-Muwatta'*, "Hajj" 32.

17 *al-Bukhari*, "Hajj" 21; *Muslim*, "Hajj" 1, 2, 5; *Abu Dawud*, "Manasik" 31.

18 *al-Muwatta'*, "Hajj" 18; *Abu Dawud*, "Manasik" 41; *at-Tirmidhi*, "Hajj" 25.

19 *al-Bukhari*, "Hajj" 21; *Muslim*, "Hajj" 1, ,2 89.

20 *al-Bukhari*, "Nikah" 30; *Muslim*, "Nikah" 46; Abu Dawud, "Manasik" 39.

21 *al-Bukhari*, "Hajj" 26; *Muslim*, "Hajj" 19; *at-Tirmidhi*, "Hajj" 13.

22 For the kinds of *ihram* or *Hajj*, refer to: *al-Bukhari*, "Hajj" *35: Muslim*, "Hajj" 19, 23; *Abu Dawud*, "Manasik" 23; *at-Tirmidhi*, "Hajj" 10–12; *an-Nasa'i*, "Manasik" 50.

23 *al-Bukhari*, "Hajj" 93, 96, 99; *Muslim*, "Hajj" 45–47; *al-Muwatta'*, "Hajj" 196.

24 *Muslim*, "Hudud" 12, 13; *Abu Dawud*, "Hudud" 23; *an-Nasa'i*, "Manasik" 220.

25 *al-Bukhari*, "Hajj" 77; *Muslim*, "Hajj" 180–183; *al-Muwatta'*, "Hajj" 42

26 *al-Bukhari*, "Hajj" 38; *Muslim*, "Hajj" 13; *at-Tirmidhi'*, "Hajj" 16.

27 *al-Bukhari*, "Hajj" 18; *Muslim*, "Hajj" 31; *Abu Dawud*, "Manasik" 11.

28 az-Zaylai, *Nasbu'r-Raya*, 3:30.

29 *al-Bukhari*, "Hajj" 82; *Abu Dawud*, "Manasik" 21; *at-Tirmidhi*, "Hajj" 15.

30 *al-Bukhari*, "Hajj" 38; *at-Tirmidhi*, "Hajj" 29; *al-Muwatta'*, "Hajj" 3.

31 *at-Tirmidhi*, "Hajj" 42; *Ibn Maja*, "Iqama" 149.

32 *Muslim*, "Hajj" 37; Ibn Hanbal, 1:305

33 *al-Bukhari*, "Hajj" 80; *Abu Dawud*, "Manasik" 50; *at-Tirmidhi'*, "Hajj" 39.

34 *at-Tirmidhi*, "Hajj" 50.

35 *al-Bukhari*, "Hajj" 89–90, 133;

36 *al-Bukhari*, "Hajj" 101; *Abu Dawud*, "Manasik" 65; *at-Tirmidhi'*, "Hajj" 60.

37 *Qur'an*, 2:203; *Muslim*, "Hajj" 58.

38 *Muslim*, "Hajj" 48; *at-Tirmidhi*, "Hajj" 64; *an-Nasa'i*, "Manasik" 226.

39 *Muslim*, "Hajj" 51; *at-Tirmidhi*, "Hajj" 62.

40 *al-Bukhari*, "Hajj" 147; *Muslim*, "Hajj" 57; *at-Tirmidhi*, "Hajj" 81.

41 *al-Bukhari*, "Hajj" 59, 60; *Muslim*, "Hajj" 38, 39; *at-Tirmidhi*, "Hajj" 111.

42 *al-Bukhari*, "Hajj" 76; *Muslim*, "Ashriba" 120; *at-Tirmidhi*, "Ashriba" 12..

43 *al-Bukhari*, "Fadail al-Madina" 13; *Muslim*, "Hajj" 88; *at-Tirmidhi*, "Manaqib" 68.

44 *al-Bukhari*, "Hajj" 19, 21, 43; *Muslim*, "Hajj" 80; *at-Tirmidhi*, "Hajj" 1.

45 *al-Bukhari*, "Fadail Madina" 1; 43; *Muslim*, "Hajj" 82.

46 *al-Muwatta'*, "Hajj" 151.

47 *al-Muwatta'*, "Hajj" 159.

48 For the violations of *ihram* and the penalties required, see Ibnu'l-Humam, *Fathu'l-Qadir*, 2:224–254; Ibn Qudama, *al-Mughni*, 3:494–496; Wahba Zuhayli, *al-Fiqhu'l-Islami wa Adillatuhu*, 3:257.

49 *al-Bukhari*, "Hajj" 55, 57; *Muslim*, "Hajj" 37; *at-Tirmidhi*, "Hajj" 34.

50 For the rules whose sources are not mentioned, refer to the *Sunna acts*.

51 *at-Tirmidhi*, "Hajj" 41–42; *Ibn Maja*, "Iqama" 149.

52 *al-Bukhari*, "Hajj" 79; *Muslim*, "Hajj" 41; *at-Tirmidhi*, "Hajj" 38–39.

53 *al-Bukhari*, "'Umra" 1.

54 *al-Bukhari*, "'Umra" 1; *at-Tirmidhi*, "Hajj" 90.

55 *al-Bukhari*, "'Umra" 4; *Muslim*, "Hajj" 34; *at-Tirmidhi*, "Hajj" 95.

56 *Muslim*, "Hajj" 73.

57 *Muslim*, "Hajj" 43; *at-Tirmidhi*, "Hajj" 78; *an-Nasa'i*, "Manasik" 229.

58 *al-Bukhari*, "Hajj" 135, 137, 139; *Muslim*, "Hajj" 48, 51, 56; *at-Tirmidhi*, "Hajj" 59, 62, 64, 65.

59 *al-Bukhari*, "Hajj" 128, 129; *Muslim*, "Hajj" 53, 54; *at-Tirmidhi*, "Hajj" 73–75.

60 *al-Bukhari*, "Hajj" 130; *Muslim*, "Hajj" 56.

61 *al-Bukhari*, "Hajj" 135, 140–143; *Muslim*, "Hajj" 51; *at-Tirmidhi*, "Hajj" 59, 62.

62 *al-Bukhari*, "Muhsar" 2.

63 *al-Bukhari*, "Muhsar" 3; *at-Tirmidhi*, "Hajj" 96; *Abu Dawud*, "Manasik" 43.

64 *Muslim*, "Hajj" 60; *at-Tirmidhi*, "Hajj" 66.

65 *al-Bukhari*, "Hajj" 108–115; *Muslim*, "Hajj" 29: *at-Tirmidhi*, "Hajj" 67–69.

66 *al-Bukhari*, "'Iydayn" 5.

67 *Muslim*, "Hajj" 3; *at-Tirmidhi*, "Hajj" 73.

68 *al-Bukhari*, "Hajj" 117.

69 *al-Bukhari*, "Hajj" 122.

70 *al-Bukhari*, "Fadail al-Madina" 13; *Muslim*, "Hajj" 88; *at-Tirmidhi*, "Manaqib" 68.

71 *al-Bukhari*, "Fadlu's-Salah fi Masjid Makka wa'l-Madina" 1; *Muslim*, "Hajj" 91.

72 *al-Bukhari*, "Fadlu's-Salah fi Masjid Makka wa'l-Madina" 1; *Muslim*, "Hajj" 91.

73 *al-Bukhari*, "Fadlu's-Salah fi Masjid Makka wa'l-Madina" 2–4; *Muslim*, "Hajj" 93.

74 *an-Nasa'i*, "Masajid" 9

75 Said Nursi, *The Letters* (trans.), The Light, New Jersey, 2007, pp.239–240.

76 M. Fethullah Gülen, *Pearls of Wisdom* (trans.), The Light, New Jersey, 2006, pp. 10–12.

Chapter 7: Marriage and Family Life

1 This chapter is partly taken from various parts (edited and summarized) of Yusuf al-Qaradawi, *The Lawful and Prohibited in Islam*, trans. Muhammad Siddiqi (ASIN: 1999).

2 *al-Bukhari*, "Salah" 12; *Abu Dawud*, "Salah" 26, 84; *at-Tirmidhi*, "Salah, 227, Adab" 40; *Ibn Maja*, "Tahara" 132.

3 *Muslim*, "Hayd" 16; *at-Tirmidhi*, "Adab" 39; *Abu Dawud*, "Hamam" 3.

4 *al-Bukhari*, "Nikah" 2; *Muslim*, "Nikah" 1; *at-Tirmidhi*, "Nikah" 1.

5 M. Fethullah Gülen, *Pearls of Wisdom* (trans.), pp. 37–38.

6 *al-Bukhari*, "Nikah" 16; *at-Tirmidhi*, "Nikah" 3, 4; *Ibn Maja*, "Nikah" 46.

7 *at-Tabarani*, *Mu'jam al-Awsat*, 7:74.

8 *at-Tirmidhi*, "Birr" 62; *Abu Dawud*, "Adab" 5.

9 *al-Bukhari*, "Nikah" 10; *at-Tirmidhi*, "Nikah"13; *Abu Dawud*, "Nikah" 3.

10 *al-Bukhari*, "Nikah" 36; *Muslim*, "Nikah" 12; *at-Tirmidhi*, "Nikah" 5.

11 *al-Bukhari*, "Nikah" 42; *Muslim*, "Nikah" 9; *at-Tirmidhi*, "Nikah" 18.

12 *Abu Dawud*, "Nikah" 18; *at-Tirmidhi*, "Nikah" 14; *Ibn Maja*, "Nikah" 15.

13 *al-Bukhari*, "Nikah" 42, 43; *Ibn Maja*, "Talaq" 16.

14 *at-Tirmidhi*, "Rada" 1; *an-Nasa'i*, "Nikah" 51; *Ibn Maja*, "Nikah" 34.

15 *al-Bukhari*, "Nikah" 28; *at-Tirmidhi*, "Nikah" 31; *an-Nasa'i*, "Nikah" 14.

16 *al-Bukhari*, "Talaq," 19.

17 *al-Bukhari*, "Nikah" 32; *at-Tirmidhi*, "Nikah" 29; *an-Nasa'i*, "Nikah" 71; Abu Dawud, "Nikah" 13.

18 M. Fethullah Gülen, *Pearls of Wisdom* (trans.), pp. 41–43.

19 *al-Bukhari*, "Shahada" 8; *at-Tirmidhi*, "Nikah" 6, 15.

20 *al-Bukhari*, "Nikah" 42, 43; *Muslim*, "Nikah" 9; *at-Tirmidhi*, "Nikah" 18; *Ibn Maja*, "Talaq" 16.

21 *Abu Dawud*, "Nikah" 18; *at-Tirmidhi*, "Nikah" 14; *Ibn Maja*, "Nikah" 15.

22 *al-Bukhari*, "Iman" 24; *Muslim*, "Iman" 106; *at-Tirmidhi*, "Iman" 14.

23 *al-Bukhari*, "Nikah" 55, 69, 72; *Muslim*, "Nikah" 16; *at-Tirmidhi*, "Nikah" 10, 11.

24 *The Qur'an*, 2:228, 233; 4:4, 20–21; 65:7; *al-Bukhari*, "Nikah" 80, 81, 83, 94, 100; *Muslim*, "Nikah" 33, 37, 38; *at-Tirmidhi*, "Nikah" 42; Abu Dawud, "Nikah" 37.

25 *Abu Dawud*, "Sunna" 15; *at-Tirmidhi*, "Rada" 11.

26 *al-Bukhari*, "Nikah" 86, 87, 89, 91, 108; *Muslim*, "Nikah" 20, 21; *at-Tirmidhi*, "Nikah" 42; *Abu Dawud*, "Nikah" 37.

27 *al-Bukhari*, "Hayd" 22; *Muslim*, "Hayd" 2; *at-Tirmidhi*, "Tahara" 99.

28 *at-Tirmidhi*, "Tahara" 102; *Abu Dawud*, "Nikah" 46; *Ibn Maja*, "Tahara" 122.

29 *al-Bukhari*, "Nikah" 97; *Muslim*, "Nikah" 22; *at-Tirmidhi*, "Nikah" 39.

30 *Muslim*, "Qadar" 1.

31 This article is mainly based on Sherif Abdul-Azim, "Women in Islam Versus Women in the Judaeo–Christian Tradition: The Myth and The Reality," http://www.islamicity.com/mosque/w_islam/poly.htm

32 Billy Graham, quoted in Abd al-Rahman Doi, *Woman in Shari'a*, London 1994, 76.

33 This article is partly taken and partly edited from Hammuda Abdul-Ati, *Islam in Focus*, Kuwait: IIFSO, 1990, pp. 184–191.

34 *an-Nasa'i*, "Jihad" 6.

35 *Muslim*, "Birr" 1.

36 M. Fethullah Gülen, *Pearls of Wisdom*, 62–64.

37 *Abu Dawud*, "Talaq" 3.

38 *Abu Dawud*, "Sunna" 15; *at-Tirmidhi*, "Rada" 11.

39 *al-Bukhari*, "Talaq" 2, 3; *Muslim*, "Talaq" 1; *Abu Dawud*, "Talaq" 4; *at-Tirmidhi*, "Talaq" 1; *an-Nasai*, "Talaq" 1, 2, 3, 4, *al-Muwatta'*, "Talaq" 53.

40 *al-Bukhari*, "Talaq" 2, 3; *Muslim*, "Talaq" 1; *Abu Dawud*, "Talaq" 4; *at-Tirmidhi*, "Talaq" 1; *an-Nasai*, "Talaq" 1, 2, 3, 4, *al-Muwatta'*, "Talaq" 53.

41 *al-Bukhari*, "Talaq" 2, 3; *Muslim*, "Talaq" 1; *Abu Dawud*, "Talaq" 4; *at-Tirmidhi*, "Talaq" 1; *an-Nasai*, "Talaq" 1, 2, 3, 4, *al-Muwatta'*, "Talaq" 53.

42 *Muslim*, "Talaq" 7.

43 *al-Bukhari*, "Talaq" 3.

44 *al-Bukhari*, "Talaq" 11; *Abu Dawud*, "Talaq" 51.

45 *Muslim*, "Talaq" 4.

46 Summarized from M. F. Gülen, *The Messenger of God, Muhammad*, 159–171.

47 Ibn Sa'd, *at-Tabaqat al-Kubra*, 8:54; *Muslim*, "Rada" 34.

48 Hakim, *al-Mustadrak*, 4:16–17; at-Tabarani, *al-Mu'jam al-Kabir*, 18:365.

49 *Abu Dawud*, "Nikah" 37; *at-Tirmidhi*, "Nikah" 42.

50 *al-Bukhari*, "Adab" 68; *Muslim*, "Fadail al-Sahaba" 2.

51 The Treaty of Hudaybiya was signed between God's Messenger and the Makkans in the sixth year after the Messenger's migration to Madina. He had left Madina for Makka to do Minor Pilgrimage (*'Umra*) with around 1,400 Companions, but the Makkans did not let them do so. As a consequence, a treaty of ceasefire for ten years was signed.

52 *al-Bukhari*, "Shurut" 15.

53 *Abu Dawud*, "Sunna" 15; *at-Tirmidhi*, "Rada" 11.

54 *at-Tirmidhi*, "Manaqib" 63; Hakim, *al-Mustadrak*, 4:31.

55 *Muslim*, "Fadail" 15; Ibn Hanbal, *al-Musnad*, 3:112.

56 *Muslim*, "Fadail" 15; Ibn Hanbal, *al-Musnad*, 3:112.

57 *al-Bukhari*, "Janaiz" 44; *Muslim*, "Fadail" 15.

58 Hasan ibn Sabbah al-Bazzar, *al-Musnad*, 1:418.

59 *al-Bukhari*, "Zakah" 60; *Muslim*, "Zakah" 46.

60 *al-Bukhari*, "Adab" 18; *Muslim*, "Salah" 53.

61 *an-Nasa'i*, "Zinah" 39; Ibn Hanbal, *al-Musnad*, 5:278–279.

62 *al-Bukhari*, "Khums" 6, "Fadail" 9; *Muslim*, "Dhikr" 18.

63 This section is summarized from Said Nursi, *The Letters* (trans.), 275–277.

64 at-Tabarani, *Mu'jam al-Kabir*, 22:309; Bayhaki, *al-Sunan al-Kubra*, 3:345.

CHAPTER 8: *HALAL* (LAWFUL) AND *HARAM* (FORBIDDEN)

1 This section is basically taken (partly edited) from Yusuf al-Qaradawi, *The Lawful and Prohibited in Islam*, trans., Muhammad Siddiqi (ASIN: 1999).

2 Ibn Jarir at-Tabari, in his *tafsir*, *sura* 9, verse 31; *at-Tirmidhi*, "Tafsir" 10.

3 *al-Bukhari*, "Ashriba" 5; *Abu Dawud*, "Ashriba" 14.

4 *al-Bukhari*, "Iman" 39; *Muslim*, "Buyu'" 41; *Abu Dawud*, "Buyu'" 3.

5 *at-Tirmidhi*, "Tahara" 52; *Abu Dawud*, "Tahara" 41.

6 *Abu Dawud*, "At'ima" 32; *Ibn Maja*, "Dhabaih" 14.

7 *Muslim*, "Sayd" 3; *at-Tirmidhi*, "At'ima" 3.

8 *Abu Dawud*, "Sayd" 23; *at-Tirmidhi*, "At'ima" 4.

9 *Muslim*, "Ashriba" 39; *Abu Dawud*, "Tibb" 11; *at-Tirmidhi*, "Tibb" 7–8.

10 *al-Bukhari*, "Ashriba" 4; *Muslim*, "Ashriba" 7; *Abu Dawud*, "Ashriba" 5; *at-Tirmidhi*, "Ashriba" 1; *an-Nasa'i*, "Ashriba" 22, 23; *al-Muwatta'*, "Ashriba" 9.

11 *Abu Dawud*, "Ashriba" 5; *Ibn Maja*, "Ashriba" 10; at-Tirmidhi, "Ashriba" 3.

12 *al-Bukhari*, "Ashriba" 4; *Muslim*, "Tafsir" 7; *Abu Dawud*, "Ashriba" 1.

13 *Abu Dawud*, "Ashriba" 1; *Ibn Maja*, "Tijarat" 11; *at-Tirmidhi*, "Buyu'" 37, 58.

14 *al-Bukhari*, "Ashriba" 26; *Muslim*, "Libas" 1, 10; *Abu Dawud*, "Libas" 10.

15 *Abu Dawud*, "Libas" 32, 34.

16 *al-Bukhari*, "Libas" 5; *Muslim*, "Libas" 5, 8, 9; *Abu Dawud*, "Libas" 28.

17 *al-Bukhari*, "Riqaq" 17; *Muslim*, "Libas" 19; *an-Nasa'i*, "Zinat" 83; *Abu Dawud*, "Libas" 43.

18 *al-Bukhari*, "Ashriba" 26, 27; *Muslim*, "Libas" 1; *at-Tirmidhi*, "Ashriba" 10.

19 *al-Bukhari*, "Muharibin" 16.

20 *al-Bukhari*, "Tafsir" 37 (252); *Muslim*, "Fadail al-Nabiyy" 39.

21 *al-Bukhari*, "Manaqib" 17; *Muslim*, "Fadail al-Nabiyy" 31.

22 *at-Tirmidhi*, "Manaqib" 1; *ad-Darimi*, "Muqaddima" 27.[x]

23 *al-Bukhari*, "Iman" 7; *Muslim*, "Iman" 17.

24 *al-Bukhari*, "Adab" 81; *Muslim*, "Fadail" 13.

25 *Muslim*, "Iman" 44; *at-Tirmidhi*, "Buyu'" 74; *Abu Dawud*, "Buyu'" 52.

26 *al-Bukhari*, "Buyu'" 2, 19; Muslim, "Buyu'" 41; *at-Tirmidhi*, Buyu'" 1, 17, 70.

27 *at-Tirmidhi*, "Buyu'" 73.

28 *Muslim*, "Buyu'" 47; *at-Tirmidhi*, "Buyu'" 40.

29 *al-Bukhari*, "Buyu'" 68–71; Muslim, "Buyu'" 5–6; *at-Tirmidhi*, Buyu'" 12–13.

30 *al-Bukhari*, "Ijara" 14.

31 *Muslim*, "Buyu'" 65; *at-Tirmidhi*, Buyu'" 65.

32 *al-Bukhari*, "Buyu'" 27; *Muslim*, "Buyu'" 48; *Abu Dawud*, Buyu'" 6.

33 *Muslim*, "Iman" 47; *at-Tirmidhi*, Buyu'" 5, 42.

34 *al-Bukhari*, "Buyu'" 88; *at-Tirmidhi*,"Buyu'" 7; *an-Nasa'i*, Buyu'" 72.

35 *al-Bukhari*, "Buyu'" 17, 18; *Muslim*, "Buyu'" 25, 27; *at-Tirmidhi*, "Buyu'" 67.

36 *Muslim*, "Buyu'" 43; *at-Tirmidhi*, "Buyu'" 48.

37 *al-Bukhari*, "Buyu'" 59; *at-Tirmidhi*, "Buyu'" 10.

38 *at-Tirmidhi*, "Buyu'" 41.

39 *al-Bukhari*, "Buyu'" 20, 75; *Muslim*, "Buyu'" 9, 11, 13; *at-Tirmidhi*, "Buyu'" 8, 14, 17, 70; *Abu Dawud*, "Buyu'" 24.

40 *al-Bukhari*, "Buyu'" 54; *Muslim*, "Buyu'" 8; *at-Tirmidhi*, "Buyu'" 19.

41 *at-Tirmidhi*, "Buyu'" 74; *Abu Dawud*, "Ijara" 50; *Ibn Maja*, "Tijara" 36.

42 *al-Bukhari*, "Buyu'" 42–48; *Muslim*, "Buyu'" 10; *at-Tirmidhi*, "Buyu'" 26.

43 *al Bukhari*, "Buyu'" 24, 112; *Muslim*, "Buyu'" 34; *at-Tirmidhi*, "Buyu'" 61.

44 *al-Bukhari*, "Salam" 1; *Muslim*, "Buyu'" 46.

45 *Abu Dawud*, "Buyu'" 36, "Aqdiya" 4; *at-Tirmidhi*, "Ahkam" 9.

46 *Muslim*, "Imara" 7; *at-Tirmidhi*, "Ahkam'" 8.

47 *al-Bukhari*, "Ahkam" 5, 7; *Muslim*, "Imara" 3, 4; *Abu Dawud*, "Haraj" 2.

48 *al-Bukhari*, "Buyu'" 97; *Muslim*, "Buyu'" 49; *at-Tirmidhi*, "Buyu'" 71.

49 *al-Bukhari*, "Buyu'" 58; *at-Tirmidhi*, "Buyu'" 57.

50 *al-Bukhari*, "Buyu'" 7, 23; *an-Nasa'i*, "Buyu'" 2.

51 *al-Bukhari*, "Buyu'" 15.

52 *al-Bukhari*, "Buyu'" 15.

53 *Muslim*, "Salam" 32–33.

54 *Muslim*, "Salam" 16; *an-Nasa'i*, "Tahrim" 18; *Abu Dawud*, "Wasaya" 10.

55 *al-Bukhari*, "Tibb'" 44; *Muslim*, "Salam" 30–32; *Abu Dawud*, "Tibb" 24.

56 For comprehensive knowledge about music, the section on "*Sama and Wajd* (Whirling dance of Sufi dervishes and Spiritual Ecstasy)" in *Ihya Ulum al-Din* ("The Revival of Religious Sciences") by Imam al-Ghazali may be referred to.

57 *Muslim*, "Birr" 3; *at-Tirmidhi*, "Zuhd" 52.

58 *al-Bukhari*, "Tafsir" 3, "Shahada" 18; Muslim, "Iman" 38–39; *an-Nasa'i*, "Tahrim" 3; *Abu Dawud*, "Wasaya" 10.

Chapter 9: Prayers, Supplications, and Remembrance of God

1 Said Nursi, *The Words* (trans.), The Light, New Jersey, 2005, pp. 332–334.

2 *al-Bukhari*, "Tawhid" 15, 51; *Muslim*, "Dhikr" 1.

3 *al-Bukhari*, "Da'awat" 66.

4 *Tafsir al-Qurtubi*, in interpreting the verse.

5 *Muslim*, "Dhikr" 8.

6 *at-Tirmidhi*, "Du'a" 99.

7 *at-Tirmidhi*, "Tafsir" 9.

8 *al-Bukhari*, "Jumu'a" 27, "Da'awat" 13, 62; "Shahada" 18; *Muslim*, "Salah" 37, 69; *at-Tirmidhi*, "Du'a" 32, 76, 79, 129; *Abu Dawud*, "Salah" 17, 27.

9 *Muslim*, "Dhikr" 22; *Abu Dawud*, "Salah" 364.

10 *at-Tirmidhi*, "Du'a" 65; *an-Nasa'i*, "Sahw" 27.

11 *al-Bukhari*, Da'awat" 1; *at-Tirmidhi*, "Du'a" 117; *Abu Dawud*, "Tib" 19 (3902).

12 *at-Tirmidhi*, "Du'a" 13; *Abu Dawud*, Adab" 17.

13 *at-Tirmidhi*, "Du'a" 13; *Ibn Maja*, "Du'a" 27.

14 *al-Bukhari*, "Da'awat" 15, *at-Tirmidhi*, "Du'a" 15; *an-Nasa'i*, "Isti'adha" 17.

15 *at-Tirmidhi*, "Du'a" 14; *Abu Dawud*, Adab" 17.

16 *at-Tirmidhi*, "Du'a" 13; *Ibn Maja*, "Du'a" 27; *Abu Dawud*, Adab" 17.

17 *at-Tirmidhi*, "Du'a" 13; *Abu Dawud*, "Adab" 17.

18 *at-Tirmidhi*, "Du'a" 79; *Abu Dawud*, Adab" 17.

19 *Abu Dawud*, "Adab" 17.

20 *Abu Dawud*, "Adab" 17; Ibn Hanbal, *Musnad*, 5:42.

21 *Abu Dawud*, "Adab" 17; *Ibn Maja*, "Du'a" 14.

22 *Kanz al-'Ummal*, 2:164..

23 *Abu Dawud*, "Adab" 17; *Kanz al-'Ummal*, 2:159.

24 *al-Bukhari*, "Da'awat," 5–6, Wudu" 80; *Muslim*, "Dhikr" 16; *at-Tirmidhi*, "Du'a" 16.

25 *Muslim*, Dhikr" 16; *at-Tirmidhi*, "Du'a" 19.

26 *al-Bukhari*, "Da'awat," 11; *at-Tirmidhi*, "Du'a" 21; *Abu Dawud*, "Tib" 19.

27 *Muslim*, "Dhikr" 16.

28 *al-Bukhari*, "Da'awat, 10; *Muslim*, Dhikr" 16; *at-Tirmidhi*, "Du'a" 24.

29 *al-Bukhari*, "Da'awat," 15; *Muslim*, "Dhikr" 16; *at-Tirmidhi*, "Du'a" 20.

30 *Abu Dawud*, "Adab" 17; *Ibn Maja*, "Muqaddima" 23.

31 *at-Tirmidhi*, "Du'a" 26; *Abu Dawud*, "Adab" 17.

32 *Abu Dawud*, "Libas" 1.

33 *at-Tirmidhi*, "Du'a" 108; *Ibn Maja*, "Libas" 17.

34 *al-Bukhari*, "Libas" 32.

35 *at-Tirmidhi*, "Du'a" 36; *Ibn Maja*, "Tijara" 27.

36 *at-Tirmidhi*, "Du'a" 35; *Abu Dawud*, "Adab" 17; *an-Nasa'i*, "Isti'adha" 30.

37 *at-Tirmidhi*, "Du'a" 34; *Abu Dawud*, "Adab" 17.

38 *Abu Dawud*, "Adab" 17.

39 *Muslim*, "Salah" 170; *Abu Dawud*, "Adab" 17.

40 *at-Tirmidhi*, "Du'a" 50.

41 *al-Bukhari*, "Da'awat," 26; *Muslim*, "Dhikr" 20; *at-Tirmidhi*, "Du'a"40.

42 *at-Tirmidhi*, "Du'a" 40.

43 *Abu Dawud*, "Adab" 17; Ibn Hanbal, 5:42.

44 *at-Tirmidhi*, "Du'a" 82.

45 Ibn Hanbal, *Musnad*, 1:391.

46 *Abu Dawud*, "Salah/Witr" HN: 1533.

47 at-Tabarani, *Mu'jam al-Kabir*, 10:258.

48 *al-Bukhari*, "Tafsir," 65.

49 *at-Tirmidhi*, "Du'a" 111.

50 *Abu Dawud*, "Salah/Witr", the final *hadith*.

51 *al-Bukhari*, "Adhan" 89; *Muslim*, "Dhikr" 14.

52 Ibn Hanbal, *Musnad*, 6:147.

53 *al-Bukhari*, "Adhan" 155.

54 Ibn Hanbal, *Musnad*, 5:191; al-Tabarani, *Mu'jam al-Kabir*, 5:119.

55 Ibn Hanbal, *al-Musnad*, 5:191; at-Tabarani, *al-Mu'jam al-Kabir*, 5:119.

56 at-Tabarani, *al-Mu'jam al-Kabir*, 8:264.

57 *Muslim*, "Dhikr" 17; *Abu Dawud*, "Witr" 13; *at-Tirmidhi*, "Du'a" 69.

58 *at-Tirmidhi*, "Du'a" 23; *an-Nasa'i*, "Sahw" 61.

59 *at-Tirmidhi*, "Tafsir (38)" 2, 4; Ibn Hanbal, *al-Musnad*, 5:243.

60 at-Tabarani, *al-Mu'jam al-Kabir*, 23:316; Hakim, *al-Mustadrak*, 1:701.

61 *Abu Dawud*, "Witr" 26; *an-Nasa'i*, "Sahw" 60.

62 *Muslim*, "Dhikr" 17; *at-Tirmidhi*, "Du'a" 73.

63 Ibn Hanbal, *Musnad*, 4:181; al-Tabarani, *Mu'jam al-Kabir*, 2:33.

64 *at-Tirmidhi*, "Du'a" 89.

65 *Muslim*, "Salah" 5, 15; *an-Nasa'i*, "Sahw" 54.

66 *al-Bukhari*, "Da'awat" 32.

67 *at-Tirmidhi*, "Du'a" 101.

INDEX